THE POLITICS OF LANGUAGE

the politics of language

Conflict, Identity, and Cultural Pluralism in Comparative Perspective

CAROL L. SCHMID

OXFORD
UNIVERSITY PRESS

2001

OXFORD
UNIVERSITY PRESS

Oxford   New York
Athens   Auckland   Bangkok   Bogotá   Buenos Aires   Calcutta
Cape Town   Chennai   Dar es Salaam   Delhi   Florence   Hong Kong   Istanbul
Karachi   Kuala Lumpur   Madrid   Melbourne   Mexico City   Mumbai
Nairobi   Paris   São Paulo   Shanghai   Singapore   Taipei   Tokyo   Toronto   Warsaw

and associated companies in
Berlin   Ibadan

Copyright © 2001 by Carol L. Schmid

Published by Oxford University Press, Inc.
198 Madison Avenue, New York, New York 10016

Oxford is a registered trademark of Oxford University Press

Library of Congress Cataloging-in-Publication Data
Schmid, Carol L.
     The politics of language : conflict, identity, and cultural pluralism in comparative
perspective / by Carol L. Schmid.
         p.   cm.
     Includes bibliographical references and index.
     ISBN 0-19-513775-2; ISBN 0-19-513776-0 (pbk.)
     1. United States—Languages—Political aspects.   2. Nationalism—United States.
3. Pluralism (Social sciences)—United States.   4. Canada—Languages—Political aspects.
5. Switzerland—Languages—Political aspects.   I. Title.
P119.32.U6 S35   2000
306.44'973—dc21   00-020664

9 8 7 6 5 4 3 2 1

Printed in the United States of America
on acid-free paper

For
Peter and Michael Schmid
who inspired this book

And the memory of
Madeleine Schmid-Stöhr
and
Howard Brotz

ACKNOWLEDGMENTS

Many individuals have assisted in bringing this work on the politics of language in the United States, Canada, and Switzerland to completion. James Crawford introduced me to the topic of language politics in the United States at a meeting of "English Plus" in the early 1980s. John Horton provided early guidance on questions of language politics and the overlapping cleavages of race, ethnicity, and class. I have had much appreciated comments from several colleagues, including Kenneth McRae, Jurg Steiner, and Edward Tiryakian. Both Ed and Jurg read major portions of the manuscript and offered helpful advice on the Canadian and Swiss chapters. Ron Greene gave the entire manuscript a detailed reading and made many constructive suggestions.

In Canada, Raymond Breton, Wsevolod Isajiw, and Marc Boucher enriched my understanding of the Canadian language situation. The Canadian Embassy awarded me a Faculty Research Grant that enabled me to complete the chapter on language relations in Quebec and Canada. In Switzerland, Hanspeter Kriesi provided unpublished survey data on language relations. Martin Kohli of the Free University of Berlin also provided valuable insights on Swiss society.

At Oxford University Press, Peter Ohlin provided helpful advice and support throughout the entire editorial process. On short notice, Matilda Kirby-Smith created all the figures for the book. I especially express my appreciation to my husband, Peter, who is fluent in several languages. He provided inspiration and collaboration throughout this study and painstakingly made all the tables for the book. Finally, the book would not have been possible without the fellowship and discussions of my many friends at Old Town, especially John and Paul.

Several grants and organizations have supported my work. The National Endowment for the Humanities has been especially supportive through an NEH Fellowship for College Teachers and a Summer Research Grant. An NEH Seminar for College Teachers on "Nationalism, National Identity, and Modernity," ably led by Edward Tiryakian at Duke University, provided insight into the relationship between current language politics and national identity and cultural nationalism. During the early stages of this work, I was also awarded a National Science Foundation Pilot Grant and an American Sociological Association Grant on Problems of the Discipline. In addition, I also thank the Southwest Voter Research Institute for providing extensive information on Hispanics and for allowing me to use unpublished survey data. The library staff at Guilford Technical Community College, Duke University, the University of Toronto, and the Schweizerische Sozial Archiv provided unfailing courtesy and efficiency.

I thank the National Clearinghouse on Bilingual Education at George Washington University, the National Immigration Forum, the Institute for Advanced Studies in Culture, St. Martin's Press, and Oxford University Press Canada for permission to reprint tables and figures in the book.

CONTENTS

THE POLITICS OF LANGUAGE

1

INTRODUCTION

The Politics of Language, National Identity, and Cultural Pluralism in the United States

I first became interested in language relations during a stay in Switzerland in 1970–71. Having grown up in California, I found it fascinating to live in the midst of four language communities. I was struck by the orderly and matter-of-fact way in which linguistic and cultural differences were treated in this small multicultural society. My interest in questions of linguistic coexistence and conflict was reawakened upon moving to Canada, another multilingual society. In Canada, by contrast, matters of language and culture excited the temperaments and sentiments of both linguistic groups. Against this backdrop, I decided to pursue the study of language conflict in the United States. Although the United States has always been home to several non-English languages, the English-Only movement resurfaced in the 1980s after lying dormant for almost half a century.

Few areas of the country have been left untouched by the post-1965 immigration and language minorities. Even the South has seen a surge of immigration in the 1990s from Asian and Hispanic countries. Excluding Texas and Florida, which already had large numbers of Hispanic residents prior to the 1990s, the nine other Southern states (Alabama, Arkansas, Georgia, Louisiana, Mississippi, North Carolina, South Carolina, Tennessee, and Virginia) are expected to see their Latino population increase by 112 percent from 1990 to 2000, according to Census Bureau projections. The Asian population is projected to grow by 72 percent in these nine states, while the region's population is only expected to increase by 14 percent (Sack, 1999).

In the small city of High Point, North Carolina, best known for the Furniture Market, one elementary school has nine different language groups represented. In the Guilford County, North Carolina public schools during the 1999/2000 academic year, there were sixty-five different languages spoken. As of July 1998, over 161,000 Hispanics were living in North Carolina, a 110-percent increase over 1990. When I moved to the Triad region of North Carolina in the early 1980s language diversity meant regional dialects. Foreigners were Yankees born outside the South. In less than a decade, this situation changed significantly. Main streets and small strip malls became home to an array of Hispanic and Asian restaurants and ethnic stores. Neighborhoods that were divided between black and white now feature an array of new immigrant groups, speaking a myriad of languages. The growth of limited English-speaking populations (LEPs) has created adjustment problems across the region and anti-immigrant sentiment. There is a need for interpreters and Spanish-language training in school systems, courts, police departments, hospitals, and social service agencies.

American Factors Contributing to Language-Based Conflict

The conditions producing today's language conflict are the basic concern of this book. Events coalescing at the end of the nineteenth century linked loyalty, American national identity, and the English language. Language alone has rarely been the major source of conflict in American society; instead, it has been the proxy for other conditions that have challenged the power relations of the dominant group(s). The contention of this study is that bilingual education and the usage of non-English languages in the public realm has become a substitute for tensions over demographic and cultural change, increased immigration from third world countries, new linguistic-based entitlements, and changing attitudes toward racial and ethnic assimilation. These three sets of conditions have fueled the English-Only movement from the 1970s into the new millennium.

Demographic and cultural change have exacerbated the language controversy, especially in the last three decades of the twentieth century. The United States experienced a large wave of immigration in those decades, one which has called attention to the country's linguistic diversity and multicultural makeup. Since 1980, the number of language-minority Americans has increased more than four times the rate of the overall population. By 1990, nearly one in every six school-aged student regularly spoke a language other than English at home. The minority language population is highly concentrated in a few states. By the mid-1990s, almost 7 percent of the U.S. elementary and secondary students were classified as "limited English proficient." In California, however, which leads the nation in limited English-speaking students, one-fourth of the school enrollment is composed of students whose native language is other than English. In the Los Angeles public school district, nearly half the students—and 60 percent of elementary students—are listed as limited English-speaking (Crawford, 1997a; Schrag, 1999). With the rise in non-English speaking newcomers, "bilingualism" was portrayed as a menace to national unity. In the last two decades of the twentieth century, there has been no more potent symbol of the tension between natives and immigrants than bilingual education. As most of the limited English speakers are people of color, this fact has also fueled the controversy.

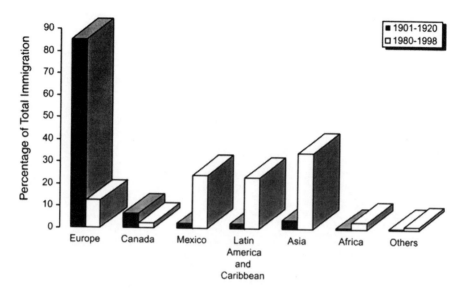

Figure 1.1   Region of Origin of Immigrants, 1901–1921 and 1981–1998. *Source*: U.S. Immigration and Naturalization Service, Statistical Yearbook. 1996 (Washington, D.C.: U.S. Government Printing Office, 1997); table 2 and U.S. Immigration and Naturalization Service 1998 Annual Report (Washington, D.C.: U.S. Government Printing Office, 1999), table 2.

At the dawn of the twentieth century, about 90 percent of immigrants to the United States were from Europe. Between 1820, when immigrant arrivals were first recorded, and 1880, most immigrants were from northern and western European countries. Ireland, Germany, and the United Kingdom led in the number of newcomers. By the end of the nineteenth century and the beginning of the twentieth century, new arrivals to the United States still came from Europe, but the source of immigration shifted to southern and eastern Europe. Large numbers of newcomers were recorded from Italy, Austria-Hungary, Poland, and Russia. By the time of the 1910 Census, immigrants made up nearly 15 percent of the U.S. population (Martin and Midgley, 1994). This was a time of language restriction and nativist movements.

When war erupted in Europe, immigration slowed and remained low throughout World War I. When immigration started to increase in the 1920s, it was sharply curtailed by restrictive immigration legislation and by the Great Depression. Easing of legal restrictions started after World War II, but immigration stayed relatively low until the mid-1960s, when changes in immigration law allowed larger flows of newcomers. In 1965, Congress abolished the national origins quota system, which had favored northwestern Europeans, limited eastern Europeans and those from Mediterranean countries, and virtually excluded Asians. Starting in 1965, family reunification gained precedence over country of origin as a criterion for granting visas. With this change in immigration law, the composition of immigrants changed noticeably (see Figure 1.1 and Table 1.1).

Table 1.1   Immigration by Region/Country of Last Residence

Decade	Total	Europe	Canada	Mexico	Latin America	Asia	Africa	Others
					No. of Immigrants (% of Total)			
1821–1830	143,439	69	2	3	3	0	0	23.0
1831–1840	599,125	83	2	1	2	0	0	11.7
1841–1850	1,713,251	93	2	0	1	0	0	3.1
1851–1860	2,598,214	94	2	0	0	2	0	1.1
1861–1870	2,312,824	89	7	0	0	3	0	0.7
1871–1880	2,812,191	81	14	0	1	4	0	0.4
1881–1890	5,246,613	90	7	0	1	1	0	0.3
1891–1900	3,687,564	96	0	0	1	2	0	0.5
1901–1910	8,795,386	92	2	1	2	4	0	0.5
1911–1920	5,735,811	75	13	4	3	4	0	0.3
1921–1930	4,107,209	60	23	11	3	3	0	0.2
1931–1940	528,431	66	21	4	6	3	0	0.5
1941–1950	1,035,039	60	17	6	12	4	1	1.4
1951–1960	2,515,479	53	15	12	13	6	1	1.0
1961–1970	3,321,677	34	12	14	26	13	1	0.8
1971–1980	4,493,314	18	4	14	26	35	2	0.9
1981–1990	7,338,062	10	2	23	25	37	2	0.6
1991–1998	7,605,088	15	2	25	22	31	4	1.0

Source: U.S. Immigration and Naturalization Service, Statistical Yearbook, 1996 (Washington, D.C.: U.S. Government Printing Office, 1997), table 2 and U.S. Immigration and Naturalization Service 1998 Annual Report (Washington, D.C.: U.S. Government Printing Office, 1999), table 2.

Over 90 percent of immigrants to the United States at the end of the twentieth century were from non-European countries. Mexico, the Philippines, China, Korea, and Vietnam were the top five countries of origin for new immigrants during the 1980s (Martin and Midgley, 1994). Between 1961 and 1995, approximately 2,050,000 immigrants came from Asia and 4,240,000 immigrated from Mexico (U.S. Immigration and Naturalization Service, 1997: table 2, p. 24). The rate of increase in the minority population was nearly twice as fast in the 1980s as in the 1970s. Thus, increased immigration has fostered the perception that newcomers are no longer learning English.

Much of this surge was among Hispanics. The percentage of Hispanics increased 61 percent between 1970 and 1980, 53 percent between 1980 and 1990, and 27 percent between 1990 and 1996. This was compared to only 9 percent, 7 percent, and 4 percent during the same time periods among the total non-Hispanic population. Immigration and high birthrates contribute to the young age structure of Hispanics, relative to the average United States population. The biggest difference between Latinos and non-Hispanic whites is in the proportion of children and elderly. In 1996, more than one-third of Latinos were children under 18, compared with nearly one-fourth of whites. At the other end of the age spectrum, only 5 percent of Hispanics were 65 and over, compared to 14 percent of whites (Pinal and Singer, 1997:13, 17).

Hispanic women tend to have larger families than other Americans in general. This is particularly true of recent immigrants, perhaps reflecting the norms of their native countries. Throughout the 1980s, Hispanic birth rates have been about 50 percent higher than for other Americans.[1] Latinos accounted for 8 percent of the total U.S. population in 1988, but 11 percent of those under 15. In 1988, the median age in the United States as a whole was 32.2 years, compared to only 25.5 years of age among Hispanics (Pinal and Singer, 1997; Valdivieso and Davis, 1988: 3).[1]

A second set of conditions that fueled the language controversy is related to new linguistic-based entitlements. At the same time, Spanish speakers are seen as the target of much hostility and are believed to gain most from language legislation. Perhaps because Hispanics are increasing relative to other immigrant groups, English-Only advocates argue that for the first time a majority of immigrants speak one language—Spanish (Califa, 1989: 312–13). For this reason, most attempts to protect English, although neutral with respect to non-English languages, have been targeted at Spanish speakers (Liebowicz, 1985: 522).

Senator Ralph Yarborough of Texas conceived the Bilingual Education Act of 1968 as a special entitlement for Mexican Americans rather than as a program to serve all linguistic groups, although its original intent was to provide federal aid for schools experimenting with bilingual approaches. With the new act, Senator Yarborough hoped to break the cycle of injustice and poverty in the Southwest. Before the bill was passed, with very little opposition, it was amended to cover all students of limited English-speaking ability, whatever their mother tongue (Crawford, 1992).

Senator Yarborough drew a distinction between voluntary immigrants—who made a deliberate choice to give up their language and culture and assimilate into the American melting pot—and Mexican Americans—who were annexed during time of war, and who were forcibly made to give up their language and culture (Crawford, 1992). This distinction did not appear in the legislation, however. The Bilingual Education Act was not clear in addressing who was supposed to benefit from it. The legislation could be interpreted in more than one way. Some ethnic elites believed the intention was to maintain minority cultures. Others thought that it was primarily a temporary measure to ease the pain of integration in the dominant culture. Because of the ambiguity of the Bilingual Education Act, heated discussion developed between those ethnic leaders advocating minority self-expression and counterforces that believed that education in languages other than English should be for as short a period as possible. This debate, however, did not emerge for more than a decade after the bill was passed.

Another piece of federal legislation that legitimized the use of more than one language was the 1975 amendments to the Voting Rights Act of 1965. The original law suspended the literacy requirements for voting in those Southern states that had systematically disenfranchised African Americans. A related provision prohibited literacy tests for voters who had completed the sixth grade on U.S. soil in a school where the primary classroom language was other than English. The main beneficiaries of this section were Puerto Ricans. A 1921 amendment to the New York state constitution denied the franchise to anyone unable to read English. This law was originally directed against Yiddish-speaking Jews. The 1975 amendments, which were extended by Congress for fifteen years in 1992, narrowly increased the right of language minorities to vote in their mother tongue. The law specified that wherever 5 percent of the voting-age citizens of a political subdivision were members of a "single language minority," and where the illiteracy rate of the minority language group was higher than the national average, election materials were to be provided in that language.[2]

A final major factor in the resurgence of language-based conflict in the United States relates to changing attitudes toward racial and ethnic assimilation. In the final three decades of the twentieth century, after passage of the 1965 immigration legislation, the notion of America as a melting pot was challenged. Many groups were frustrated by the failure to achieve full assimilation, equal status, and economic equity. In response to the civil rights movement, American social and legal systems moved in the direction of increased civil rights and protection for groups and individuals, and these led to several opposing movements, including the development of nativist organizations for the advancement of Official English, referendums restricting access to social services for newcomers, state laws making English the official language, court cases, and prejudice toward non-English speakers. By November 2000, 25 states passed laws making English the official language, more than at any time in American history.[4] In education, the workplace, the voting booth, and other arenas of government entitlements, the courts were forced to arbitrate the civil rights of language minorities. Many Americans felt threatened by the impeding shift in political power relations and resent paying taxes to benefit immigrants and their children. In general, there has been a sense of vulnerability that has torn away at America's sense of security and identity.

A significant portion of the population has the perception that the linguistic hegemony of English in the United States is at an end and that many non-English speakers, encouraged by government policies, retain their native tongues. This sense of insecurity and attempt to redefine the American identity has manifested itself in several ways. Many groups push for stricter immigration requirements. There is an escalation of conflict between foreign and domestic ethnic groups. Perhaps, most visibly, there has been an increase in language policy movements. The 1995 referendum in Canada over sovereignty in Quebec has brought more attention to issues of language in the United States and intensified the growing sense that the linguistic and political unity of America is seriously threatened.

The renewed hostility toward language minorities in the last two decades of the twentieth century caught Americans by surprise. Language was again at the forefront of a new form of ethnic confrontation and cultural nationalism. In response to this perception of linguistic instability, a number of groups, such as U.S. English and English First, have openly advocated the establishment of legislation that will ensure the status of English in the United States by legislating it as the official language of the country. The intent of most Official English laws is to enjoin the government from providing services in languages other than English. A critical question is why laws declaring English as the "official" language have suddenly appeared on both the federal and state levels, when the United States has existed without federal official language legislation for more than two hundred years.

How is language conflict related to the search for a national identity and cultural nationalism, which has been gripping many states at the end of the millennium?

National Identity, Language, and Nationalism

The United States is conspicuous by its absence from most studies of nationalism (Grant, 1996),[3] particularly the way language has defined national identity. Whereas the roots of the current wave of cultural nationalism are very similar in the United States and many countries of western Europe, the way in which they are played into the national consciousness depends on the stage already set in terms of an "imagined community" (Anderson, 1991; Brubaker, 1992). The "imagined" linguistic homogeneity of the United States has influenced the current search for an American identity. In 1977, Mackey observed, "The popular image of the United States as a nation united by one language and one culture has always been illusory. It is an ideal engendered by the now outmoded values of nineteenth-century nationalism" (Kloss, 1977: vii). This myth has resurfaced at the end of the twentieth century.

Language has become increasingly important in mobilizing ethnic groups. Most theorists agree that language is an important factor in modern nationalism. Benedict Anderson (1991) sees language as essential to the origin of nationalism. The principal material precondition for nationalism is what he calls "print-capitalism," meaning commercial printing on a widespread scale. Print-capitalism spreads the idea of the nation and the ideology of nationalism, both within one nation and to other parts of the world. Printing standardizes languages as it aids the development of capitalism and the state. Through this medium, the publishing of dictionaries and literature strengthens vernacular languages more generally. In this way, nations are "imagined" by many people, and linguistic nationalism takes root.

The importance of language in nationalist movements is largely confined to Europe and its former colonies, and, to a lesser extent, the Middle East. The notion that nations are really language groups and that nationalism is a linguistic movement is therefore primarily a Western idea. The idea of a national language developed in Europe, particularly Germany and France, as the touchstone of nationality and national culture. Anthony Smith believes that language follows the growth of nationalistic fervor; it does not create it. For nationalists, language becomes a means of justifying their convictions (Smith, 1971: 149–50).

Joshua Fishman (1989) argues that language becomes part of the secular religion, binding society together. Language is a powerful instrument for promoting internal cohesion and providing an ethnic or national identity. It contributes to values, identity, and a sense of peoplehood. A common vernacular also establishes effective boundaries between "ingroups" and "outgroups." Furthermore, language is an important variable in power relations between dominant and subordinate groups. In Noam Chomsky's (1979: 191) words, "questions of language are basically questions of power."

The English-Only movement in the United States is an example of the renewal of cultural nationalism in countries that had experienced nationalism before the

Second World War and were thought to be immune from its influence (Smith, 1991: 138). Unlike earlier waves of ethnic nationalism, based on ethnic autonomist and separatist movements, a new wave of cultural nationalism is primarily concerned with a redefinition of national identity. This movement is evident in settler states— in Anglo Canada and the United States, as well as in Western Europe—especially in Germany, France, Britain, and Switzerland—countries that are faced with integrating significant numbers of immigrants, migrants, and foreign workers.

Perhaps the central difficulty in the study of nations and nationalism has been the problem of finding adequate and agreed definitions of the key concepts (Hutchinson and Smith, 1994: 3–4). In the context of this book, nationalism takes on a special meaning. I am concerned primarily with the cultural content of nationalism. Thus, I shall define cultural nationalism as an ideology and form of behavior, one which includes a cultural doctrine and social movements aimed at maintaining identity on behalf of a population that believes itself to be a nation— whether real or imagined. This can be differentiated from a political definition of nationalism, which is primarily concerned with the political process of forming nations and nation-states and movements for attaining and maintaining autonomy—as one can observe, for example, in Quebec and Puerto Rico. The aim of cultural nationalists as opposed to political nationalists is the moral regeneration of societies, such as that in the United States (Hutchinson, 1994: 124).

The concept of national identity, which is closely associated with nationalism, is essentially subjective (see Renan, 1970; Weber, 1978). As used in this book, national identity refers to a sense of belonging to—but not necessarily reinforced by— a common culture, customs, language, heritage, and political institutions. At the same time, national identity consists of a sense of distinctiveness from other people who may or may not share certain of these characteristics. Cultural pluralism relates to the willingness on the part of some dominant groups to permit cultural and linguistic variability within the range still consonant with national unity and security. This is frequently the immediate policy of an ultimate assimilationist approach. The current discussion over language rights and cultural pluralism is a debate about national identity and what it means to be an American in the late twentieth and early twenty-first century. In the American context, controversy over Official English and bilingualism is about competing models of Americanism.

Despite a general perception that non-English-speaking immigrants are streaming uncontrollably into the United States, resulting in increased nationalistic and nativistic sentiment, few works have examined why language relations are a major source of political schism. At the end of the twentieth century, the political, social, and legal aspects of speaking non-English languages connected to a number of issues, including racial politics and civil rights, immigration policy, ethnic diversity, cultural pluralism, and national identity. These issues have generated some of the most important domestic debates of the late twentieth century. Thus, at the beginning of the new millennium, it is particularly important to analyze and understand this largely forgotten chapter in American politics. According to Werner Sollars (1997), language continues to be a blind spot in the debates about cultural pluralism in the United States. Serious discussion of language diversity and language conflict requires answers to a number of pertinent questions:

- What are the roots of language policy and conflict in the United States? Were they present prior to the nation's founding, or are they of more recent origin?
- Is the push toward "English-Only" a new movement, or is it merely ethnic intolerance clothed in a new form? How is it similar or different from the Americanization movement that came before it?
- To what extent is there a right to work or to be educated in languages other than English? Is the United States becoming a "tower of Babel" with the right to be able to work and be educated in tongues other than English?
- To what extent do attitudes differ between Hispanics and Anglos on language issues and core values? Is the situation in the United States comparable to that in Canada, a bilingual confederation confronted with separation because of ethnic and linguistic tensions?
- How can we explain recent cases of language conflict in Puerto Rico and California? Is language becoming the new dividing line in American society?

Organization of the Book

The second chapter of *The Politics of Language* traces the historical roots of American language policy. Starting with the attitudes of the founding fathers, it sketches the development of early language policy. The founding fathers were pragmatists on the language question. The Continental Congress accommodated politically significant groups of non-English-speaking immigrants in an attempt to gain their support and to promote loyalty toward the cause of independence. During the first century and a half of American history, forced linguistic assimilation was more likely among non-white groups than among white immigrants.

Linguistically differentiated ethnic groups have emerged primarily through conquest and immigration. Conquered ethnic groups, which have been predominantly groups of color, fared much worse in the United States than white immigrant groups. The federal government pursued a goal of cultural as well as physical containment toward Native Americans. English was imposed on Puerto Ricans through a policy of "Americanization." Despite an initial majority population of Mexican-Americans, both California and New Mexico were only admitted as states when English speakers were the dominant group. Cultural nationalism in the United States roughly coincides with the nineteenth-century tide of romantic nationalism and ethnic identification in Europe.

The third chapter analyzes the politics of exclusion, emphasizing a comparison of the Americanization movement in the early part of the twentieth century with the contemporary English-Only or Official English movement in the last two decades of the twentieth century. Opposition to immigrants is not a new phenomenon; every new group of immigrants that has come to the United States has been denounced at the time of their entry. In time of high immigration, economic insecurity, and high unemployment, there is a particularly low tolerance for group differences. The United States has followed cyclical patterns of welcoming and dramatically rejecting language minorities and immigrants. When times are good and there is a shortage of unskilled labor or other gaps in the labor market immigrants are more accepted than in bad economic times. When the economy slumps, native citizens are more likely to condemn large immigrant groups for taking away "our" jobs and using public welfare. There is a general perception that citizens are losing ground while paying taxes to benefit those defined as the "other." Americans are particularly concerned about providing welfare benefits for immigrants. Many Americans, especially in states with a high proportion of immigrants, such as California, feel threatened by a shift in political power and are dissatisfied with the public schools.

The fourth chapter analyzes the legal status of languages other than English. The legal effect of state Official English laws remains unclear. Many of the state laws are very broad. Thus far, courts have ruled that they are primarily of symbolic value. If the laws are strictly enforced, they could deprive language minorities of important rights in the workplace, voting booth, and the education arena. In general, English-Only forces have been more successful in using the laws politically than in the courtroom. For example, in California, the passage in 1986 of Proposition 63—the Official English constitutional amendment—was employed to pressure the governor into vetoing bilingual education legislation. Proposition 227, which was passed by a significant majority of California voters in 1998, severely restricted bilingual education classes in the state. Many issues concerning language minorities are misunderstood. Is there an entitlement to speak and be served in languages other than English? Do citizens have the right to vote in a language other than English? Must the federal government publish tax, social security, and other information in "foreign" languages? Are states obliged to offer bilingual education?

The fifth chapter examines group perceptions and attitudes among Anglos and Hispanics toward bilingualism and making English the official language, as well as attitudes of Americans toward bilingualism and immigration. By analyzing current polls on Hispanic and Anglo attitudes toward second language learning and maintenance, a clearer picture will emerge with respect to the complex interrelationship between language and ethnic identity.

Chapter 6 is devoted to Canada, with special emphasis on Quebec. Grappling with questions of language diversity, Americans are prone to draw superficial parallels with Canada. U.S. English, an organization committed to making English the official language of the United States, has exploited this ignorance of the Canadian language situation. In a booklet published by U.S. English, entitled *Democracy or Babel?* (Peña, 1991), the author draws an analogy between Quebecois separatists and calls for bilingualism from some Hispanic leaders. Without understanding the Canadian situation, it is easy to equate language diversity with conflict and language homogeneity with domestic peace.

Canada and the United States differ significantly in language relations. As Canada developed from colony to country, the French language became more entrenched, even though English maintained a dominant position. The United States was home to many languages, but English became the undisputed national language, making the United States—unofficially—a unilingual state. While comparisons are frequently drawn between the large Spanish-speaking populations in the United States and the French-speakers in Canada, they fail to consider the different positions of the minority languages in the two countries.

Chapter 7 analyzes language policy in Switzerland. Unlike the United States, both Canada and Switzerland recognize official multilingualism. The two countries, however, have made widely divergent accommodations to maintaining more than one language and provide interesting contrasts to the United States. Switzerland has been a stable plurilingual country for over one and a half centuries. By examining these two plurilingual advanced democracies, this study will address some of the social, political, and legal alternatives and dilemmas facing the United States as it enters the twenty-first century. An examination of the American experience with multilingualism in comparative terms, including its strengths and weaknesses, makes for a more insightful understanding of that experience.

The penultimate chapter analyzes three recent cases of language conflict. Each became a substitute for a political agenda far beyond language itself. In the 1990s, the English-Only movement gained widespread political momentum, often with racial overtones. After the Oakland School District announced that Ebonics was the normal language of many African Americans in the district, the resolution generated outrage, misconceptions, and public outcry. The Oakland Board of Education was accused of classifying Ebonics-speaking students as bilingual so it would be able to apply for more federal funds. Race, class, and language quickly become distorted in the public mind.

U.S. English, the nation's largest English-Only lobby, testified before Congress on Puerto Rican self-determination. The issue was whether an island where 98 percent of the population speaks Spanish should adopt English as their sole official language. Lack of speaking English, identification as "Puerto Ricans" rather than as "Americans," and possible conflict between Puerto Rican and U.S. culture were suddenly linked together. If Puerto Rico would be admitted as a state, they announced, we could be creating our own Quebec. How long would it be before the 329 languages spoken in the United States also demanded equal treatment? In California, a June 1998 primary ballot measure that largely eliminated bilingual education in public schools received overwhelming support. Is the nation's dominant language endangered by the encroachment of other tongues? Are we experiencing creeping multilingualism in the United States? Chapter 8 examines the politics and facts behind bilingual education in California at the end of the twentieth century.

The concluding chapter provides a framework for understanding language politics in the United States. Historical forces at the end of the nineteenth century set the stage for the recent linguistic conflict by identifying accentless English as an essential component of loyalty to the nation and American identity. Many other factors have fueled the late-twentieth-century version of cultural nationalism, including massive international population movements; rapid, fundamental, and socioeconomic transformations; an attack on welfare state programs; and nativistic elites who have been able to promote a vague program and legislation based on a mythical monolingual past.

2

HISTORICAL BACKGROUND OF LANGUAGE PROTECTION AND RESTRICTION

English-Only legislation first appeared in 1981 as a constitutional English Language Amendment. The measure has never come to a congressional vote, however. Since 1991, English-Only advocates have promoted a statutory form of Official English, which would apply only to the federal government (Crawford 2000). The Constitution of the United States does not contain a provision giving official status to English. Neither the Articles of Confederation nor the Constitution made English the "official" or "national" language of the United States, nor has any subsequent federal law explicitly legislated English as an official language (Kloss, 1977: 28–33). There have been several recent attempts to pass Official English legislation. English may be the common, de facto national language of the United States; however, it has never been the exclusive language of the country. Chapter 2 provides a historical interpretation of the rising dominance of English—in spite of the fact that, in its short history, the United States has probably been host to more bilingual people than any other country in the world (Hakuta, 1986). The founding fathers and later policy makers held ambivalent attitudes toward languages other than English, ranging from pragmatic acceptance to deliberate policies of forced extermination and assimilation.

Views of the Founding Fathers

During the Colonial period, German, Spanish, and French colonists—among others—brought their language and culture with them to the New World. There also were numerous Native American languages already spoken in the Americas. In the early period of the United States, between 1770 and 1820, the founding fathers proposed different solutions and held diverse attitudes toward those who spoke languages other than English. The choice of a single language during this early period as the official mode of communication in the new nation was never legislated (Heath, 1976). Although the authors of the Constitution ultimately decided not to endow English with a special legal status, they assumed that English would develop as a common language in the United States.

Germans were the nation's largest non-English-language-speaking group at the beginning of the Republic; therefore, they attracted the most attention from the founders of the new country. In several writings, Benjamin Franklin expressed alarm at the increase in Pennsylvania of the German-speaking population, which accounted for approximately one-third of that colony's population. In letters to James Parker, a colonial printer, and Peter Collinson, a British member of Parliament, he berated the increase in numbers and ignorance of the new German immigrants: "The Observation concerning the Importation of Germans in too great Numbers into Pennsylvania is, I believe a very just one. This will in a few Years become a German Colony: Instead of their Learning our Language, we must learn their's, or live as in a foreign country" (letter to Parker on March 20, 1751, cited in Labaree [1961: 120]).

Franklin was particularly concerned with the inability of the Germans to assimilate and subscribe to independence, as well as to the American political culture of the colonies.

> Not being used to Liberty, (they) know not how to make modest use of it. . . . Few of their children in the Country learn English; they import many Books from Germany; and of the six printing houses in the Province, two are entirely English; two half German half English, and two entirely English; They have one German Newspaper and one half German. Advertisements, intended to be general are now printed in German and English; the Signs in our Streets have inscriptions in both languages, and in some places in only German: They begin of late to make all their Bonds and other legal Writings in their own Language, which (though I think it ought not to be) are allowed good in our Courts, where the German business so increases that there is continued need of Interpreters; and I suppose in a few years they will also be necessary in the Assembly, to tell one half of the Legislators what the other half say . . . (letter to Collinson, May 9, 1753, cited in Labaree, [1961: 494])

In his *Observations on the Increase of Mankind*, Franklin's concern in 1755 with the large German-speaking population of Pennsylvania is again evident: "Why should the Palatine boors be suffered to swarm in our Settlements, and by herding together, establish their Language and Manners to the exclusion of ours? Why should Pennsylvania, founded by the English, become a Colony of *Aliens*, who will shortly be so numerous as to Germanize us instead of our Anglifying them?" (Wagner, 1981: 31).

James Crawford (1989: 29) observed that Franklin was apparently embarrassed by his xenophobic remarks and subsequently deleted this passage from later editions of his writings. Franklin, like many of his compatriots, held an ambivalent view toward language minorities. In 1738, he founded one of the earliest German-language newspapers in America, *Die Philadelphische Zeitung*, although it failed after two issues. Toward the end of his life, perhaps because the threat of Germanization had dwindled, Franklin became a supporter of German-language higher education (Weaver, 1970).

Another founding father, Thomas Jefferson, took a different view toward language minorities. He was a firm believer in the importance of language learning. At William and Mary College in Williamsburg, he learned to read Greek, Latin, French, Italian, and Spanish (Lipscomb, 1904: vol. 19, 246). In a letter to T. M. Randolph Jr. from Paris in July 1787, Jefferson encouraged Randolph to learn French and Spanish—French because of its obvious importance in diplomatic affairs and scientific publications, and Spanish because "our connection with Spain is already important, and will become daily more so. Besides this, the ancient part of American history is written chiefly in Spanish" (Lipscomb, 1904: vol. 6,167).[1] Although Jefferson believed in the utility of modern language learning, he also was concerned that immigrants coming from absolute monarchies would be unable to adjust to America and would transmit their language to their children. The founders needed and wanted immigrants to conquer the continent, but they wanted them, in the phrase of John Quincy Adams, "to cast off the European skin" (Rischin, 1966: 47). In 1807, Jefferson (then president) proposed settling thirty thousand Americans in the newly acquired Louisiana Territory to prevent the area from retaining the French language and legal code system (Baron, 1990). By contrast, Jefferson believed that Germans, because of their inability to speak English, would make ideal candidates for settling the Western lands. In a letter to Colonel Richard Claiborne on August 8, 1787, he observed that the best tenants for Western lands would be "foreigners, who do not speak the language." Since they were unable to communicate with others, "they confine themselves to their farms and their families, compare their present state to what it was in Europe, and find great reason to be contented." Jefferson believed that the Germans were best suited for this role, as well as the best for the landlords, because they were the most available and "do best for themselves" (Lipscomb, 1904: 253). Jefferson was a staunch believer in white Anglo-Saxon supremacy, as were several other leading figures in the revolutionary generation (Ellis, 1997: 297).

Benjamin Rush, a member of the Continental Congress and a signer of the Declaration of Independence, was the most vigorous proponent of the maintenance of languages other than English. A strong supporter of a German college in Pennsylvania, he resisted the argument "of some narrow-minded people" who argued that if the Germans had a college of their own it would be a way of maintaining their language in the country. He believed that by "teaching and learning in their own language" the Germans would acquire a more rapid knowledge of the English language. Furthermore, he hoped that the German language would not be completely lost to Pennsylvania: "It will be the inlet into the state of all the learning of one of the wisest nations of the world" (Butterfield, 1951: 365).

Rush appeared to anticipate the argument made by many current opponents of bilingual education. With respect to the objection that a German college would "tend to render the Germans a distinct people from other citizens of the state," he responded that it is "*ignorance* and *prejudice* only that keeps men of different countries and religions apart." Rush believed that a German college would remove these prejudices and open the eyes of the Germans to the importance of the English language. In fact, he took it for granted that one of the first teachers that would be appointed for the German college would be a professor of the English language (Butterfield, 1951: 365, 366).

Part of Rush's support of a German college was no doubt opportunistic. He was eager to win German support for the Republican party in Pennsylvania. This, however, was not his only motivation. In general, Rush was a friend of the German immigrants. Benjamin Rush served as a charter trustee of Franklin College in Lancaster. Leaders such as Rush recognized that if government legally pressured groups to give up their native languages, the resistance of such groups would provoke hostility rather than legitimate the ideas of democracy and republicanism.

Many myths surround the importance of languages other than English. One myth has it that only one vote kept German from being the national language in the late-eighteenth-century legislature. The "Muhlenberg legend," however, greatly exaggerated the claims of German. The accurate history of this incident is that a group of Virginia Germans requested that some laws of the United States be issued in both German and English. A congressional committee favored the proposal, but when it came to a House vote, it was rejected 42 to 41. Frederick August Muhlenberg may have cast the deciding vote, although congressional records failed to record this (Heath, 1976). Other legends—circulated during the Revolution and in the mid-nineteenth century—suggested that French would become the language of the United States. A British etymologist, Sir Herbert Croft, wrote in a letter in 1797 that Americans had considered "revenging themselves on England by rejecting its language and adopting that of France (Heath and Mandabach, 1983: 94). As Heath and Mandabach observe, "In spite of these myths portraying French, German, or Latin as the national tongue, there was never serious doubt about the issue, and there was never any official declaration of the status of English" (1983: 94).

Most of the founding fathers probably considered language an individual matter in the new Republic, as long as the newcomers did not want to retain the use of their language for a prolonged period of time. It is likely that the founding fathers were pragmatists on the language question. The Continental Congress accommodated politically significant groups of non-English-speaking immigrants in an attempt to gain their support and to promote loyalty toward the cause of Independence (Crawford, 1989; Health, 1976). The Articles of Confederation were printed in German, and at different times federal documents appeared in French, German, Dutch, and Swedish (Kloss, 1977).[2]

The new federal Constitution was completely silent about a national or official language. In fact, the matter was never debated in the Continental Congress. Nevertheless, the ambivalence expressed by the founding fathers toward foreigners revealed a dilemma, one which has persisted through the end of the twentieth century. There continues to be a struggle between the notion that foreigners constitute a definite asset to society (or at least cause it no undue strain) and the counterview that foreigners threaten society because of their preservation of native ways—including use of their home language—and therefore encourage dissension and social division. The founding fathers and individual colonialists often expressed both points of view and in so doing illustrated the dualism built into the American experience.

It is significant that the authors of the Federalist papers—John Jay, James Madison, and Alexander Hamilton—did not even mention what would now be called ethnic and linguistic diversity. Even though the first census in the United States showed that the English and their descendants constituted slightly less than half of the population, Madison said nothing about ethnicity or cultural pluralism in his two essays on diversity (Fuchs, 1990). The clearest evidence that the authors of the Federalist papers assumed that all immigrants would assimilate to the English language and the American way of life appears in the Second Federalist Paper. John Jay wrote, "Providence has been pleased to give this one connected country to one united people—a people descended from the same ancestors, speaking the same language, professing the same religion, attached to the same principles of government . . . " (Rossiter, 1961: 38).

Attempts to Standardize the American English Language

As early as 1780, John Adams predicted that English would occupy a dominant role among world languages, "because the increasing population in America . . . will . . . force their language into general use, in spite of all the obstacles that may be thrown their way" (Baron, 1990: 2). To guarantee this outcome, Adams believed that English should be standardized to retain the purity of the language. While on a diplomatic mission to Europe during the Revolutionary War, he wrote "A Letter to the President of Congress," dispatched from Amsterdam on September 5, 1780, which proposed establishing an English-language academy (Adams, 1992: 31–33). Adams desired to establish a "public institution for refining, correcting, improving and ascertaining the English language." He hoped that such an institution would have a beneficial effect on the union of the states and would serve as a standard for all persons in the new country. Adams believed English was destined to be "in the next and succeeding centuries more generally the language of the world than Latin was in the last or French is in the present." The language academy carried with it another political mission as well, which included the dissemination of American views of "liberty, prosperity and glory" (Adams, 1992: 32). Like many of his European contemporaries, Adams was convinced that "the form of government has an influence upon language, and language in turn influences not only the form of government, but the temper, sentiments, and manners of the people" (Baron, 1990: 28). Therefore, Adams saw the need for the American language and government to be codified and expanded to other nations (Heath, 1976).

Adams's proposal met with little success. It never emerged from the congressional committee. The Continental Congress was not convinced of the importance of the academy to American goals. In general, nationally sponsored cultural institutions and other centralizing institutions faced severe obstacles during the early years of the republic (Heath, 1976). The idea of government regulating American speech was deemed to be incompatible with the spirit of freedom of speech in the United States (Marshall, 1986).

Noah Webster also tried to promote language standardization through his *American Spelling Book* issued in 1783 and *American Dictionary of the English Language* published in 1828. Webster sought to establish a system of American—as opposed to British—English in the New World: "Great Britain, whose children we are, and whose language we speak, should no longer be our standard; for the taste of her writers is already corrupted, and her language on the decline" (Webster, 1992: 34). He believed that only through the establishment of schools and some uniformity in the use of books could one preserve the purity of the American tongue. Webster's efforts at standardization of the American language were comparatively unsuccessful at that time in American history. Webster's *American Dictionary* sold only twenty-five hundred copies, and his work drew little praise during his lifetime (Heath, 1976).

Despite Webster's inability to convince the American public to adopt his spelling books, grammars, and dictionaries as models of correctness during his lifetime, his impact was still considerable. Perhaps his most important legacy was to begin establishing the connection between language and Americanism. This nexus between language and nationality, however, was not firmly laid until the end of the nineteenth century, and is an important factor in the recent upsurge of linguistic nationalism in the United States today. But there is also another tradition in the United States, which tolerated—and perhaps even promoted—languages other than English.

The Early Bilingual Tradition

During the nation's first century there was, in general, a laissez-faire attitude toward language issues. In the early years of the republic, two early themes surfaced with respect to language policy—pragmatism and universalism (Heath, 1976, 1981). Non-English speakers from Europe typically established parochial schools and churches in which German, Swedish, Norwegian, and other languages were spoken. In the late seventeenth century, bilingualism was common among members of both the working classes and the middle professional and business classes, especially in New York, Pennsylvania, New Jersey, and Delaware. German-speaking Americans in Philadelphia operated schools as early as 1694. In the mid-eighteenth century, newspaper advertisements made frequent mention of black and white runaway servants with proficiency in more than one language (Crawford, 1989; Read, 1937).

In some rural areas where Germans were heavily concentrated, lessons in public schools were conducted entirely in German. This pattern was evident in parts of Wisconsin, Ohio, Pennsylvania, Missouri, Minnesota, and the Dakota Territory (Perlmann, 1990). The German-language schools were a reasonable—and probably an inevitable—response in areas with few English-speaking settlers and teachers rather than a conscious effort at bilingual or monolingual non-English schools (Schlossman, 1983).

Most of the earliest school laws made no mention of the language to be employed in the public schools. If the language question was raised, political pressure at the polls was important. The Germans in Ohio, for example, gave support to the Democrats in the 1836 election. Charging that they had paid taxes for public school support and that the Democratic party owed them recognition, the Germans fought to exercise influence on the course of study in the Ohio public schools. The Germans did not want English to be excluded but for German to be taught as well. In response to this demand, the Ohio legislature passed a law that allowed German to be taught in those districts where a large German population resided (Faust, 1909).

As the number of newcomers increased in response to an open immigration policy in the 1830s and 1840s, Midwestern states began to accommodate the new waves of immigrants. Bilingual instruction was common throughout the mid-nineteenth century in both private and public schools. It was explicitly authorized by law in states such as Ohio (English-German, 1839) and Louisiana (French-English, 1847) (Kloss, 1977: 84). The German influence in Pennsylvania was so substantial that German schools received public funding well into the nineteenth century (Conklin and Lourie, 1983).

In the mid-1800s, public and private German-English schools were also operating in cities such as Baltimore, Cincinnati, Cleveland, Indianapolis, Milwaukee, and St. Louis (Crawford, 1989). By 1900, according to Heinz Kloss (1977), six hundred thousand children—approximately 4 percent of public and parochial school students—were receiving instruction at least partly in German. Writing in 1909, Albert Faust noted that the Lutheran synods collectively had over twenty-one hundred schools, about twenty-five hundred teachers, and over one hundred thousand pupils, who spent at least part of their day learning German. In several cities, programs were developed that bore at least some resemblance to late-twentieth-century bilingual programs. In Cincinnati, where native Germans constituted nearly two-thirds of all the foreign-born residents in 1900 (Faust, 1909) some schools had a German-English curriculum, with a half day spent on German-language instruction and a half day spent on everything else, including English language instruction. The program was primarily intended for the early grades, but was available through the sixth grade. In Indianapolis, German was taught for one period a day in the early grades, then used as the language of instruction for geography and American history in grades five through eight. Although the programs were not without their critics, the Cincinnati program existed for three-quarters of a century (from the 1840s to World War I) and the Indianapolis program for about thirty-five years (from 1882 until World War I). These dual-language programs, however, were unique. Most major American cities did not adopt the Cincinnati model. School programs involving the German language were usually restricted to one period a day of instruction—from twenty minutes to an hour a day (Perlmann, 1990).

German schools proliferated in other parts of the country. The first bilingual public school in New York City was established in 1837. In 1838, German Lutheran parochial schools, which had instruction in German, were converted to public schools in Pennsylvania. In 1886, the Chicago board of education succumbed to pressure from the politically powerful German immigrants and decided to set up a

German-language school in each area of the city. In 1870, a German school that taught exclusively in German was founded in Denver. Oregon, Maryland, Iowa, Kentucky, Ohio, Minnesota, and Nebraska had laws that allowed bilingual education at least in some instances (Rothstein, 1998: 104–105).

In addition to a substantial bilingualism tradition, there were also strong forces toward linguistic assimilation, both voluntary and involuntary. As early as the mid-eighteenth century, for example, the Dutch often lost their mother tongue and adopted English by the second or third generation On a trip up the Hudson in 1744, Andrew Hamilton observed the passengers spoke such a medley of Dutch and English, which he described as a "Tower of Babel." In 1750, Peter Kalm, a Swedish botanist, noted that the majority of those of Dutch descent, were quickly succumbing to the English language. The younger generation scarcely ever spoke anything but English, and many became offended if they were taken for Dutch because they preferred to pass for English (Wertenbaker, 1937). Linguistic assimilation was also evident in a petition submitted by the parishioners of one New York City church in 1762, in which the minister was asked to speak English. Kalm observed the same tendency of the Swedes to voluntarily adopt English, often by the second generation (Wright, 1957: 49). Another observer in Maryland found that "contrary to the expectations of those who believed that the diverse origins of American would beget a polyglot tongue, the language of the immediate descendants of so promiscuous an ancestry was 'perfectly uniform" (Krauss, 1949: 261).

Not all groups adopted English as rapidly. The Dutch and Swedes appear to have voluntarily adopted the English language in two or, at the most, three generations. The Germans, by contrast, maintained their culture and language much longer. This was especially true where there were sizable German-speaking communities such as in Pennsylvania and some Midwestern states, reinforced by new immigration. Language maintenance was related to the recentness of immigration, as well as to the size and concentration of the German-speaking population. During the Revolutionary period, the German immigrant population swelled to over a quarter of a million (Castellanos, 1992).

The German schools raised issues about the process of transition to English in a way that is similar to bilingual programs today. Debates about language maintenance as compared to the sink-or-swim approach were common. The issues raised by bilingual education were typically resolved in the area of ethnic politics rather than through sound educational policy. The discussions did not focus on the psychological advantages or disadvantages of bilingual training for children. These were not the central issues. According to Joel Perlmann, "The issues had to do with being a good American and creating a good America: issues of national self-image, the national future, views of immigrants, and the immigrants' view of themselves" (1990: 31). Some Americans thought that the best policy for Americanizing the immigrant was to deny German a place in the schools. Others maintained that permitting German instruction would keep the Germans in the public schools and ease their transition to American culture. The Germans themselves were very vocal in their belief that their children should be taught in their own language in the public schools.

Forced Language Assimilation: The Color of Language Politics

Indigenous Languages

In contrast to the experience of white linguistic minorities, for Native Americans, assimilation to English was coerced. From the onset, Europeans did what they could to eradicate Native American languages. The colonists set out to "civilize" and Christianize the Indians, forcing them to assimilate to Western civilization and to speak English. In 1802, Congress made provisions for the expenditure of funds, not to exceed $15,000 per year, to promote "civilization among the aborigines." This action stood as the only indication that Congress recognized responsibility for Indian education for over a decade. Then, in 1819, Congress enacted a provision allowing the president to employ "capable persons . . . for teaching (Indian) children in reading, writing, arithmetic . . . for the purpose of . . . introducing among them the habits and art of civilization" (Leibowitz, 1971: 64).

During the next fifty years, these schools continued to be maintained either exclusively by missionaries or with the joint support of missionaries and the federal government. Provisions in 1802 and 1819 made no specific mention of the English language. Both provisions, however, attempted to promote "civilization." There was an implicit assumption that the English language was the "civilized" tongue and the Native American languages were "barbaric" languages.

Because the Native Americans were thought of as "uncivilized," it was not inconsistent with this policy to move them off their land into more "civilized circumstances." Writing in 1817, President James Monroe stated that "The hunter or savage state requires a greater extent of territory to sustain it than is compatible with the progress and just claim of civilized life . . . and must yield to it" (Senate Special Subcommittee on Indian Education and Welfare; quoted in Leibowitz, 1971: 69). Initiated by President Andrew Jackson in 1830, Congress adopted the Indian Removal Act, which forcibly removed tribes west of the Mississippi River.

Confinement of Native Americans on reservations was the cornerstone of federal Indian policy during the nineteenth century. The story of the Nez Percé is typical of federal treatment of Native Americans, especially in the Western territories. The first treaty with the Nez Percé was signed in 1855, granting them the majority of their traditional territory. This treaty only lasted a few years. With the discovery of gold in 1860, a large influx of white prospectors, speculators, and settlers invaded Nez Percé land. In 1862, the Nez Percé Indian federal agent urged negotiation of a new treaty "which would secure peace between the Nez Percé and the crowds of whites who have gone upon their reservation in search of the gold which there abounds" (Report of CIA 1862, quoted in Park, 1982: 55). Because the federal government was unable to keep white settlers and prospectors off Nez Percé territory, in 1863 a new treaty that reduced the tribe's reservation to about 10 percent of the acreage allowed in the 1855 treaty was negotiated. This reduction in reservation size was defended as a means of opening and securing additional territory for white settlers and as a "measure necessary to protect Indians from the evils resulting from unregulated contact with whites." Both the treaties of 1855 and 1863 "were based on the desire to make the tribe more subject to management so a policy of forced assimilation could be carried out" (Park, 1982: 55).

Forced assimilation also included the extermination of Native American languages. In 1868, the "Peace Commission," composed of the Commissioner of Indian Affairs and a group of generals—including General Sherman—set the tone for later Native American language policy. The commission report noted that Indians had to learn the English language in order to reduce conflict between whites and Native Americans and to achieve the benefits of civilization.

> Now by educating the children of these tribes in the English language these differences would have disappeared and civilization would have followed at once. Nothing then would have been left but the antipathy of race, and that, too is always softened in the beams of a higher civilization. . . . Through the sameness of language is produced sameness of sentiment and thought, customs and habits are molded and assimilated in the same way, and thus in the process of time the differences producing trouble would have been gradually obliterated. . . . In the difference of language today lies two-thirds of our trouble. (Prucha 1973: 198)

Beginning in the 1870s, the United States government began forcing Native American children into boarding schools and punishing them for using their own dialects (Park, 1982). The goal of the schools run by the Bureau of Indian Affairs (BIA) was to break up the use of Indian dialects and to substitute the English language. In 1887, the BIA made this policy clear, announcing: "Instruction of Indians in the vernacular is not only of no use to them but is detrimental to the cause of education and civilization and will not be permitted in any Indian school. . . . The impracticability, if not impossibility of civilizing Indians of this country in any tongue but our own would seem obvious" (Baron, 1990: 165).

The boarding school dominated Native American education for the next fifty years. Only a few mission schools taught in a combination of English and native languages. In most cases only English-speaking teachers were employed. Often Indian children were punished if they lapsed into native languages (Baron, 1990). By the 1920s, there were seventy-seven Indian boarding schools, "whose express purpose was the complete assimilation of Native American children, remolding their conception of life and their attitudes toward the land" (Hernández-Chávez, 1994: 145). Children from different tribes were forcibly taken from their parents and transported great distances. Tribal religions and culture, as well as native languages, were suppressed. Native American children were taught to speak, read, and write—as well as dress and act—like white children. The consequence of these government policies was cultural disintegration, a legacy that is associated today with Native American poverty, alcoholism, and educational failure (Reyhner, 1992: 61–62; Spring, 1996).

At the end of the twentieth century, there were about two hundred different Native American North American languages still spoken by the indigenous population, out of over three hundred precontact languages. The viability of most of these languages, however, remains in question. Michael Krauss (1996) estimates that 175 of the 210 languages spoken in the United States (the other thirty-five are spoken only in Canada) only about twenty, or 11 percent, are still being taught to children by their elders in the traditional way. In Canada, which has been somewhat more tolerant of non-English languages, about 30 percent of the indigenous languages are still spoken by children. The other 89 percent of Native American languages in the United States have experienced varying degrees of language devastation. Krauss labels continuing language transfer from parents to children "Category A." It is now the smallest category in North America.

According to Krauss (1996), Category B has about thirty languages that are still spoken by the parental generation. The parents theoretically could speak their native language to their children but generally do not. Categories C and D are the largest categories. Category C consists of languages spoken only by the middle-aged or grandparent generation. Category D languages are spoken only by a few of the very oldest people. Together, the last two categories encompass almost 75 percent of native speakers.

Although native languages are spoken to some degree in approximately thirty of the fifty states, there are few areas where they are still viable languages. In Hawaii, until recently, no one under the age of seventy could still speak Hawaiian, except for residents of one small very isolated private island. There were only around two hundred Hawaiian-speaking residents (this included about thirty children). Until Hawaii was taken over by the United States at the beginning of the twentieth century, Hawaiian was a powerful and prestigious language. There have been recent attempts to revive the Hawaiian language in preschools, as well as in a few elementary schools and high schools. In 1996, 1,208 students were enrolled in Hawaiian-language immersion programs in eleven schools, and thirty-five hundred were in nonimmersion programs (Krauss, 1996; Reyhner, 1998). It remains to be seen how successful these experimental projects will be. Joshua Fishman (1991) argues that school-based efforts are secondary or tertiary to the key process of intergenerational mother tongue transmission, which can only successfully be carried out in the home, family, and community.

In Alaska, only two out of twenty languages are still spoken by children. In the entire Northwest and Pacific Coast region, there are no indigenous languages spoken by children. In the rest of the United States, some Cherokee is still spoken in Oklahoma, and Choctaw is spoken by a small population of adults and children in Mississippi. Only in the Southwest, primarily in Arizona and New Mexico, are many Native American languages relatively vital and viable (Krauss, 1996; U.S. Bureau of the Census, 1993a).

A rapid shift to English is evident even for communities such as the Navajo and Apache, with the most viable indigenous languages, that have historically been more isolated and slower to become bilingual. Krauss (1996) places both of these languages in Category A of indigenous languages that are threatened but still spoken by children. Among the Navajo language, loss is fairly recent. As late as the 1930s, 71 percent of Navajos spoke no English as compared with 17 percent of Native Americans as a whole. While Navajo claims the largest number of speakers of any indigenous language in the United States—about 160,000 speakers, the absolute and relative proportions of Navajo speakers have drastically declined in the second half of the twentieth century.[1] A 1992 tribal survey suggests that language erosion is even more rapid among the youngest children. In 110 schools on or near the reservation, 32 percent of kindergartners spoke Navajo well, as compared to 73 percent who spoke English well. Only 16 percent spoke better Navajo than English

(Crawford, 1998; Holm and Holm, 1995). The same trend with regard to language erosion and loss is apparent among the white Mountain Apache tribe in Arizona. In a small tribal survey conducted in the mid-1990s, Bernadette Adley-SantaMaria (1997) found the greatest difference in Apache language ability was between the oldest and youngest age groups.[2]

Many American indigenous communities are addressing this crisis through experimental language and cultural renewal programs. It is difficult to ascertain the effectiveness of these programs. Native American bilingual/bicultural education has fluctuated in response to federal funding and language policies and to other pressing priorities such as health care, basic education, job training, and economic development. In the those few long-running programs that have provided indigenous language–English bilingual maintenance programs, substantial success has been recorded. The students at the Rock Point Community School in Arizona, which first offered a bilingual/bicultural program in English and Navajo in 1967, have consistently done as well or better than other students on English-language standardized tests at almost all grade levels in reading, language arts, and math. In addition, they have continued to improve in Navajo language skills and to maintain higher attendance rates (Reyhner, 1990; Rosier and Holm, 1980). Like true immigrant bilinguals (see chapter 3), Native American bilinguals also surpass their monolingual peers. Those fully bilingual in English and their indigenous tongue are a small minority. Increasingly, most young Native Americans will grow up speaking only English, learning at best a few words of their ancestral tongues (Crawford, 1998).

Language Colonialism and the Case of Puerto Rico

A strong central government also reduced the importance of other non-English tongues at the beginning of the twentieth century. The history of relations with Puerto Rico, Hawaii, the Philippines, and the other territories of the United States is one of American intervention in matters of language. "The need to consolidate the nation's territorial gains and solidify its political processes seems to have played an important role in the drive toward cultural and linguistic homogeneity," observed Josué González, a former director of the federal Office of Bilingual Education and Minority Language Affairs (Crawford, 1989: 23). After the United States acquired Puerto Rico in the Spanish-American War in 1898, federal authorities mandated English as the language of instruction on the island (Language Policy Task Force, 1978). There was a conscious policy of "Americanization," with the intent of converting the island's Spanish speakers into anglophones. The principle vehicle of this change was the public education system (Negron de Montilla, 1971).

In 1899, Victor Clark, the interim director of Puerto Rican schools, recommended that English replace Spanish as the language of instruction, maintaining that it would be just as easy to teach Puerto Ricans English as it would be to replace their patois with standard Castilian Spanish. When this policy failed, he advocated teaching both English and Spanish. This initial policy of bilingualism also was supported by the next commissioner of education for Puerto Rico, Martin Brumbaugh. Brumbaugh's successors, however, imposed a policy calling for English as the official language for instruction in the schools (Osuna, 1949). From the start, the Bureau of Education, under the military regime, aimed at reshaping Puerto Rico's school system along American lines. According to the military law, one teacher of English had to be employed in each city or town with a grade school. Teachers whose mother tongue was not English were expected to learn English. New teacher candidates were required to be examined in English (Negron de Montilla, 1971).

This policy of Americanization between 1903 and 1949 also emphasized patriotic exercises, including flag raising, saluting, and singing national songs. The main focus during the first half of the twentieth century was to promote English and discourage Spanish in the schools. Spanish was taught as a classroom subject, but the medium of instruction continued to be English. The object of this educational policy, which was called the "Filipino Plan," was "to convert the Puerto Ricans into an English-speaking people" (Martínez, 1976: 56). To assure compliance with this policy, the U.S. Congress passed the "Foraker Act" (1900–1917), which mandated that the Puerto Rican governor and the commissioner of education were to be appointed by the president of the United States, with advice and consent of the U.S. Senate.

Agitation from the Puerto Rican legislature spurred some changes in educational policy. In 1916, the U.S. Commissioner of Education compromised and allowed Spanish instruction in grades one through four, Spanish and English in grade five, and only English thereafter. This policy lasted until the late 1940s (Crawford, 1989). In the 1910s, members of the Puerto Rican legislature attempted to terminate English instruction in the public schools, offering English only as a course rather than the required language for most subjects. When the speaker of the territorial House of Representatives founded a private Spanish university-level institute, Education Commissioner Juan Huyke (1921–1930) denied school accreditation. He regarded Spanish higher education as a threat to the government's language and education policies. Huyke insisted that "our schools are agencies of Americanism. They must implant the spirit of America in the hearts of our children" (Barreto, 1995: 70).

In 1935, the Massacre of Río Piedras left several students and Puerto Rican nationalists dead. The late 1930s and 1940s marked a period of heightened Puerto Rican nationalism. In 1937, after the Massacre of Ponce, the United States retrenched on the language issue—which had been liberalized with respect to Spanish instruction by Commissioner of Education José Padín—to encompass Spanish instruction in grades one through eight. Only two years after reinstating Spanish instruction, Commissioner Padín was forced to leave his post. President Franklin D. Roosevelt appointed a new commissioner, José Gallardo, and reemphasized the U.S. desire to make Puerto Rico an English-speaking territory. Roosevelt wrote to Gallardo that Puerto Ricans would profit from "the unique historical circumstance which has brought them the blessings of American citizenship by becoming bilingual," but he emphasized that bilingualism will be achieved "only if the teaching of English throughout the insular education system is entered into at once with vigor, purposefulness, and devotion, and with the understanding that English is the official language of our country" (Osuna, 1949: 391).

The fifty-year vacillation between English and Spanish created extreme chaos and helped fuel a nationalist movement that still exists in Puerto Rico. The language conflict helped solidify the broader nationalist struggle. Language conflict was seen by many as a political struggle between U.S. imperialism and independence forces. Resistance was directed against bilingualism. The imposition of English became a symbol for the Americanization of the population. As Dennis Baron (1990: 179) observed, "Language in Puerto Rico has always been more a political issue than an education one, tied up with issues of statehood or independence, cultural pluralism and Americanization."

Despite continued attempts to Anglicize the Puerto Rican population, American policies were, for the most part, unsuccessful. Puerto Rico's location inhibited the type of linguistic contact found in New Mexico and in Quebec. Puerto Rico was a linguistically homogeneous Spanish-speaking territory when it was claimed by the United States in 1898. Its acquisition did not promote or encourage new settlements by anglophones. The island's location, 855 miles southeast of the southern coast of Florida, acted as a significant obstacle to settlement and language contact. The few Americans who did migrate to Puerto Rico in the first half of the twentieth century were primarily colonial administrators. Another hindrance to Anglophone settlement was Puerto Rico's high population density. At the time of the Spanish-American War, almost one million Puerto Ricans lived on the island that was less than thirty-five hundred square miles in size (Barreto, 1995).

Language Conflict and the Western Territories

The geographic and demographic condition of Puerto Rico differed from those of the Western territories, which were vast and sparsely populated. After the Mexican-American War of 1848, Mexico ceded a vast territory—including California, Arizona, New Mexico, and parts of Colorado—and also approved the prior annexation of Texas. All citizens of Mexico residing within this territory automatically became U.S. citizens, as long as they did not leave the territory within one year of the treaty ratification. English-speaking Americans encountered Hispanics who had preceded them in the Southwest by more than a century.

Examples from California and New Mexico illustrate how political coercion eliminated any opportunity for the United States to formally recognize Spanish as a second language. The original California State Constitution was drafted in a context of linguistic equality, even though only eight of the forty-eight delegates to the 1849 Monterey Constitutional Convention were native speakers of Spanish. The convention elected an official translator, and all resolutions and articles were translated before being voted upon. The final constitution was simultaneously published in Spanish and English; furthermore, it provided that all laws would be published in English and Spanish (Kloss, 1977: 181–182; Leibowitz, 1971: 46–47).

By the end of 1848, there were approximately fifteen thousand residents in California, half of whom were of Mexican descent. The Gold Rush of 1849 rapidly changed this situation, and within a year the population expanded to approximately ninety-five thousand people, almost all Anglo-Americans. By 1850, when California became a state, the Hispanic population was reduced to less than 20 percent of the population. The Gold Rush not only initiated a massive increase in the English-speaking population but also resulted in a struggle over land. Both of these trends operated to the detriment of the Spanish-speaking natives (Conklin and Lourie, 1983; Leibowitz, 1971).

Taking advantage of their greater numbers and political power, Anglos ignored the rights granted to the Mexicans. In the early 1850s, California passed statutes suspending the publication of the state laws in Spanish. There also were new laws requiring court proceedings to be in English. In addition, there was a discriminatory tax against foreign miners, effectively driving Hispanic competition out of the gold fields and wresting land from them in a foreign legal system administered in English (Conlin and Lourie, 1983; Schmid, 1987).

The rise of English in California was so rapid that by 1855 the California Bureau of Public instruction decreed that English was the only medium of public education. In 1870, a statute was enacted providing that "all schools shall be taught in the English language." Never again would Spanish be accorded official status. The Constitution of 1879 dropped all official use of Spanish, maintaining that government business would be "conducted, preserved, and published in no other than the English language" (Baron, 1990: 17). The California constitution was amended in 1894 to restrict the vote to those who could read and write English. It also required that all official proceedings in all branches of government be conducted and published "in no other than the English language" (Leibowitz, 1971: 49–50). Leonard Pitt summarizes the plight of the Californios (the Mexican-origin Californians) during the period from 1846 to 1890 at the hands of the Anglos: "It was he who first guaranteed the Californians full citizenship; he who agreed to treat them as equals and not as conquered people; he who broke his word by declaring open season on the rancheros" (1966: 284).

At the time of statehood, 18 percent of all education in the state was private and Catholic. These private schools were largely composed of students of Spanish descent and were taught in Spanish under the direction of the padres. The schools initially were state-supported. In 1852, however, a new law prohibited religious schools from sharing in state funds. Despite these laws, Southern California remained a Spanish-speaking region for some time. Spanish newspapers and bilingual schools flourished into the 1870s. There also were Spanish-speaking judges, elected officials, and community leaders (Leibowitz, 1971). The segregation of Mexican American children in the public schools of California was fairly well established by the mid-1920s. It was done, however, primarily through the assignment of school districts rather than by state law, and it was never uniformly applied. In California, some districts chose not to segregate children of Mexican descent; even in segregated districts, some children of Mexican descent were allowed to attend white schools (Wollenberg, 1976). In the second half of the twentieth century, Spanish was reduced from an official language to one on the periphery. Spanish speakers from then on in California would only have the choice of learning English or remaining a minority outside mainstream society.

The situation in New Mexico seems, at first sight, to be historically similar to that in Quebec (which eventually led Canada to accept official bilingualism; see chapter 6 for an analysis). Spaniards settled in northern New Mexico before 1600, two centuries prior to the arrival of the Anglos. Ceded to the United States in 1848, English speakers remained a minority until after 1900. Only about one-hundred Anglos settled in the state before 1846, and most of these married into prominent native families (Leibowitz, 1971). Unlike California, competition for resources did not come for another three decades in New Mexico, because there was never a large farm or gold rush influx of population.

Schools in the New Mexico territory operated primarily in Spanish, more than four decades longer than in California. According to the 1874 Annual Report of the territorial school authorities, the public school population of New Mexico was 5 percent English, 69 percent Spanish, and 26 percent bilingual. The two earliest school laws in the state, in 1863 and 1869, lacked any language provisions. As late as 1884, a school law that recognized public Spanish-language elementary schools was passed in New Mexico. According to this statute, "each of the voting precincts of a country shall be and constitute a school district in which shall be . . . taught reading, writing . . . in either English or Spanish or both, as the directors may determine" (Kloss, 1977: 311). In 1889, 30 percent of schools were still administered in Spanish (Conklin and Lourie, 1983: 64–65).

Liberalism and leniency prevailed toward the Hispanic population for almost another decade. Spanish speakers shared political and economic power with Anglos, and the Spanish version of bilingual territorial laws generally took precedence over the English in disputed cases. Translation to English was required, however, for communication with Washington, D.C. The great preponderance of Hispanics in the population made Spanish the de facto language of government (Hernández-Chávez, 1994).

Gradually, Anglo-Americans from the east, who were unsympathetic toward Mexican culture and language, came to dominate the territory. In 1891, a statute was passed requiring all schools in New Mexico to teach in English (Kloss, 1977: 312). As in the case of Native Americans and Mexicans in California, the emphasis on English-language instruction was part of the broader struggle over land, which was developing between the English-speaking white settlers and the Mexican Americans in New Mexico. It is estimated that Mexican Americans lost approximately two million acres of private land and 1.7 million acres of communal land (Leibowitz, 1971: 52).

In 1876, both the House and Senate committees on the territories recommended passage of a statehood bill; however, three members of the House committee opposed statehood. The minority report observed that the territory was populated "by a people nine-tenths of whom speak a foreign tongue, most of whom are illiterate, and the balance with little American literature." The report went on to emphasize the undesirability of the Hispanic population by comparing them to uncivilized Indians: "Few are pure-blooded or Castilian . . . the rest being a mixture of Spanish or Mexican and Indian" living in a "condition of ignorance, superstition, and sloth that is unequaled by their Aztec neighbors, the Pueblo Indians" (Baron, 1990: 96).

Again in 1902, a special congressional committee recommended that statehood be postponed until domestic immigration sufficiently "Americanized" the population in the New Mexico territory (Conklin and Lourie, 1983). In the petitions for statehood, Eduardo Hernández-Chávez (1994: 147) noted, "the fact that Spanish was the normal language in all facets of New Mexico society loomed always as the primary consideration." Race and religion (almost all Mexicans in New Mexico Territory were Catholic) also played an important role. Unlike other states, New Mexico waited sixty-four years for statehood. Approximately fifty petitions were made before New Mexico finally became a state.

The U.S. government refused to grant statehood to New Mexico until 1912, when Anglos finally outnumbered Hispanics, thereby putting an end to any challenge by Spanish to the preeminence of English in American life and to the possibility of official bilingualism at the state level (Schmid, 1987). With statehood and an Anglo majority, Spanish declined precipitously in public use. The New Mexico Enabling Act of 1910 provided that schools were to be conducted in English. Officials and legislators were required to know English, although laws continued to be published in both English and Spanish for the next twenty years. Several state statutes promoted English as the language of the classroom. By 1921, Spanish had ceased being used in the schools, and by 1935 it was no longer an official language in the legislature (Baron, 1990; Kloss, 1977).

In some schools, the speaking of Spanish was strictly forbidden, both in the classroom and on the playground. "Spanish detention," punishment for speaking Spanish on school grounds, was inflicted on Mexican American children in the Southwest as late as the 1960s (U.S. Civil Rights Commission, 1972). More than language instruction, however, was involved. In 1937, New Mexico spent $51 per pupil in the predominantly Anglo counties and less than $35 in the Spanish-speaking counties (Leibowitz, 1971). Thus, even though New Mexico maintained Spanish longer than the other western territories, it basically followed the same pattern as the other states with English as the only official language.

Summary

A review of the early history of the United States reveals a basic political (and linguistic) inequality between white citizens and non-white citizens (Takaki, 1987: 29). A similar distinction is made by Alejandro Portes (1990: 161), who noted that while ethnic groups come into to being in three ways—conquest, immigration, or political settlements (such as we shall see in the case of Switzerland)—U.S. history does not register a single case of "negotiated" ethnicity. Linguistically differentiated ethnic groups have therefore only emerged through the two other alternatives: conquest and immigration.

In the early republic, language was considered an individual matter, as long as white immigrant groups did not want to sustain their language or threaten the dominant elites. To achieve loyalty to the revolutionary cause, the Continental Congress published key documents into German and French. John Adams tried unsuccessfully to establish an English Academy to serve as a standard for all persons in the new country. Noah Webster attempted to promote language standardization through his *American Spelling Book* issued in 1783 and *American Dictionary of the English Language* published in 1828. Webster's books, however, did not sell well during his lifetime, and it took another half century or more before the nexus between the English language and loyalty to the American nation would be firmly planted in the American conscious.

Conquered ethnic groups, on the other hand—who in the late-nineteenth and early-twentieth centuries were groups of color—were never allowed the freedom to maintain their languages. The federal government pursued a goal of both cultural and physical containment toward Native Americans. The main consequence of these practices, from the point of view of language, was the establishment, beginning in 1879, of a system of boarding schools whose express purpose was the forced assimilation of Native American children. Ronald Wardhaugh (1987) concluded that Spanish has always been under attack in the United States. English was imposed on Puerto Ricans through a policy of "Americanization." The purpose of this policy was to convert the Island's Spanish speakers into anglophones. The principal vehicle for this change was the public education system. Because of the distance from the mainland and lack of English-speaking settlers, however, the policy ultimately failed. Despite an initial majority population of Mexican Americans, both California and New Mexico were only admitted as states when English speakers were the dominant group, a process that took much longer in New Mexico than in California. White settlers, prospectors, and speculators overran Native American and Mexican land and subjugated much of the population. Language laws and practices that restricted Native American and Spanish speakers were not passed in the interests of the people but rather for the convenience of the state and English-speaking elites.

Michael Lind (1995) argued in *The Next American Nation* that, from a historical perspective, there was a progression from a more exclusive sense of who could become an American to a more inclusive one. He saw a progression from Anglo-America to Euro-America to Multicultural America. In terms of language minorities, this was not the case. National identity increasingly became identified with speaking English. Conflict with Native Americans and colonialization of Puerto Rico and Hawaii, as well as confrontation with Mexico and massive waves of immigrants from southern and eastern Europe, sealed the relationship between American identity, loyalty to the nation, and accentless English.

With the exception of brief periods in American history, languages other than English in the United States have been tolerated rather than embraced. To win their loyalty, German Americans were allowed to maintain their language, although the founding fathers and subsequent leaders held an ambivalent attitude toward German and other immigrant languages—especially where there were large concentrations of non-English speakers. The toleration of German Americans turned to hostility and contempt prior to World War I (as we shall see in the next chapter). The history of language policy in the United States through the last decades of the nineteenth century was characterized by the imposition of English and the restriction of other languages over a wider range of institutions.

3

IMMIGRANT EXCLUSION AND LANGUAGE RESTRICTION IN THE TWENTIETH CENTURY

High levels of immigration in the United States have typically led to two trends: an increase in various strains of xenophobia, and a crusade to "Americanize" the new immigrants. As John Higham observed, "When neither a preventative nativism nor the natural health of a free society seemed sufficient to cope with disunity, a conscious drive to hasten the assimilative process, to heat and stir the melting pot, emerged" (1967: 235). Both the post-1965 era and the period of Americanization campaigns—defined as the decades between the 1890s and the 1920s—aimed at the "new immigration" from southern and eastern Europe (Graham and Koed, 1993), shared a significant upsurge of newcomers, who were thought to be significantly different from the native-born population and incapable of being assimilated. The debates that raged over immigration and language policy expose the extent of the anxiety about who was to be included in the nation, which has compelled a reexamination of what it means to be an American.

The first part of this chapter briefly analyzes the nature of post-1965 immigration and compares it with earlier immigrant waves in the twentieth century. The second part of the chapter traces the various strands of the current ideology of exclusion and compares it with the earlier "Americanization movement." Finally, a cultural and economic framework is presented to explain the rise of an ideology of exclusion and resistance to new immigrants in the United States.

High Levels of Immigration and the Heating up of the Melting Pot

The period from the late nineteenth century through World War I was a time of high immigration and a crusade to "Americanize" the new immigrants. In 1911, a federal commission issued a forty-two-volume study of the foreign-born population, alleging that the "new immigrants" were less skilled and educated, more clannish, slower to learn English, and generally less desirable as citizens than the "old immigrants" (Handlin, 1957). A 1919 article in the *American Journal of Sociology* also echoed this theme, observing that "unlike the earlier immigrants, many of the latecomers manifested no intention of making America a permanent home and no desire of becoming Americans" (Hill, 1919: 611).

The "new immigrants" came from those regions of Europe—the Russian Empire, Austria-Hungary, Italy, and the Balkans—that were comparatively poor and had a less democratic tradition than the "old immigrants," who came from the British Isles, Germany, Holland, and other sections of northwestern Europe. This first wave of newcomers had a common fund of social mores and practices and a somewhat similar socioeconomic and political experience. In addition, most of the first wave of immigrants were Protestant, whereas the second wave tended to be Catholic and Jewish.

The new immigrant groups began to migrate to the United States in significant numbers as early as 1875, when approximately 10 percent of the total number of immigrants came from eastern and southern Europe. Each year thereafter the percentage increased, until by 1896 it reached 57 percent, and, by 1902, over 76 percent. From 1873 to 1910, it has been estimated that approximately 9,306,000 immigrants from southern and eastern Europe migrated to the United States (Hartmann, 1948: 15). At the turn of the twentieth century, the nation's already high immigration increased dramatically, doubling between 1902 and 1907 (Landes, Cessna, and Foster, 1993). This new wave of immigrants provided a great source of unskilled labor for America's growing industries. To fuel these industries, the immigrants settled in the great industrial and urban centers of the northeastern seaboard region, as well as in the Midwest, where opportunities for finding employment were most favorable. Immigrants gathered in such centers as the New York—New Jersey metropolitan area, Boston, Pittsburgh, Buffalo, Cleveland, Chicago, the Pennsylvania anthracite and bituminous coal fields, and a score of other communities, propelled by both voluntary and involuntary forces (Hartmann, 1948). The already crowded conditions existing in the urban areas forced the newcomers to occupy some of the poorest and least desirable residential areas. By the time World War I began, one-fourth of all Philadelphians, one-third of all Bostonians and Chicagoans, and four-fifths of all New Yorkers were of foreign birth or parentage (Landes, Cessna, and Foster, 1993). High residential concentration plus their large numbers made them even more visible to the native population.

Today's "new era"[1] immigration waves represent a significant departure from the past. This stems in part from the change in national origins, with most of the newcomers arriving from Latin America and Asia, not from Europe. The context in which immigration occurs also differs from the earlier waves of immigrants. Newcomers in the early part of the twentieth century were more likely to find an expanding economy that needed unskilled labor. Recent immigrants entered an economy that disproportionately rewarded the highly skilled. Current skill and education levels required by the marketplace are very different from those required in the past. The changes in the economy threatened the mobility of both immigrant and significant segments of the citizen population. Furthermore, the new era immigration is more global in its impact, with the flow and composition of immigrants determined by recent global and national economic and political transformations (Abelmann and Lie, 1995; Ong, Bonacich, and Cheng, 1994).

In the last several decades of the twentieth century, the main source of immigrants to the United States has been shifting away from Europe and toward Asia and South and Central America. Half of the newcomers between 1955 and 1964 came from Europe, with most of the remainder arriving from North America, primarily Mexico, the Caribbean, and Central America. The proportion arriving from Europe in the ten years from 1965 to 1974 had dropped to barely 30 percent while the percentage arriving from Asia increased dramatically to 22 percent and the percentage coming from Mexico and Central America increased by 40 percent (Landes, Cessna, and Foster, 1993). Immigration increased significantly around 1965 after a lull of almost four decades. The rate of increase in the immigrant population was nearly twice as fast in the 1980s as in the 1970s (see Figure 3.1). Much of the surge was among Hispanics, who comprised 48 percent of immigrants during the 1980s. In 1991, newcomers from Mexico comprised almost 42 percent of the total immigrant population (U.S. Immigration and Naturalization Service, 1997). By 2015, they are expected to surpass the African American population (Population Reference Bureau, 1999). According to Barry Edmonston and Jeffrey Passel (1994: 42), this new era immigration from Asia and Latin America is shifting the racial composition of the United States, making it more diverse politically and economically and more multiracial. As a consequence, black Americans constitute an increasingly smaller portion of the American minority population.

Much like the immigrants who came before them, the most recent wave of newcomers are highly concentrated among a few states and metropolitan areas. California, New York, Florida, Texas, Illinois, and New Jersey contain nearly three-fourths of the foreign residents counted in the 1990 Census. California, a traditional destination for immigrants from both Asia and Latin America, contained one-third of the U.S. foreign-born population in 1990. Although many immigrants are from rural backgrounds, 90 percent live in metropolitan areas, many of which are experiencing economic decline. Nearly five million Hispanic Americans live in the Los Angeles Consolidated Metropolitan Statistical Areas (CMSA), while nearly three million live in New York. Close to a million Hispanics live in the CMSAs of Miami, San Francisco, and Chicago (U.S. Bureau of the Census, 1993c).

Language and Racial Restriction and the Ideology of Exclusion

The first English-language requirement for naturalization was adopted with the explicit purpose of limiting the entrance into the United States of southern and

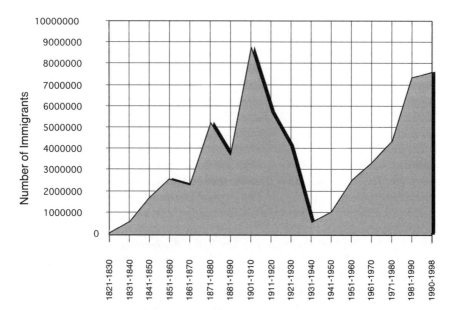

Figure 3.1   Immigration to United States by Decade. *Source*: U.S. Immigration and Naturalization Service, Statistical Yearbook, 1996 (Washington, D.C.: U.S. Government Printing Office, 1997), table 1 and U.S. Immigration and Naturalization Service 1998 Annual Report (Washington, D.C.: U.S. Government Printing Office), table 2.

eastern Europeans. During the war, the idea of expulsion as an alternative to assimilation was frequently discussed. In 1916, the National Americanization Committee, which worked closely with the federal bureau of education, sponsored a bill in Congress to deport all aliens who would not apply for citizenship within three years. The U.S. Congress, by way of the Revenue Act of 1918, doubled income tax rates on "nonresident" aliens—an ill-defined term, but one clearly intended to increase the rate of naturalization. In 1919, fifteen states decreed English as the sole language of instruction, an Oregon law required foreign-language newspapers to publish English translations, and a California law mandated that foreigners pay a special poll tax of $10.20 (Graham and Koed, 1993; Higham, 1967).

In the 1850s, Germans were 36.6 percent of all immigrants; in the 1860s, they were 34 percent of the newcomers; in the 1870s, they were 25.6 percent of the immigrant population, and in the 1880s, they were 27.7 percent of the decade immigrant wave (DeSipio and de la Garza, 1998: 19). As one of the largest language minorities in the United States, German Americans came under immediate suspicion. The large increase in German speakers in all likelihood made the population more visible. Between 1850 and 1880, the number of foreign-born Germans whose mother tongue was German increased from 15 to 60 percent, largely as a result of immigration (Kloss, 1977: 13). After the United States entered World War I, measures were taken in many states against the German population. According to Carl Wittke (1936: 163):

[The war] precipitated a violent, concerted movement to eradicate everything German from American civilization. . . . Mob rule broke out in many parts of the United States, and the German-American element trembled with fear before the excesses of an enraged public. German music, German literature, German church services, German singing societies, the use of the German language, practically everything that could be labeled with the hated German name . . . came under the ban, as the passions threatened to divide the American population permanently into a pro and an anti-German group.

In 1917, an amendment to the Espionage Act, requiring every foreign-language paper to submit precise English translations of all articles containing news on the war, was submitted to Congress. The primary purpose of the amendment was to provide effective censorship for the foreign-language press, most notably for German-language papers. Although there was some protest against the law, it went into effect on October 15, 1917. The law had a dampening effect on German-language newspapers in the United States. By 1920, ten papers, which had previously been printed in German, appeared exclusively in English. Although there were few arrests, several editors were interned as alien enemies. The editor of the *Cleveland Echo*, a socialist paper, was arrested for not filing a translation of an article that attacked the American Protective League (Wittke, 1936).

German schools had enjoyed a privileged position in the curricula of some school systems. The hysteria of the war changed this situation, however. Petitions were circulated to eliminate German from the curriculum. Almost immediately, the number of students taking German in the schools dropped significantly. For example, in the Cincinnati high schools in the fall of 1918, fewer than thirty students elected to take German. On April 1, 1919, Governor James Cox urged the adoption of a law to abolish the teaching and use of German in the public, private, and parochial elementary schools of Ohio as "a distinct menace to Americanization and a part of a plot formed by the German government to make the school children loyal to it" (Wittke, 1936: 181).

Patriotic societies in various parts of the United States attempted to prohibit the use of German in public life. In Staunton, Illinois, a "vigilance corps" of the State Council of Defense posted placards demanding that all speak English. Similar measures were attempted in Diller, Nebraska, and in Milford and Cleveland, Ohio. In South Dakota, the Council of Defense prohibited the use of German in sermons, public addresses, and the schools and over telephones. The governor of Iowa, W. L. Harding, issued a proclamation requiring English as the language of public, private, and church schools, as well as public addresses and conversations on trains and over telephones. In Findlay, Ohio, the city council imposed a fine of $25 for speaking German on the streets. Similar incidents occurred in small towns and German farming communities in Iowa and South Dakota. Orders forbidding the speaking of German were extended to religious services. Mob violence occasionally occurred. Crowds broke into the desks of high schools in scores of American cities and burned all the German books that could be found (Wittke 1936: 186–189).

Through immigration and nationality laws, the federal government ranked populations into hierarchies of assimilability, in which some groups were regarded as more likely to "fit in" than others (Carter, Green, and Halpern, 1996). The nativitist Workingmen's Party led a movement for a new state constitution in California in 1878–1879. The constitutional convention adopted provisions banning Chinese from employment in many work places. Under pressure from California and other western states, the U.S. Congress passed an act to suspend Chinese immigration in 1882. Fundamental to the opposition of the Chinese and other undesirable groups was the antagonism of race, which was reinforced by economic competition (Sandmeyer, 1939).

The reconstitution of national identity was articulated through concepts of race, language, country of origin, and religion. The debate over immigration policy helped expose the extent of anxiety over who was to be included in the nation. This started a process by which the federal government codified, in immigration laws, racist and nationalist discourse. Over the next two decades, the principle of exclusion by race was extended to several groups that were thought to be unassimilable. The exclusion of Japanese workers was accomplished by the Gentleman's Agreement of 1907. Immigrants from southern and eastern Europe were also racialized. See Table 3.1 for a historical summary of restrictions on immigration and naturalization.

Immigration restrictionists were motivated by a variety of factors, including ideological commitments to white supremacy, acceptance of Social Darwinistic thinking, vote-getting demagoguery, and the belief that the increase in immigration that took place from 1890s onward, particularly from southern and eastern Europe, would threaten the nation's ability to absorb and "Americanize" the newcomers (Carter, Green, and Hapern, 1996). Wartime intolerance of German Americans, coupled with language and ethnic and racial antagonism, combined to create an atmosphere conducive to the revision of America's once liberal immigration policy.

Language Acquisition and Racial Inferiority

The nativism of the late nineteenth and early twentieth centuries was also influenced by racial eugenics. It was promulgated in many articles in the mass media by some members of the American elite. Madison Grant, for example, argued that the Nordic race was being destroyed by the millions of inferior immigrants from southern and eastern Europe. In his view, the Nordic race was intellectually, culturally and politically superior to all other races. In the early 1900s, many Americans of northern European descent described themselves as "white men," believing themselves to be superior and completely different in racial terms from southern and eastern Europeans. American eugenicists were obsessed with racial miscegenation and feared if they allowed more racially inferior southern and eastern Europeans in the country that this would destroy the superior Nordic race (Feagin, 1997).

By the early twentieth century, the prevailing scientific community believed there was a close relationship between lack of English and lower intelligence. The

Table 3.1   Restrictions on Immigration and Naturalization Law

Decade	Year	Restriction Imposed
1790s	1790	Naturalization is authorized for "free white persons" who have resided in the United States for at least two years and swear loyalty to the U.S. Constitution. The racial requirement would remain on the federal books until 1952, although naturalization was opened to certain Asian nationalities in the 1940s.
	1798	The Alien and Sedition Acts authorize the president to deport any foreigner deemed to be dangerous and make it a crime to speak, write, or publish anything "of a false, scandalous and malicious nature" about the president or Congress. An amended Naturalization Act imposes a 14-year residency requirement for prospective citizens; in 1802, Congress would reduce the waiting period to five years, a provision that remains in effect today.
1880s	1882	The Chinese Exclusion Act suspends immigration by Chinese laborers for ten years; the measure would be extended and tightened in 1892 and a permanent ban enacted in 1902. This marks the first time the United States has restricted immigration on the basis of race or national origin.
1890s	1891	To the list of undesirables ineligible for immigration, Congress adds polygamists, "persons suffering from a loathsome or a dangerous contagious disease," and those convicted of "a misdemeanor involving moral turpitude."
1900s	1906	The first language requirement is adopted for naturalization: ability to speak and understand English.
	1907–8	Under a so-called Gentlemen's Agreement, the United States promises not to ban Japanese immigration in exchange for Japan's pledge not to issue passports to Japanese laborers for travel to the continental United States (although they remain welcome to become agricultural workers in Hawaii). By a separate executive order, President Theodore Roosevelt prohibits secondary migration by Japanese from Hawaii to the mainland.
1910s	1917	Over President Wilson's veto, Congress enacts a literacy requirement for all new immigrants: ability to read 40 words in some language. Most significant in limiting the flow of newcomers, it designates Asia as a "barred zone" (excepting Japan and the Philippines) from which immigration will be prohibited.
1920s	1921	A new form of immigration restriction is born: the national-origins quota system. Admissions from each European country will be limited to 3% of each foreign-born nationality in the 1910 census. The effect is to favor Northern Europeans at the expense of Southern and Eastern Europeans. Immigration from Western Hemisphere nations remains unrestricted; most Asians will continue to face exclusion.
	1924	Restrictionists' decisive stroke, the Johnson-Reed Act, embodies the principle of preserving America's "racial" composition. Immigration quotas will be based on the ethnic makeup of the U.S. population as a whole in 1920. The new national-origins quota system is even more discriminatory than the 1921 version. "America must be kept American," says President Coolidge, as he signs the bill into law. Another provision bans all immigration by persons "ineligible to citizenship"—primarily affecting the Japanese.
1940s	1943	To appease a wartime ally, a token quota (105) is created for Chinese immigration. Yet, unlike white immigrants, whose quotas depend on country of residence, all persons of "Chinese race" will be counted under the Chinese quota, regardless of where they reside.
1950s	1950	The Internal Security Act, enacted over President Truman's veto, bars admission to any foreigner who might engage in activities "which would be prejudicial to the public interest, or would endanger the welfare or safety of the United States." It excludes or permits deportation of noncitizens who belong to the U.S. Communist Party or whose future activities might be "subversive to the national security."

Table 3.1 (continued)

Decade	Year	Restriction Imposed
	1952	The McCarran-Walter Act retains the national-origins quota system and "internal security" restrictions, despite Truman's opposition. For the first time, however, Congress sets aside minimum annual quotas for all countries, opening the door to numerous nationalities previously kept out on racial grounds. Naturalization now requires ability to read and write, as well as speak and understand, English.
1960s	1965	The United States finally eliminates racial criteria from its immigration laws. Each country, regardless of ethnicity, will receive an annual quota of 20,000, under a ceiling of 170,000. Up to 120,000 may immigrate from Western Hemisphere nations, which are still not subject to country quotas (an exception Congress would eliminate in 1976). Annual ceilings for quota admissions would be raised over the years, most recently to 700,000 in 1990.
1980s	1986	The Immigration Reform and Control Act gives amnesty to millions of undocumented residents. For the first time, the law punishes *employers* who hire persons who are here illegally. The aim of employer sanctions is to make it difficult for the undocumented to find employment. The law has a side effect: employment discrimination against those who look or sound "foreign."
1990s	1990	The Immigration Act of 1990, raises the limit for legal immigration to 700,000 people a year.
	1996	A persistent recession in the U.S. in the early 1990's, among other reasons, leads to calls for new restrictions on immigration. The Illegal Immigration Reform and Immigrant Responsibility Act is passed, toughening border enforcement, closing opportunities for undocumented immigrants to adjust their status, and making it more difficult to gain asylum. The law also establishes income requirements for legal immigrants. In the Personal Responsibility and Work Opportunity Act, Congress makes citizenship a condition of eligibility for public benefits for most immigrants.
	1997	A new Congress mitigates some of the overly harsh restrictions passed by the previous Congress. In the Balance Budget Agreement with the President, some public benefits are restored for some elderly and disabled immigrants who had been receiving them. With the Nicaraguan Adjustment and Central American Relief Act, Congress restores an opportunity for certain war refugees living in legal limbo to become permanent residents.
	1998	Congress continues to mitigate some of the nativist provisions passed by the Congress in 1996. The Agricultural Research, Extension, and Education Reform Act restores more public benefits to some immigrants. The Noncitizen Benefit Clarification and Other Technical Amendments Act restores public benefits to an additional group of long-time resident immigrants. The Haitian Refugee Immigration Fairness Act resolves the legal limbo status of certain Haitians refugees, and allows them to become permanent U.S. residents. The American Competitiveness and Workforce Improvement Act significantly raises the number of skilled temporary foreign workers U.S. employers are allowed to bring to the United States.

Source: National Immigration Forum, "Chronology: Changes in Immigration and Naturalization Law." 1999 (http://www.immigrationforum.org/Facts/ChronRestrict.htm) 28 July 2000. By permission of the National Immigration Forum.

only question was that of causality: Did the immigrants' lack of intelligence cause their lack of English ability or vice versa? H. H Goddard, who translated the Binet IQ test into English, administered the IQ test to thirty Jewish immigrants at Ellis Island in 1917. Of the thirty participants, he found that twenty-five of them were "feebleminded." At the start of World War I, Goddard convinced the army to test approximately two million draftees, many of whom were foreign-born and had very limited proficiency in English. In one of the most influential analyses of these data, published in 1923, Carl Brigham concluded that, "the representatives of the Alpine and Mediterranean races in our immigration are intellectually inferior to the Nordic race." The underlying cause of the nativity differences according to Brigham was race rather than language (Portes and Rumbaut, 1996: 197–198).

Bilingualism came directly under attack. Beginning in the 1920s, bolstered by new psychometric tests, the majority of psychological studies consistently found evidence that bilingual children suffered from a language handicap. In comparison with monolingual children, bilingual youth were found to be inferior in intelligence test scores and on a range of verbal and nonverbal linguistic abilities. Nature rather than nurture was implemented as the cause of the low IQ among bilingual immigrant schoolchildren (Portes and Rumbaut, 1996). Collectively, these findings gave support to attempts to vastly reduce the number of newcomers. The findings also provided justification to reduce bilingual and foreign language instruction. A poll of twelve hundred public school systems by March 1918 found that about one in seven school districts had already dropped German. In the South, the proportion was much higher—almost four in ten (Higham, 1967: 208).

Efforts to shut off immigration overlapped with the extension in Congress of Jim Crow legislation into the District of Columbia. Many of the key Southern officials responsible for segregating streetcars and public amenities in the capital helped to spearhead the effort to bar certain types of immigrants from entering the country. The 1917 Burnett Act—also known as the Literacy Act—was the culmination of these longstanding efforts to codify racist and nationalist ideology to groups thought to be unassimilable. Much of the debate surrounding the Burnett Bill took the form of Southern senators and congressmen urging their fellow members of Congress to adopt successful methods of "racial" separation and control. This conception of the immigration problem was not an exclusively Southern construct, however. West coast representatives, who warned of the "yellow peril" of the Chinese and Japanese, also played a pivotal role in the passage of the Burnett Act: "Like their counterparts from Dixie, these officials pointed to their region's intimate knowledge of the deleterious effects of other 'races' and claimed authority based upon years of local restrictionist campaigning and legislation" (Carter, Green, and Halpern, 1996: 141; see also Higham, 1967). In general, opposition to immigration was cast in racial terms, with language, religion, color, and country of origin as important signifiers. Central to the argument were judgments about the likely adoption of an American identity, which during this period meant cultural proximity to the Anglo-Saxon foundation on which the nation was built.

The Immigration Restriction League, formed in Boston in 1894 primarily by British Americans, tried to curtail immigration by pressing the U.S. Congress to pass literacy restrictions. Language played a pivotal role in the final form of the

Burnett Act. The ability to read a simple passage in some language was the primary administrative means of determining suitability to live in the United States. Proponents of this provision, influenced by the Dillingham Commission, believed that literacy was an accurate measure of intelligence and a reliable indicator of the capacity for citizenship. There was an assumption made that the ability to read was a useful means to distinguish between foreigners likely to adapt to "American ways" and those who were unassimilable. Undoubtedly, there was also the belief that the literacy law would distinguish between "unfit" southern and eastern Europeans and the more "desirable" northern Europeans. While the bill barred certain Asiatics, it failed to stop the large wave of newcomers from southern and eastern Europe (Hutchinson, 1981). Over the next few years, the sentiment for further restrictions increased, coinciding with the Red Scare and fear of postwar unemployment.

The decades of the Americanization movement culminated in legislation in 1921 and 1924 that created the national origins quota system, effectively closing the gates to mass immigration. The 1921 Immigration Act limited admissions from each European country to 3 percent of each foreign-born nationality in 1910, with an annual maximum of 350,000 entrants. The consequence was that northern Europeans were favored at the expense of southern and eastern Europeans. Higham observed that the 1921 Act "proved in the long-run to be the most important turning point in American immigration policy. It imposed the first sharp and absolute numerical limits on European immigration. It established a nationality quota system based on the pre-existing composition of the American population —an idea which has survived in one form or another through all subsequent legislation" (1967: 311).

Large-scale evasion quickly emerged, with estimates of illegal entrants ranging from one hundred thousand a year to one thousand a day (Keller, 1994: 229). In 1924, the Johnson Act superseded the 1921 legislation. It was even more extreme —it reduced the number of immigrants by using the 1890 Census as a benchmark, lowering quotas from 3 percent to 2 percent. The 1924 act also excluded certain immigrants—that is, Chinese and Japanese—as ineligible for citizenship. Furthermore, it provided for an examination of prospective immigrants overseas, and it put the burden of proof of admissibility on the would-be immigrants (Hutchinson, 1981). By the 1920s, the anti-immigrant hysteria had taken on major proportions; immigrants in many states were prohibited from practicing certain jobs or professions, including medicine, engineering, and law. Immigration restriction marked the conclusion of an era of nationalistic and nativistic legislation in the mid-1920s. Language and immigration issues then lay largely dormant as a public issue for the next half century.

Language and cultural differences are again the focus of a new nativism in the last two decades of the twentieth century. Recent organizing has targeted the language and culture of newcomers to the United States, particularly Spanish speakers. Increased immigration and concentration of newcomers in a few states and metropolitan areas has fostered the perception that immigrants are no longer learning English. Language rights and antiforeigner sentiment have emerged as important domestic issues in the second half of the twentieth century. Between

1970 and 1990, the U.S population grew by 20 percent, while the Asian and Hispanic populations grew by 385 percent and 141 percent, respectively. During this period, nine million new American immigrants were added from countries in Asia and Latin America. Asian Americans now make up 3 percent of the population, with Hispanics comprising 9 percent of the total population (Feagin, 1997). Individuals from Mexico are the largest single block of immigrants. They comprised 13.7 percent of the legal newcomers during the 1960s, 14.2 percent during the 1970s, and 14.0 percent during the 1980s (DeSipio and de la Garza, 1998: 20); that number expanded to 25.4 percent between 1991 and 1998 (U.S. Immigration and Naturalization Service, 1997, 1999).

In addition to changing demographics, other factors have contributed to the recent emergence of language as a source of conflict in the political arena. These include immigration reform, limited government recognition of bilingualism, and a heightened sense of nationalism and patriotism. In 1965, the national origins system and the explicit exclusion of Asians were abolished. Furthermore, the Immigration and Nationality Act Amendments of 1965 repealed the national origins quotas, established a 7-category preference based on family unification and skills and imposed a ceiling on immigration from the Western Hemisphere for the first time in American history. Settlement patterns exacerbated the language conflict, as the growth of the Hispanic and Asian communities are heavily concentrated in a few areas. The recent entry of so many immigrants who speak languages other than English makes them more visible and distorts perceptions of how well immigrants are learning English and adapting to the United States. Both English-language ability and income tend to increase with time spent in the country (Fix and Passel, 1994).

Another important factor was the limited legal recognition of languages other than English (this will be discussed in chapter 4). The Bilingual Education Act reversed our 200-year-old tradition of a laissez-faire attitude toward language. It seemed to contradict ingrained assumptions about the role of second languages and the melting pot in American society. The goals of the act were unclear, so it was variously interpreted as a remedial effort, enrichment program, and possibility to maintain one's own language and culture through the public schools (Crawford, 1989).

Finally, declining economic conditions and current events seem to have fueled a new search for a national identity. According to Joshua Fishman (1988: 132), the English-Only movement represents middle-class Anglo fears and anxieties manifested by the creation of "mythical and simplistic and stereotyped scapegoats." The causes of Anglo insecurity are the perceived loss of American leverage on the world scene over the last twenty years, the uneven performance of the American economy for a significant portion of the American population, and the loss of social mobility for the next generation. As Donald Horowitz observed (1985), language is an especially salient symbolic issue because it links political claims with psychological feelings of group worth.

Nativists now—as in the past—have stressed four major themes. A common theme is the complaint that certain "races" are intellectually and culturally inferior and should not be allowed into the country, at least not in substantial numbers.

Nativists have often regarded immigrant groups as racial "others" quite different from the Euro-American majority. A second and related theme views those who have immigrated from racially and culturally inferior groups as problematical in terms of their complete assimilation to the dominant Anglo culture. A third theme, articulated most often in troubled economic times, is that "inferior" immigrants are taking the jobs and disrupting the economic conditions of native-born Americans. A fourth theme, also heard most often in times of fiscal upheaval, is that immigrants are creating serious government crises, such as corrupting the voting system or overloading school and welfare systems (Feagin, 1997: 13–14).

An examination of the recent wave of nativism reveals many common conditions similar to the Americanization movement of the earlier part of the twentieth century, including a large and sustained immigration inflow, economic uncertainty and job insecurity, and significant cultural, ethnic, social, and linguistic disparities between the newcomers and the older citizen population (Muller, 1997). As in the early decades of the twentieth century, contemporary nativists blame many problems on the new immigrants. They find convenient scapegoats for the crisis in public institutions, including schools, healthcare, and welfare, as well as high crime rates in poor immigrant quarters and the trend toward higher taxes.

Complaints about a breakdown in the process of assimilation are especially prevalent during periods of high immigration, economic restructuring and recession, providing fertile soil for the growth of nativism, along with negative nationalism. This trend has not abated, even though the new immigrants do not directly affect the vast majority of American workers, most of whose jobs are not directly threatened by the newcomers (Commission on Behavioral and Social Science and Education, 1997). Several studies indicate that objective self-interests and economic conditions seem to be less important in shaping popular attitudes than the intensity of feelings toward a group or political symbol (Tatalovich, 1995).

Several theories about status and politics have been developed to explain conservative responses to public issues. English-Only campaigns conform to the pattern of such movements in that they attempt "to maintain structures of order, status, honor, or traditional social differences or values" (Lo, 1982: 108). According to the notion of status preservation, declining groups seek to maintain their eroding position by identifying with extremist and nativist causes (Lipset and Raab, 1978). Another approach also emphasizes status politics, arguing that supporters of right-wing movements were either falling in status or rising in status; this included immigrant groups anxious to demonstrate their Americanism (this approach is characterized by essays in Daniel Bell [1964] and Richard Hofstadter [1967]). A final theory postulates that status symbolism rather than angry responses to changes in status are of primary importance in swelling the ranks of conservative movements. Using this approach, J. R. Gusfield (1963) found that the American temperance movement reflected identification with a threatened lifestyle, a symbolic clash between two cultures—dry, abstaining Protestant middle classes versus wet, immigrant, primarily Catholic workers who opposed the abolition of alcohol. An adaptation of this perspective has recently been employed by Jack Citrin, Beth Reingold, Evelyn Walters, and Donald P. Green (1990: 536), who conclude that "an important reason for the popularity of the Official English movement is the pervasive public desire to reaffirm an attachment to a traditional image of Americanism that now seems vulnerable."

The Rise of U.S. English: Myths and Facts about English-Language Proficiency among U.S. Immigrants and Their Children

"U.S. English" is the largest, most aggressive, and most successful of the political groups promoting English as the official language in the United States. It has grown rapidly, from three hundred members in 1983 to four hundred thousand members nationwide as of 1990, with about half of these members in California (Schmid, 1992b). In 2000, U.S. English claimed to have 1.4 million members and to be one of the fastest growing interest groups in the country (U.S. English, 2000b). The activities of U.S. English include lobbying for a federal constitutional amendment to make English the official language of the United States, restricting government funding for bilingual education to short-term transitional programs, and supporting state and national Official English statutes (Schmid, 1992b). U.S. English has helped finance and has given legal support to most states that have passed Official English legislation since the early 1980s.

By 2000, voters or legislators had enacted English-Only legislation in twenty-five states[2] (see Table 3.2), and nowhere has such an initiative been defeated at the polls. In 1986, California voters, by a margin of 73 to 27 percent, adopted a constitutional amendment declaring English the state's official language. In November 1988, voters in the states of Arizona, Colorado, and Florida passed English-Only amendments to their state constitutions by 51 percent in Arizona,[3] 61 percent in Colorado, and 84 percent in Florida.

An important factor that sparks anti-immigrant sentiment in the United States and provides support for U.S. English and other restrictionist groups is the perception that new immigrants are unwilling or unable to learn English as readily as earlier waves of immigrants. The lack of English proficiency has been blamed for numerous economic, social, and health problems encountered by immigrants and by society as a whole. Economists argue that English proficiency is a form of human capital, and that limited knowledge is associated with lower earnings, less schooling for adolescents, and communication barriers with healthcare providers (Espenshade and Fu, 1997).

Not since the beginning of the twentieth century has language received as much attention in the United States. Language battles in the 1980s and 1990s—like their counterparts in the 1900s—appealed to patriotism and unity, often casting language minorities into the role of outsiders who deliberately chose not to learn English. Unlike the earlier period, when these issues tended to be more localized, the late 1990s has seen a campaign orchestrated at the national level. While the stated goal of U.S. English is to establish English as the official language in the United States, its connections to immigration restriction groups suggest a more far-reaching agenda.

The Federation for American Immigration Reform (FAIR) and U.S. English possess many common roots. Dr. John Tanton, a Michigan ophthalmologist, en-

Table 3.2   States with Official English Legislation and Year Passed (as of 1999)

State	Year	Type of Legislation
Alabama	1990	Constitutional amendment adopted by voter initiative
Alaska	1998	Constitutional amendment adopted by voter initiative, stayed by injunction March 1999
Arizona	1988	Constitutional amendment adopted by voter initiative
(unconstitutional)	(1998)	Ruled unconstitutional by federal district and appellate courts, decisions vacated in 1997 by the U.S. Supreme Court, held unconstitutional by the Arizona Supreme Court in 1998
Arkansas	1987	Statute
California	1986	Constitutional amendment adopted by voter initiative
Colorado	1988	Constitutional amendment adopted by voter initiative
Florida	1988	Constitutional amendment adopted by voter initiative
Georgia	1986	Nonbinding resolution
Hawaii	1978	Constitutional amendment recognizing English and Native Hawaiian as official languages
Illinois	1923	Statute
	1969	"American" was silently replaced with English
Indiana	1984	Statute
Kentucky	1984	Statute
Mississippi	1987	Statute
Missouri	1998	Statute
Montana	1995	Statute
Nebraska	1923	Constitutional amendment
New Hampshire	1995	Statute
North Carolina	1987	Statute
North Dakota	1995	Statute
South Carolina	1987	Statute
South Dakota	1995	Statute
Tennessee	1994	Statute
Utah	2000	Statute
Virginia	1981	Statute, revised in 1996
Wyoming	1996	Statute

Source: Adapted from James Crawford, 1999. "Language Legislation in the U.S.A." 2000 (http://ourworld.compuserve.com/homepages/jwcrawford/langleg.htm) 31 July 2000; "State by State: The 2000 Election," 2000. *New York Times* November 7.

vironmentalist, and population-control activist, launched FAIR in the late 1970s. FAIR is a Washington, D.C.–based lobby that advocates tighter restrictions on immigration. FAIR has proposed reducing the current level of about one million legal immigrants per year to three-hundred thousand or fewer (Seper, 1995). Prior to organizing FAIR, Tanton served as president of Zero Population Growth. Former Senator S. I. Hayakawa of California and Tanton organized U.S. English in 1983 as an offshoot of FAIR. U.S. English, by highlighting the cultural impact of immigration, was able to bolster FAIR's demands for stricter control of the nation's borders. Until mid-1988, according to federal tax returns, U.S. English was a project of U.S. Inc., a tax-exempt corporation that also channels large grants to FAIR, Americans for Border Control, Californians for Population Stabilization, and other immigration-restrictionist groups. While FAIR did not hesitate to target Hispanic newcomers, particularly undocumented Mexicans, U.S. English focused on language and

Table 3.3   Language Spoken at Home and Ability to Speak English for Persons Five Years Old and Over, 1990

			English Ability (%)			
Rank	Language	Total	Very Well	Well	Not Well	Not at All
United States		230,445,777				
English only		198,600,798				
Total Non-English		31,844,979				
1	Spanish	17,339,172	52	22	18	8
2	French	1,702,176	72	19	9	0
3	German	1,547,099	75	18	6	0
4	Italian	1,308,648	67	22	10	1
5	Chinese	1,249,213	40	30	21	9
6	Tagalog	843,251	66	27	7	1
7	Polish	723,483	63	23	12	2
8	Korean	626,478	39	31	25	5
9	Vietnamese	507,069	37	35	23	5
10	Portuguese	429,860	55	22	17	6
11	Japanese	427,657	48	31	19	2
12	Greek	388,260	69	20	10	1
13	Arabic	355,150	66	23	9	2
14	Hindi	331,484	71	20	7	2
15	Russian	241,798	46	27	21	6
16	Yiddish	213,064	71	21	7	1
17	Thai (Laotian)	206,266	38	34	23	5
18	Persian	201,865	62	26	10	3
19	French Creole	187,658	47	30	19	30
20	Armenian	149,694	50	24	17	9

Source: U.S. Bureau of the Census, Language Spoken at Home and Ability to Speak English for United States, Regions and States: 1990 CPH-L-96 and 133 (Washington, D.C.: U.S. Government Printing Office, 1993), table 5.

avoided immigration issues (Crawford, 1989: 54, 66; 1992: 153). Both organizations supported California's constitutional amendment that declared English to be the state's official language. In this way, the two sister organizations were able to increase their social and economic influence.

Most attempts to protect English, although facially neutral, have been targeted at Spanish speakers (Liebowicz, 1985: 522). Spanish is the largest single non-English language spoken (see Table 3.3) and has the largest number of limited English proficient students (Table 3.4). U.S. English has recently depicted Spanish-speaking communities in the United States as having unprecedented linguistic rates of language and cultural maintenance. Tanton, in a memo leaked to the press, warned of a Hispanic "political takeover" through immigration, language maintenance, high birthrates, and cultural maintenance.

> *Gobernar es poblar* translates to "govern is to populate" . . . In this society where the majority rules, does this hold? Will the present majority peacefully hand over its political power to a group that is simply more fertile. . . . How will we make the transition from a dominant non-Hispanic society with a Spanish influence to a dominant

Table 3.4   Language Groups and Number of Limited English
Proficient (LEP) Students, 1991–1992

		LEP Students	
Rank	Language	Number	%
1	Spanish	1,682,560	79.9
2	Vietnamese	90,922	3.9
3	Hmong	42,305	1.8
4	Cantonese	37,742	1.7
5	Cambodian	37,742	1.6
6	Korean	36,568	1.6
7	Loatian	29,838	1.3
8	Navajo	28,913	1.3
9	Tagalog	24,516	1.1
10	Russian	21,903	0.9
11	Creole (French)	21,850	0.9
12	Arabic	20,318	0.9
13	Portugese	15,298	0.7
14	Japanese	13,913	0.6
15	Armenian	11,916	0.5
16	Chinese (unspe.)	11,540	0.5
17	Mandarin	11,020	0.5
18	Farsi	8,563	0.4
19	Hindi	7,905	0.3
20	Polish	6,747	0.3

Source: National Clearinghouse for Bilingual Education, "What are the Most Common Languages for LEP Students?" 1995 (http://www.ncbe.gwu.edu/askncbel/fac/05toplangs.htm)
28 July 2000. By permission of the National Clearinghouse on Bilingual Education.

Spanish society with a non-Hispanic influence? . . . As whites see their power and control over their lives declining, will they simply go quietly into the night? Or will there be an explosion? . . . We're building in a deadly disunity. (Tanton, 1988 cited in Crawford, 1992: 111)

The focus on language differences and opposition to bilingualism is seen by many political and social scientists as thinly viewed hostility and resentment toward Hispanics and other minority language groups (Alatis, 1986; Heath and Kraser, 1986; Judd, 1987; Marshall, 1986). The loss of a common language is an oft-repeated theme of U.S. English (de la Peña, 1991). There is little evidence, however, to support this claim. Many myths exist surrounding language proficiency and the speed at which new immigrants and their children are learning English.

Despite widespread belief that immigrants are less likely than older waves of newcomers and their children to learn English, current studies do not support this commonly held opinion. In 1990, 14 percent of the nation's population spoke a language other than English in the home, but only about 6 percent did not speak English at all (see Table 3.3). In one of the best designed studies looking at language shift, drawing on the 1976 Survey of Income and Education, Calvin Veltman (1988: 44) concluded that data "certainly do not indicate that hispanophone immigrants resist the learning of English; in fact, the data indicate very rapid move-ment to English on the part of Spanish immigrants." He found that more than three-fourths of any given age group of immigrants will come to speak English on a regular basis after approximately fifteen years of residence. Even more important, approximately 70 percent of the youngest immigrants and 40 percent of those aged 10 to 14 (at the age of arrival) will make English their usual language. Despite sig-nificant differences according to age, education, nationality group, year of immi-gration, and English knowledge prior to immigration, according to a detailed 1989 study (Portes and Rumbaut 1996), added years of U.S. experience improved the skills of most immigrants. New immigrants, especially those from Asian and Latin American countries, may encounter initial problems during the first few years with the English language. However, based on the evidence of the study, "fears that America's newcomers are failing to learn English appear to be greatly exaggerated" (Espenshade and Fu, 1997: 302).

In a recent study of 1990 census data for the five Southwestern states, a similar pattern of intergenerational shift from Spanish to English was observed. While the Spanish-origin population increased by 140 percent between 1970 and 1990, the number who reported using Spanish in the home was just 111 percent across the two decades. Despite the magnitude of the increase, during the same time, lan-guage loyalty rates (defined as the proportion of Spanish speakers within the His-panic population) decreased dramatically. The proportion of Spanish speakers fell from 94.4 percent to 82.6 percent between 1970 and 1990. The decrease was even greater among the younger school-age population. The ability to speak Spanish declined from 83.6 to 71.9 percent in this younger group. Language loyalty rates were found to be in even steeper decline in traditionally established Chicano com-munities. Hernández-Chávez (1997) concluded that the numerical increases in Spanish speakers in the Southwest were due almost exclusively to immigration rather than Spanish maintenance.

Portes and Rumbaut, in the Children of Immigrants Longitudinal Study, fol-lowed a large sample of teenagers along the two coastlines of Miami and Fort Lauderdale in south Florida and of San Diego in California. The sample comprises seventy-seven nationalities—including Mexicans, Filipinos, Vietnamese, Cambo-dians, Laotians, and other Asian and Latin American nationalities in San Diego and Cubans, Haitians, Jamaicans, Nicaraguans, Colombians, and other Latin American and Caribbean groups in south Florida. Over 90 percent of the children of immigrants in the sample reported speaking a language other than English, pri-marily with their parents. In 1992, 73 percent of the total sample preferred to speak English to their parent's native tongue, including 64 percent of the foreign-born youth and 81 percent of the U.S.-born youth. By 1995, among the same sample of youth, 88 percent preferred English, including 83 percent of the foreign-born and 93 percent of the U.S-born. This result also held true for the Mexican-origin group in San Diego living on the border with Mexico. The rapidity in which English tri-umphs and foreign languages atrophy, according to Rumbaut, is why the United States has been historically called a language graveyard (Alba, Massey, and Rum-baut, 1999: 11–12).

Even highly educated parents who make a conscious effort at transferring Spanish to their children do not stand much of a chance of maintaining Spanish. Nativist fears that Spanish will surpass English are entirely unfounded: "Results of the study indicate that only in places where immigrant groups concentrate and manage to sustain a diversified economic and cultural presence will language survive past the first generation. In the absence of policies promoting bilingualism, even these enclaves will be engulfed, in all probability, in the course of two or three generations" (Portes and Schauffler, 1994: 659). The irony of Proposition 227 in California, which effectively eliminates most bilingual education in public schools, is that what is at risk is not English but the preservation of some fluency in the immigrants' home language.

Evidence from past studies in the United States, Canada, and other societies points to the positive association of bilingualism with intellectual development (see Hakuta, 1986; Peal and Lambert, 1962). Current evidence from the Children of Immigrants Longitudinal Study found that fluent bilinguals outperformed both limited bilinguals and English monolinguals. Fluent bilinguals retained a strong advantage over both groups, even after other predictors were controlled. The fluent bilinguals scored higher on standarized reading and mathematics tests, and their grade point averages were significantly higher. Among second-generation youths in the sample, fewer than one-third were fluent in their parents' tongue and English. Unfortunately, education in the United States strongly encourages immigrant children to lose their fluency in the languages they speak at home. This policy is in agreement with nativist ideals and organizations such as U.S. English and the California antibilingual education "Save the Children" campaign, but is at odds with the interests of individuals and a global economy (Portes and Hao, 1998).

David E. Lopez (1996), in his study of language maintenance in Los Angeles, observed that class status rather than language is the major dividing line between Hispanics and Anglos and Asians: "Immigration and the intergenerational inheritance of status are the powerful forces that will continue to maintain and exacerbate ethnic and racial differences in the Los Angeles area" (Lopez, 1996: 160). By contrast, he predicts that language use and preferences will play a minor role in ethnic segmentation, even though language use continues to be an important symbolic resource in the struggle for political and ethnic rights in Southern California.

New Era Immigration: New Cracks in the Melting Pot

Concerns over assimilation and national cohesion has shaped both the "new immigration" of the early twentieth century and the "new era post-1965 immigration." Both periods promoted an ideology of exclusion against new immigrant communities. This ideology included a persistent belief that the new wave of immigrants was unable to be assimilated in the American culture and was slower to learn English than the groups that came before them. Both periods have experienced legislation to correct this situation through enactment of English-Only laws and attempts to limit immigration.

A number of things are different today from what they were in the period between 1880 and 1920. The first important difference is that the United States is more of a welfare state than when the first "new immigration" took place. Therefore, the debate and measures of exclusion have also changed. Healthcare, schools, and welfare state programs are more extensive and more expensive, which means each "new era" newcomer is a greater potential drain on the system than were the newcomers in the 1880s (Glazer, 1995: E3). Legislation not only threatens to limit immigration but also to cut off services and welfare benefits for legal and illegal immigrants who reside in the United States. Increasingly, politicians and the general public ask whether new immigrants should be supported, and to what extent and at what cost to public budgets.

Most notable of recent legislation challenging the provision of services is Proposition 187 in California. Proposition 187, the so-called Save Our State initiative, promised to bar undocumented aliens from nonemergency care at public clinics and all other state social services. In addition, it restricted the children of these immigrants, about three hundred thousand students, from attending public schools, and it required police, school administrators, social service agencies, and public and private healthcare workers to report to the federal Immigration and Naturalization Service (INS) anyone they "reasonably suspected" of being an illegal immigrant (Jost, 1995: 99). *Time* magazine described Proposition 187 as "one of the most sweeping restrictions on aliens ever enacted in the United States" (Hornblower, 1994: 68). The 1994 referendum was a thermometer of the hostility building toward undocumented workers, particularly Hispanics, in California.

The outcome of the vote was closely split along ethnic lines. The vote was 59 percent in favor and 41 percent opposed to Proposition 187. Non-Hispanic whites make up only 57 percent of California's population, but they comprise 80 percent of eligible voters; they voted 2 to 1 for Proposition 187. Latinos, who make up one-quarter of the population, represented only 8 percent of the November voters; Hispanics opposed the measure 3 to 1. A narrow majority (53 percent) of Asians and African Americans, Catholics (51 percent), and Jews (55 percent), according to a *Los Angeles Times* exit poll, opposed it. White Protestants, by contrast, overwhelmingly supported the measure (Zipperer, 1995:43).

This result seems to confirm J. R. Gusfield's (1963) view of a symbolic clash between a dominant and minority culture. The result also gives support to Joshua Fishman's (1988) view of Anglo—particularly Protestant—fears and anxieties and a search for a scapegoat to explain a threatened way of life. Many areas of California have experienced an economic recession, declining tax base, and deteriorating schools and social services. One of the problems is the high concentration of undocumented workers in California. The INS estimates that, in 1992, 60 percent of the illegal Mexican immigrants in the United States resided in California (Martin and Midgley, 1994).

Immediately after the vote, the governor of California, Pete Wilson, moved to bar illegal immigrants from receiving prenatal services and entering nursing homes—thus, he claimed, freezing $90 million a year in funds for legal residents. Wilson was quick to exploit public sentiment against immigrants and old minorities, strongly endorsing Proposition 187 and supporting the elimination of all state affirmative action programs. In other states with large populations of recently arrived legal and illegal immigrant populations—such as Arizona, Florida, Illinois,

New York, and Texas—supporters began pushing for laws similar to Proposition 187 (Ayres, 1994: A42). In spite of popular support of the referendum, most of its provisions are yet to be enforced. Proposition 187 has intensified a renewed national and legal debate over the comparative costs and benefits of immigration.

The Personal Responsibility and Work Opportunity Act of 1996 (PRWORA) has in part followed California's lead. It severely restricts welfare and public benefits for both legal and illegal aliens. Until fall 1997, when PRWORA came into force, immigrants usually received the same benefits, such as food stamps and Supplementary Security Income (SSI), as did citizens. New immigrants entering the United States on or after August 22, 1996 are now excluded from most federal benefits for the first five years they are in the United States unless they are refugees, are veterans of the U.S. Armed Services, or had worked for at least ten years in the United States. At the time the new welfare law was passed, about 1.5 million legal immigrants were receiving welfare benefits. Most lost these benefits; however, amendments in 1997 and 1998 restored SSI and food stamps for legal residents who resided in the United States on or before August 22, 1996, to remain eligible (Martin and Midgley, 1999).

A little-known provision of the 1996 immigration law went into effect on December 19, 1997. The legislation resulted in a significant reduction in legal immigration. The new law required that any American or legal permanent resident wishing to sponsor a family member from abroad must prove that he or she earns at least 125 percent of the federal poverty level. While the requirement appears neutral with respect to different nationalities, unlike the more severe 1921 and 1924 legislation that created the national-origins quota system, the new requirement has a disproportionate effect on certain nationalities. Over half (57.1 percent) of Mexicans and Central Americans under this provision are unable to reunite with close family members (see Figure 3.2). According to the INS, this figure is almost twice that of Asian immigrants (29 percent) and of all Americans (28 percent) (National Immigration Forum, 1997b). Many of these Latino working families suffer not from unemployment or underemployment but from overemployment at poverty wages.

A third difference between the two major waves of immigration relates to the health of the public schools. The nation's public schools, one of the institutions central to transmitting the national culture, are currently "caught in a crisis that makes them far less effective than in the earlier period of immigration" (Graham and Koed, 1993: 26). Many middle- and upper-middle-class families have left the public schools for private institutions, especially in metropolitan areas. This trend and the declining economic fortunes of many cities have left metropolitan school districts strapped for resources. One of the current problems with respect to language services in the schools is the high concentration of immigrants who have limited English proficiency. Figure 3.3 indicates that there has been a steady increase in Limited Proficient English (LEP) students from 1986 through over the 1996–1997 school year. All three states with the largest LEP populations in 1997—California (1,381,393), Texas (513,634), and New York (247,087)—have also reported recent substantial increases in their LEP populations (National Clearinghouse for Bilingual Education, 1998: figure 1).

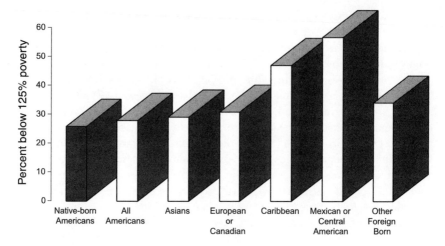

Figure 3.2 Percentage of American Families Unable to Sponsor an Immigrant (Under the New 125%-of-Poverty Rules). *Source*: The Urban Institute by the National Immigration Forum 1997a (http://immigrationforum/Press/102097pr.htm) 28 July 2000. By permission of the National Immigration Forum.

The fourth major difference between the two twentieth-century waves of immigration waves has to do with class and with racial and ethnic backgrounds of the newcomers. The socioeconomic status of America's "new era" immigrants is more heterogeneous than that of the previous "new immigrants." Although most immigrants come to the United States with lower educational attainments than natives, today a higher percentage are university educated. There are a large number of highly skilled doctors, engineers, computer specialists, and others who find employment in the United States. In California's Silicon Valley, one-third of all engineers and microchip designers are foreign born. Each year, one-third to one-half of the student winners of the Westinghouse Science Talent Search, one of the most prestigious high-school competitions, come from immigrant families.

The wide educational differences among immigrants from different countries has led Michael Fix and Jeffrey S. Passel (1994) to call the educational distribution "hourglass shaped." At the low end of the hourglass are immigrants from Latin America, 40 percent of whom have less than nine years of education compared with 20 percent of Europeans and Canadians and 15 percent of Asians. At the top of the hourglass are the 15 percent of Asians who have advanced degrees versus 9 percent of European immigrants, 4 percent of Latin American immigrants, and 7 percent of natives. Recent immigrants—those who arrived between 1980 and 1990—are more likely (24 percent) than natives (20 percent) to have a college degree (Fix and Passel, 1994: 33–34).

In this way, the current immigration is beneficial in ways the older European immigration was not. Alejandro Portes and Rubén Rumbaut (1996) observe that the turn-of-century immigrants were in a uniformly disadvantageous position. With few exceptions, their individual education and occupational skills were modest, and they confronted a generally unfavorable context on arrival. Although the

U.S. government allowed them in, they did not assume any responsibility for their well-being. In general, employers hired them but assigned them to the lowest paid jobs. Many of the same conditions exist today. The law does provide more protection on the basis of race, religion, and nationality than was the case for the earlier wave of twentieth-century immigrants (see Schmid, 1992). These protections, however, are increasingly under attack. U.S. English is mounting a renewed legal attack and nationwide drive to make English the official language of the United States. In addition, state and federal legislation has severely limited welfare benefits to aliens.

Finally, the proportion of racial minorities is greater now than it was in the early twentieth century. In 1960, the top five countries for legal immigration to the United States were Mexico, Germany, Canada, the United Kingdom, and Italy. In 1998, Mexico maintained the lead, but the next four were China, India, the Philippines, and the Dominican Republic; the top European country, in fourteenth place, was the former Soviet Union. The central division in the United States has traditionally been between "white" and "nonwhite." The new era immigration from Asia and Latin America adds a new dimension to racial relations and tensions in the United States. Will the gradual incorporation of nonwhite immigrants and their children change racial fault lines in American society?

Nazli Kibria (1995: 312–313) suggests that the successful incorporation of Jewish and Italian immigrants and their children into the middle class in the United States involved a process of movement from "nonwhite" to "white." Economic growth and the gradual perception of the majority group that the newcomers were not so different than they, as well as a lull in immigration, facilitated this transition.

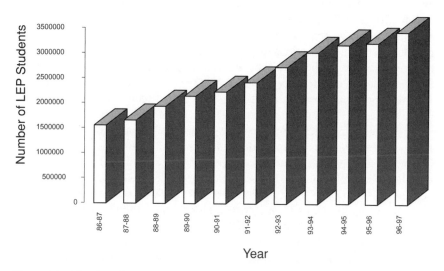

Figure 3.3   Number of LEP Students, 1986–1997. *Source*: Reynoldo Macías, "How Has the Limited Proficient Student Population Changed," National Clearinghouse for Bilingual Education, 1999 (http://www.ncbe.gwu.edu/askncbe/faqs/08leps/htm) 28 July 2000. By permission of the National Clearinghouse on Bilingual Education.

These conditions are more difficult to imagine, given the current economic context and the non-European origins of the majority of new era immigrants. Competition between minority and majority groups over limited government resources, combined with the often unequal treatment of groups, does little to encourage cooperation. Furthermore, books such as Peter Brimelow's (1995) *Alien Nation: Common Sense about America's Immigration Disaster* have sharply focused the immigration debate on the issue of the racial and ethnic background of the newcomers. Brimelow voices concern over the growing tide of non-European immigration.

As we have seen, the ideology of exclusion in the late twentieth century bears many differences from nativism and efforts to Americanize foreigners in the early part of this century. These include (1) the expansion of the welfare state and the reduction of welfare state services to immigrants; (2) the health of American schools and specific targeting of bilingual education in schools; (3) greater racial and educational diversity of the post-1965 wave of immigrants; and (4) a new racial fault line between those of European and non-European backgrounds. The concluding section analyzes the roots of the current attempt to exclude immigrant minorities from the broader American community.

Summary: Economic and Cultural Factors Contributing to Immigrant Exclusion and Language Restriction

Opposition to immigrants is not new. Every new group of immigrants that has come to the United States has been denounced at the time of their entry (Simon, 1984). In time of high immigration and economic insecurity, there is a particularly low tolerance for differences. Boundaries are drawn, dividing the populace into "us" and "them." Chapter 5 shows that attitudes and prejudices toward immigrants appear to be more negative in the first half of the 1990s than in the previous decade, when similar questions were asked. Economic, cultural, and symbolic factors have exacerbated the conflict between citizens and new immigrant communities and escalated the ideology of exclusion at the end of the twentieth century.

One important factor contributing to the sense of economic insecurity is the radical transformation of the American labor market. The demand for labor is being affected by restructuring forces stemming from the nature and pace of technology, stiff international competition, and a major shift away from manufacturing toward services (Briggs and Moore, 1994: 35). The number of jobs available to unskilled laborers nationwide has been cut in half—from 60 percent in 1950 to 30 percent in 1994. In five years, only 15 percent of the workforce will be unskilled; the remainder will require training beyond high school, though not necessarily a college degree (Folk, 1995: B8).

Roberto Suro (1994), in *Remembering the American Dream*, focuses on the consequences of migration to the United States from Latin America, especially Mexico. A major difference between the early and late immigration is related to the structure of opportunities for upward mobility available for the children of immigrants, especially Hispanics. Suro concludes that these opportunities are more limited in the 1990s than in the 1920s, while the costs of staying poor are much higher than before. A growing industrial economy with an appetite for low-skilled labor, and a four decade lull (1921–1965) between immigration waves made the assimilation of low-skilled foreigners easier a century ago than today. He notes the key issue of the 1990s and beyond—rather than entry at the border—is the integration of the children of immigrants, whose achievements would ultimately be the measure by which the success of their wave of immigration is gauged. At the end of the 1990s, the Hispanic high school dropout rate is 50 percent compared with 20 percent for the population as a whole. English-Only legislation and attacks on bilingual education and the welfare state programs have done little to remedy this result.

Since the post-1965 wave of mass migration began, the proportion of immigrants whose occupations at the time of arrival were in the professional, technical, or managerial occupations has declined sharply, although these occupations have sustained the greatest growth during this period. The occupations of a preponderance of new immigrants have been in blue-collar jobs (operatives, laborers, and farmworkers) or low-wage personal service jobs. In urban areas, where most immigrants are concentrated, poorly educated newcomers compete with the sizable pool of low-skilled citizen workers for a declining number of jobs in the low-skill sector of the labor market. This trend exacerbates the negative view of immigrant minorities (Briggs and Moore, 1994: 41–44).

Direct economic competition alone does not explain the ideology of exclusion. A 1995 survey of state residents, the first since the election to gauge a cross-section of California adults, found that a majority believed that the passage of Proposition 187 in November 1994 was a good thing. This result included 60 percent of whites, 52 percent of blacks, 30 percent of Latinos, and 49 percent of Asians. Although blacks are probably more likely to face competition from immigrants, a larger proportion of white Californians support the denial of services to illegal immigrants (Feldman, 1995).

A second factor that helps explain the recent rise in the ideology of exclusion against immigrant minorities is the general perception that citizens are losing ground (see Fishman, 1988; Lipset and Raab, 1978) while paying exorbitant amounts for immigrants. Americans are particularly concerned about providing welfare benefits for immigrants. In December 1994, 53 percent of Americans favored a law in their state that would eliminate education, health, and welfare benefits for illegal immigrants and their children. In addition, 56 percent favored cutting all aid to immigrants who entered the United States legally until they had lived here at least five years (Jost, 1995: 100). Many of these provisions have been integrated in the 1996 Immigrant Responsibility Act as part of the new welfare law.

A third factor that has exacerbated the ideology of exclusion against new immigrant communities is a symbolic clash of lifestyles. There is undeniably a clash between two cultures. An anti-immigrant attitude is not confined to a small group who are experiencing status inconsistency. Like flag burning—and the Pledge of Allegiance—this issue is largely symbolic. This helps explain the widespread appeal of the English-Only movement and the movement to reduce services to immigrants, both illegal and legal. Social movements create their own symbols of identification. The data points to a clash between two cultures—one white and predominantly middle- and lower-middle-class—versus the other—immigrant, primarily of working-class and recent non-English-speaking backgrounds. One can vividly see this clash in communities such as Monterey Park, which changed rapidly from a predominantly Anglo community in the 1960s to a minority Anglo city in the 1980s.[4] The conflict between opponents and proponents of Official English in Monterey Park included the appropriate language of business signs, the number of non-English language books in the public library, anti-immigration politics, and slow versus rapid growth (Horton, 1995).

Finally, conservative movement organizations such as FAIR, U.S. English, and the Save Our State campaign in support of Proposition 187, along with the battle over bilingual education in California have taken advantage of the widespread public concern with the growth, ethnic composition, cost, and rate of assimilation of new wave immigrants. Politicians, particularly Republicans, have encouraged the ideology of exclusion to bolster their own standing. The Republican governor of California, Pete Wilson, and Ron Unz, a prior Republican gubernatorial hopeful, have been particularly successful in exploiting the immigrant and language issues, moving the immigrant, bilingual education, and affirmative action debates to the federal arena. Republican congressional members have sponsored several Official English bills. Patrick Buchanan, a presidential candidate in 1992, 1996 and 2000 insisted that America was losing its "white European culture" (Briggs and Moore, 1994: 85). In Washington, D.C., Republicans in the House of Representatives pushed legislation to deny federal welfare benefits to many legal immigrants. "People should not expect to come to this country with their hands out to receive benefits paid for by taxpaying Americans," Texas House Republican Bill Archer told reporters on January 13, 1995 (Jost, 1995: 100).

The ideology of exclusion in the late twentieth century is best explained by a combination of factors. These include anti-foreigner attitudes fueled by a rapid influx of immigration, the radical transformation of the labor market, and the perceived costs of legal and illegal immigration in an expanded welfare state. Symbols that equate the exclusive use of English with being a "true American" have also increased the conflict between immigrant and "natives." Finally, a theoretical framework must take into account the recent ascendancy of anti-immigrant organizations such as U.S. English, FAIR, and Save Our State, as well as the Republican politicians who have campaigned to eliminate bilingual education and other services, and who have politicized mass prejudices against new immigrant minority communities in the United States.

The next chapter examines the legal rights of non-English-speaking minorities in the United States. To what extent are the rights to education, particularly bilingual education, protected in America? Do citizens have the right to vote in a languages other than English? Must the federal government publish tax, social security, and other information in "foreign" languages? Do linguistic minorities today have more rights than those at the turn of the century?

4

LANGUAGE RIGHTS AND THE LEGAL STATUS
OF ENGLISH-ONLY LAWS

The recent English-Only movement has produced state resolutions, statutes, and constitutional amendments establishing English as the "official" language. English-Only rules are aimed at eliminating governmental services in languages other than English. In the workplace, English-Only rules require employees to refrain from speaking languages other than English on the employer's premises (Mealey, 1989). Proponents of these measures argue that the purpose of this legislation is to promote national unity and protect the only common bond that holds our divergent society together (Leibowicz, 1985). As of 2000, twenty-five states and forty cities had passed some form of law declaring English the official language.[1] U.S. English and other proponents of Official English claim that such laws are only intended to restrict governmental services in languages other than English (Chen, 1992). As English is indisputably the primary language of the United States, declaring English the official language appears harmless. However benign the declaration of an "official" language seems, such laws may have severe discriminatory repercussions.[2]

Restrictive language practices also have appeared in the workplace. Employer rules, which prohibit minority-language workers from speaking in their native languages to coworkers, are widespread (Mealey, 1989). While Title VII of the Civil Rights Act of 1964 outlaws employment discrimination based on race, color, religion, sex, or national origin, the statute does not expressly prohibit discrimination on the basis of language. An important question is to what degree language is construed by the courts as national origin discrimination, which is an area protected by Title VII.

Official English legislation gives rise to numerous legal issues. Despite its obvious importance, there has been relatively little scholarly attention directed toward the issue of language rights in the United States. This chapter analyzes the issues raised by English-Only rules, state constitutional laws and statutes, and workplace rules restricting services and discourse to the English language. The first part reviews the historical and social conditions that have influenced the rise of the recent English-Only laws. The second section reviews the major equal protection and First Amendment cases on language rights. In the third section, English-Only laws in the workplace are discussed. The courts have been severely split in their interpretation of Title VII and whether laws requiring English to be spoken on the job violate the 1964 Civil Rights Act. Finally, four of the most important statutory protections for non-English speakers—the Bilingual Education Act of 1968, Title VI of the Civil Rights Act of 1964, the Equal Educational Opportunities Act of 1974, and the federal Voting Rights Act as amended in 1975 and subsequent years—are examined.

Early Language Restriction under the Constitution

Between 1820 and 1840, over 750,000 German, British, and Irish immigrants arrived in the United States. During the next twenty years, 4.3 million more came from those countries. About one-third were from German-speaking countries. Immigrants fled their native countries to escape economic problems and to seek political freedom (Martin and Midgley, 1994). To accommodate this population, by the middle of the twentieth century, public and parochial German schools were operating in many cities. Heinz Kloss (1977) estimates that 4 percent of the school population—more than six hundred thousand public and parochial elementary students—were receiving instruction exclusively or partly in German. Linguistic differences helped create negative stereotypes and aroused antipathy against the newcomers. For the first time in American history, an ideological link was forged between language and loyalty to the American nation. By 1919, twenty-three states had enacted laws restricting instruction in foreign languages (Ross, 1988). Many of these states mandated English as the exclusive language of instruction in the primary grades.[3]

Language Rights and the U.S. Constitution

There are few Supreme Court decisions on language rights. The few cases, which have vindicated the rights of language minorities, have not been based exclusively on language. The most obvious source of constitutional protection against government-sponsored language-based discrimination is the Equal Protection Clause of the Fourteenth Amendment.

On the eve of World War I, the fear of Germans as the largest, most cohesive ethnic group, made their language especially susceptible to special prohibition. In 1923, the Supreme Court had to strike down the most extreme of these laws. In

Meyer v. Nebraska (1923), the U.S. Supreme Court reversed a conviction of a Nebraska schoolteacher. Robert Meyer was charged with the crime of teaching a Bible story in German at a private school to a ten-year-old child. The Nebraska statute prohibited the teaching of any language other than English to a child who had not passed the eighth grade.

The Court determined that the right to teach a language and the right of parents to engage a teacher to instruct children in a foreign language are among the liberties protected against state infringement by the due process clause of the Fourteenth Amendment: "Mere knowledge of the German language cannot reasonably be regarded as harmful. Heretofore it has been commonly looked upon as helpful and desirable. Plaintiff in error taught this language in school as part of his occupation. His right thus to teach and the right of parents to engage him so to instruct their children, we think, are within the liberty of the Amendment." The Court went on to note: "The protection of the Constitution extends to all, to those who speak other languages, as well as to those born with English on the tongue. Perhaps, it would be highly advantageous if all had ready understanding of our ordinary speech, but this cannot be coerced by methods which conflict with the Constitution" (*Meyer v. Nebraska* 1923: 400-401).

On the same day that *Meyer* was decided, the United States Supreme Court struck down similar statutes in Ohio and Iowa (*Bartels v. Iowa* 1923). Nebraska, Iowa, and Ohio all attempted to show that there was a legitimate need for language laws, and that they were within the police power of the states. Furthermore, the three states argued that the statutes were needed to ensure that school children were educated into loyal and patriotic citizens. The Nebraska brief argued that the legislation was designed "to prevent children reared in America from being trained and educated in foreign languages and foreign ideals before they have had an opportunity to learn the English language and observe American ideals" (Ross, 1988: 175).

In *Meyer*, the decision was based primarily on the due process right of parents to rear their children without state interference. The Supreme Court relied on *Meyer* three years later to declare unconstitutional a Philippine statute in *Yu Cong Eng v. Trinidad* (1926). That statute required Chinese merchants to keep their books in English, Spanish, or a local dialect, thereby prohibiting them from using the only language they understood. The Court held that the law was invalid "because it deprives Chinese persons—situated as they are, with their extensive and important business long established—of their liberty and property without due process of law, and denies them the equal protection of the laws" (*Yu Cong Eng v. Trinidad* 1926: 524-525). Essentially, the Court found that this was a form of national origin discrimination against Chinese, although it did not articulate a constitutional right to use one's native language per se.

Application of the Equal Protection Clause and Language Rights

The U.S. Supreme Court applies a "strict scrutiny" standard of review to classifications that infringe on rights considered "fundamental," or classifications that single out "suspect classes" (Tribe, 1978). Strict scrutiny has been interpreted as applying not only to discrimination on the basis of race but also to discrimination based on national origin.[4] Strict scrutiny also has been applied to categorizations impinging on fundamental rights such as privacy, marriage, voting, travel, and freedom of association.

An intermediate level of scrutiny is applied to classifications that implicate the rights of "quasi-suspect" groups, such as classifications on the basis of sex or illegitimacy. Under an intermediate level of scrutiny, a statutory classification is validated if it substantially furthers a legislative purpose. Classifications that do not implicate either specially protected rights or specially protected persons are granted broad deference by the courts by the "rational basis" standard. The courts will uphold the law so long as it has a rational or reasonable basis (Tribe, 1978).

The U.S. Supreme Court has not resolved the question of whether language-based discrimination constitutes a "suspect" class. A number of legal scholars have argued that language-based discrimination should be afforded strict scrutiny or at least intermediate-level scrutiny (Califa, 1989; Moran, 1981; Official English: Federal Limits, 1987). They have emphasized the need for strict scrutiny because of the close relationship to national origin discrimination. Like racial minorities, non-English speakers have suffered a history of discrimination (including voting and access to political power), have been stigmatized by government action and have suffered economic and social disadvantage.

In general, the courts have rejected an equal protection challenge to language minorities unless the case involves a very close relationship to national origin discrimination or involves rights considered fundamental. More common is the reasoning in *Soberal-Perez v. Heckler* (1983), a second circuit case, which rejected an equal protection challenge for the failure to provide information in Spanish to Social Security recipients and applicants: "The secretary's failure to provide forms and services in the Spanish language does not, on its face, make any classification with respect to Hispanics as an ethnic group. The classification is implicitly made, but it is one of English-speaking versus non-English-speaking individuals, and not made on the basis of race, religion, or national origin. Language, by itself, does not identify members of a suspect class" (*Soberal-Perez v. Heckler* 1983: 41).

In addition to the second circuit, the sixth and ninth circuits have employed similar reasoning and have continued to hold that language is not synonymous with nationality. In the sixth circuit's decision in *Frontera v. Sindell* (1975: 1219), the court ruled that the Civil Service Commission, in conducting its examination in English, did not discriminate against a Spanish-speaking applicant on account of his nationality. The Equal Protection Clause does not require that the state attack all aspects of a problem; "[i]t is enough that the State's action be rationally based and free from invidious discrimination." In *Carmona v. Sheffield* (1973), the ninth circuit held that the failure to provide information in Spanish regarding unemployment insurance benefits did not violate equal protection under the rational basis test. Again, in *Pabon v. MacIntosh* (1982), the court concluded that classes held only in English are not a violation of the Equal Protection Clause in the absence of a suspect classification or a fundamental right. Finally, in *Toure v. the*

United States (1994), a second circuit criminal case, the court held that there is no right to administrative notice in French. Citing *Soberal*, the court observed that English-language notice of administrative forfeiture of property seized from a French-speaking defendant with limited knowledge of English satisfied the requirements of due process.

The standard of judicial review under the Equal Protection Clause will continue to be a major issue in the area of language rights. The current interpretation of the equal protection analysis does not recognize language discrimination as a subset of national origin discrimination. Therefore, where language, as opposed to national origin, is at issue, English-Only laws are rarely deemed "suspect."

Current Language Restriction

Although today's Official English movement does not share the extreme goals of the Americanization movement, there are many philosophical similarities between the two movements. First, there is an implicit comparison between "new" immigrants, who are unwilling to assimilate, and "old" immigrants, who readily assimilated to American culture. Second, there is an equation of linguistic diversity with political disunity and fragmentation of the American culture. Third and finally, there is a link between English proficiency and American identity. After half a century of relative language peace, in the 1980s language again became the focus of a great deal of contention. Attempts to protect the official status of the English language in American life appeared on both the local and national levels.

English-Only proponents argue that immigrants, particularly Spanish speakers, are unwilling to learn English, unlike earlier waves of immigrants (de la Peña, 1991). English-Only advocates maintain that unless English is declared the official language of the United States, the nation will become divided along linguistic lines. Legally, there is much uncertainty about the implications of state Official English measures (Schmid, 1992b).

Despite the philosophical similarities between the Americanization and Official English movements, Califa (1989) observes that recent immigrants arrive in the United States with considerably more political empowerment than earlier immigrant groups. To what extent are there more legal protections now for non-English-speaking immigrants? Is there a constitutional entitlement to language rights, which was unavailable to earlier newcomers?

Protection of Language Rights under the First Amendment

English-Only laws imposed by the government on private businesses may violate the First and Fourteenth Amendments. The First Amendment prohibits government from abridging freedom of speech, expression, and association. The First Amendment is clearly implicated when the government directly restrains the private use of foreign languages. The primary goal of the Fourteenth Amendment is to secure equal treatment against discrete and insular minorities, specifically on the grounds of race and national origin or classifications that have an impact on fundamental rights.

Very few cases have challenged Official English laws or governmental restraints on the use of foreign languages. The few cases that have implicated the First Amendment are directly related to the 1980s English-Only movement. In *Asian American Business Group v. City of Pomona* (1989), Pomona restricted the size and language of business signs. The 1988 ordinance provided that: "on-premises signs of commercial or manufacturing establishments which have advertising copy in foreign alphabetical characters shall devote at least one half of the sign area to advertising copy in English alphabetical letters" (*Asian American Business Group v. City of Pomona* 1989: 1329).

The court held that the ordinance was unconstitutional on three major grounds (*Asian American Business Group v. City of Pomona* 1989: 1329–1332). First, the court observed that by requiring one-half of the space to be devoted to English characters, the ordinance regulates the cultural expression of the signowner, as the "language used is an expression of national origin, culture and ethnicity." Second, the ordinance as a regulation of noncommercial speech fails to meet the standard of strict scrutiny, by serving a compelling government interest. Third, the ordinance burdens the freedom of expression, which is a fundamental interest. *American Asian Business Group*, by restricting language usage, appears to be closer in its reasoning to *Yu Cong* (1926) than to the cases in which a public agency fails to offer information or tests in languages other than English. In both *Yu Cong* and *American Asian Business Group*, the state restricted the use of language and discriminated on the basis of national origin.

A second case, *Yniguez v. Mofford* (1990), challenged on First Amendment grounds on the district court level, found Arizona's Proposition 106 unconstitutional because it was too broadly worded. In 1988, the citizens of Arizona, by a ballot initiative, amended the state constitution to require all government employees and officials during working hours to "act in English and no other language" (Ariz. Const. art. 28, § 1(3)(a)(iv) & 3(1)(a). The Arizona Amendment would have prohibited government officers and employees from using a foreign language in the performance of official duties. A bilingual state employee, Maria-Kelley F. Yniguez, who processed medical malpractice claims, challenged the Arizona constitutional amendment, which was approved by 50.5 percent of the voters, shortly after adoption. Ms. Yniguez spoke Spanish and drafted documents in Spanish when dealing with Spanish-speaking Arizonans. When the amendment took effect, Ms. Yniguez stopped speaking Spanish on the job and filed a lawsuit.

The district court held that a state may not "require that its officers and employees relinquish rights guaranteed them by the First Amendment as a condition of public employment" (*Yniguez v. Mofford* 1990: 314). The law was ruled unconstitutional on the ground of being "overbroad." The court did not have to reach the question of whether the First Amendment bars English-Only restrictions. Nor did it have to decide the more common case in which employees in state offices would be required to cease speaking in languages other than English—for example, state employees officially commenting on matters of public concern in a language other than English or state judges performing marriage ceremonies in a language other than English.

The Ninth Circuit Court of Appeals, sitting en blanc, affirmed the district court decision in *Yniguez v. Arizonans for Official English* (1995) in a 6-to-5 ruling in October 1995. The circuit court also found that the amendment placed an unconstitutional burden on the free-speech rights on public employees and the people they served. Writing in the majority, Judge Stephen Reinhardt argued that the amendment obstructs the free flow of information and adversely affects the rights of many private citizens. He concluded that speech in any language is still speech and that the decision to speak in another language should be protected by the First Amendment. In the dissenting opinion, Judge Alex Kozinski argued that the majority was ignoring the principle that government employees have no personal stake in what they say in the course of employment. The majority approach, according to Judge Kozinski, would allow bureaucrats the right to turn every policy disagreement into a federal lawsuit. The Arizona Official English amendment was much more restrictive than Official English statutes in other states. Therefore, there is some question whether the reasoning used in *Yniguez* could be used to challenge Official English laws in other jurisdictions.

During the 1996/97 term, the U.S. Supreme Court agreed to review the Arizona law, which requires public employees to conduct government business only in English (*Arizonans for Official English v. Arizona* 1997). The Court, however, did not rule on the merits of the case.[5] The case was held to be moot on complex procedural grounds. Ms. Yniguez left her state job prior to the filing of an appeal to the ninth circuit. Rose Mofford (Arizona's governor at the time the case was appealed to the ninth circuit court of appeals) opposed the amendment and refused to appeal the district court's ruling. The case was carried forward by Arizonans for Official English, an affiliate of U.S. English. The U.S. Supreme Court expressed grave doubts as to the standing of the petitioners, which originally sponsored the ballot initiative. According to the Court, Arizonans for Official English lacked standing to pursue the appellate review under Article III of the U.S. Constitution case-or-controversy requirement. In order to have standing to defend on appeal in the place of the original defendant, the litigants must possess a direct stake in the outcome of the case (*Arizonans for Official English v. Arizona* 1997).

The highest court vacated the ninth circuit judgment and remanded the case with directions that the action be dismissed by the district court. The U.S. Supreme Court expressed no view on the correct interpretation of Article 28 or on the measure's constitutionality. This decision meant that the Arizona Supreme Court was given the opportunity to provide an authoritative interpretation of the English-Only provision in Arizona.

In April 1998, the Arizona Supreme Court, in a unanimous decision, overturned the Official English law, thereby making Arizona the nation's first state since the 1920s to have an Official English law overturned. The Arizona Supreme Court held that the law violated the First Amendment and Equal Protection Clause of the Fourteenth Amendment to the U.S. Constitution because it "adversely affects non-English speaking persons with regard to their obtaining access to their government and limits the political speech of elected public employees." "By denying persons

who are limited in English proficiency, or entirely lacking in it, the right to participate equally in the political process, the Amendment violates the constitutional
right to participate and have access to government, a right which is one of the 'fundamental principle [s] of representative government in this country" (*Ruiz v. Hull*
1998: sec. 2, sec. 50).

The court stressed that it did not suggest that government agencies were required to communicate with residents in languages other than English. "However,
the American tradition of tolerance recognizes a critical difference between encouraging the use of English and repressing the use of other languages" (*Ruiz v. Hull*
1998: sec. 22). The only requirements for bilingual materials are imposed by federal
law, such as mandates for voting materials to be provided in native languages.

The constitutionality of English-Only laws in other states are not affected by the
ruling, which is limited to Arizona. Most of the twenty-four statutes in the other
states are less prescriptive and more symbolic than the Arizona amendment. The
Arizona amendment has been identified as one of the most restrictive Official English laws to date (*Ruiz v. Hull* 1998: sec. 139). Other state Official English laws have
been challenged on narrower grounds. In Alabama, state officials are being sued
because they only provided driving tests in English. Before Alabama adopted the
English-Only law in 1990, it offered driving examinations in fourteen languages
(Terry 1998). On November 30, 1999, the eleventh court of appeals ruled that Alabama must abandon its policy of giving the written exam only in English because
this policy discriminated against the state's estimated 13,000 non-English-speaking
residents. The eleventh circuit court held that state recipients of federal funds,
which caused a disparate impact on the ability of non-English speakers to enjoy
federal benefits, violated Title VI of the Civil Rights Act of 1964 (*Sandoval v. Hagan*
1999). In Alaska, an initiative that was approved by nearly 70 percent of the voters
was stayed by temporary injunction before the legislation could go into force in
March 1999. The law required state and city officials to conduct government business only in English. The Alaska Superior Court judge held that the law was unclear and appears to threaten free-speech rights. Of particular concern to Alaska
native peoples is the extent to which it would apply to indigenous languages.[6] The
case, in August 2000, remains to be decided. In the case of *Alaskans for a Common
Language Inc. v. Kritz* (2000) it was held in June of 2000 that Alaskans for a Common Language could go forward to defend the initiative. U.S. English, however,
was found to lack sufficient standing in the case.

The main impact of English-Only laws has been primarily political, rather
than legal. Since people of color—recent immigrants from Latin and Central
America—are more likely to not speak English fluently or at all, Official English
laws have targeted this population. In the workforce, the inability to speak one's
mother tongue has primarily disadvantaged the large Hispanic population. The
next section will turn to the legal rights of non-English-speaking residents in the
workplace.

English-Only Laws in the Workplace

Coverage and Purpose of Title VII

Employees who work for private firms are generally not protected by the U.S. Constitution, which protects against abuses by government but not private entities. Although linguistic minorities lack constitutional protection, Title VII of the 1964 Civil Rights Act[7] provides some measure of protection. Title VII outlaws employment discrimination based on race, color, religion, sex, or national origin. While the U.S. Supreme Court has declared alienage—which refers to noncitizenship—to be a suspect criterion with respect to state action, this is not the case under Title VII. In *Espinoza v. Farah Manufacturing. Co.* (1973), the U.S. Supreme Court held that a private employer's refusal to hire aliens did not constitute discrimination on the basis of national origin in violation of Title VII of the Civil Rights Act.

Title VII of the Civil Rights Act of 1964 makes it unlawful to refuse to hire, discharge, or "otherwise discriminate against any individual with respect to his compensation, terms, conditions, or privileges of employment." Furthermore, it is forbidden for an employer to "limit, segregate, or classify his employees or applicants for employment in any way which would deprive or tend to deprive any individual of employment opportunities or otherwise adversely affect his status as an employee" on the basis of the prohibited criteria.

While Title VII does not expressly prohibit discrimination on the basis of language, the Equal Employment Opportunity Commission (EEOC) has issued broad guidelines in defining national-origin discrimination.[8] These guidelines include discrimination because of an "individual's or his ancestor's place of origin," or because an "individual has the physical, cultural or linguistic characteristics of a national origin group." The EEOC guidelines specifically recognize that an individual's mother tongue or primary language is an important characteristic of national origin.[9]

Narrow versus Broad Interpretation of National Origin

Language as a Matter of Individual Preference

The leading cases on whether English-Only rules constitute national origin discrimination are *Garcia v. Gloor* (1980) and *Gutierrez v. Municipal Court* (1988). The two cases disagree, employing different interpretations of the degree to which language may be considered national origin discrimination.

Garcia v. Gloor (1980) establishes the legality of English-Only rules. The Court of Appeals for the Fifth Circuit held that a bilingual employee fired for speaking Spanish on the job had not stated a claim of national origin discrimination under Title VII. Hector Garcia, a Mexican American, was employed as a salesman for Gloor Lumber and Supply. His duties included selling lumber, hardware, and supplies in both Spanish and English. The store was located in a heavily Hispanic area, and many of Gloor's customers wished to be waited on by a Spanish-speaking salesman.

Gloor Lumber had an English-Only rule prohibiting its salesmen from speaking Spanish unless they were speaking with Spanish-speaking customers. The Hispanic salesmen, with the exception of breaks, were not allowed to speak to each other in Spanish. Garcia was discharged when he spoke Spanish with another salesman during working hours. Garcia sued, claiming that his discharge constituted national origin discrimination in violation of Title VII. The court held that language discrimination does not constitute national origin discrimination. The choice of which language to speak at a particular time is a matter of individual preference: "Neither the statute nor common understanding equates national origin with the language that one chooses to speak." The court interpreted national origin as one's birthplace or the birthplace of one's ancestors. Title VII "does not support an interpretation that equates the language an employee prefers to use with his national origin" (*Garcia v. Gloor* 1980: 268, 270).

Garcia also argued that the English-Only rule had a disparate impact[10] on Hispanic Americans, even if that result was not intentional, because the rule was likely to be violated only by Spanish speakers of Latin American origin. In disparate impact cases, the employer uses employment practices that are facially neutral but in fact fall more harshly on one group than another. Therefore, although the policy or practice is applied evenly to all employees, it has a disproportionate effect on members of a particular race, color, sex, religion, or national origin. Most English-Only rules are analyzed under disparate impact theory and allege discrimination on the basis of national origin. The court failed to accept Garcia's argument, holding that there is no disparate impact if the affected employee "can readily comply with the speak-English-Only rule (and) as to him non-observance was a matter of choice" (*Garcia v. Gloor* 1980: 270).

The court concluded that a bilingual employee's desire to speak his native language is not an immutable characteristic like place of birth, race, or sex. The fifth circuit accepted Gloor's business reasons for the English-Only rule with little analysis. Gloor offered three major arguments: (1) English-speaking customers objected to conversations between employees in Spanish, which they could not understand; (2) requiring bilingual employees to speak English in the workplace, except when they served Hispanic customers, would improve their literacy in English; and (3) the rule would enable Gloor Lumber's English-speaking supervisors to supervise Hispanic employees more effectively (*Garcia v. Gloor* 1980: 269).

The fifth circuit interpreted national origin discrimination very narrowly and declined to critically examine Gloor's business reasons for the English-Only rule. While no violation of Title VII was found by the Gloor court, the Gutierrez court evaluated a similar rule enacted under similar circumstances and came to the opposite conclusion.

Language as an Important Aspect of National Origin Discrimination

The ninth circuit was the first federal court to endorse the EEOC guidelines on English-Only rules. The *Gutierrez* (1988) court struck down a rule imposed by three municipal judges that prohibited bilingual court clerks from speaking to each other in Spanish except during breaks. The court found that the English-Only policy had a discriminatory impact on Hispanics and was not justified by business necessity.

To meet the business necessity test, the court held that the employer's justification must be "sufficiently compelling to override the discriminatory impact." The challenged practice must also "effectively carry out the business purpose it is alleged to serve, and there must be available no acceptable less discriminatory alternative which would accomplish the purpose as well" (*Gutierrez v. Municipal Court* 1988: 1039–1041).

Applying this stringent test, the appeals court rejected the five major arguments put forward by the employers to justify their English-Only rule. First, the employers argued that the state and country need to have a single language system. This argument, however, was undercut by the fact that it was an important part of the clerks' duty to communicate with the non-English-speaking public in Spanish. Second, the defendants said if an English-Only rule was not imposed in the workplace, it would turn into a "Tower of Babel." This claim was contradicted by the fact that the use of Spanish was part of the normal press of court business. Third, appellants asserted that English-Only rules are necessary to promote racial harmony in the workplace. This allegation was unsupported by any evidence; in fact, racial hostility was increased between Hispanic and non-Spanish-speaking employees because the English-Only rule made the Spanish speakers feel belittled. Fourth, employers contended that the English-Only rule was necessary because several supervisors did not speak or understand Spanish and their job entailed monitoring the work of the clerks. The court observed that a more effective way of monitoring the work product of the clerks would be to hire Spanish-speaking supervisors. Finally, the appellants argued that the English-Only rule was required by the California Constitution. However, the court considered the constitutional amendment, which was passed by the voters in 1986, as "primarily a symbolic statement" that did not affect communications between coworkers in government.

Gutierrez, like *Garcia*, argued that the English-Only rule had a disparate impact on Hispanic employees. By failing to meet the rigorous business necessity standard, the court agreed that the plaintiff successfully established an adverse impact claim. The *Gutierrez* court rejected the reasoning in *Gloor*, relying on the EEOC English-Only guidelines and a broader interpretation of national origin. Because Ms. Gutierrez was no longer employed by the municipal court, however, the U.S. Supreme Court vacated the decision as moot and determined that the findings had no precedential authority.

In one of the most recent decisions to address the issue of English-Only rules in the private sector, *Garcia v. Spun Steak Co.* (1993), the court reaffirmed the *Gloor* interpretation of English-Only laws. The Spun Steak Company had a work force of thirty-three employees, twenty-four of whom were Hispanic. Two employees could speak only Spanish, and the rest had varying levels of English proficiency. The company promulgated a rule prohibiting the use of Spanish during working hours in response to complaints that Garcia and Buitrago, the plaintiffs, had harassed and insulted non-Spanish speaking employees in Spanish. In response to a claim by Garcia and Buitrago—both of whom were bilingual—that the English-Only rule had a disproportionate impact on their national origin group, the court initially conceded that if the English-Only policy caused any adverse effects, such an impact would fall disproportionately on Hispanic employees. Applying the fifth circuit's reasoning in *Garcia v. Gloor*, however, the court concluded that the English-Only rule had an adverse impact exclusively on those employees who possessed such limited English skills that they were effectively denied the privilege of conversing on the job. In contrast, "the language a person who is multi-lingual elects to speak at a particular time is . . . a matter of choice" (*Garcia v. Spun Steak Co.* 1993: 1487).

According to the reasoning in *Spun Steak*, it appears that an employer may restrict the language used at work of multilingual employees. The court rejected the EEOC guidelines, on the premise that an individual's primary language is not necessarily an important link to his cultural or ethnic identity (Locke, 1996). Current legal reasoning then, seems to contradict sociological evidence that has shown the significance of language, particularly the mother-tongue, as a "fundamental aspect" of ethnicity and national origin (see Edwards 1985, 1994; Perea 1992). The ninth circuit held that the mere existence of an English-Only rule does not create a presumption of national origin discrimination. Contrary to the EEOC guidelines, which presumed that an English-Only policy created a discriminatory work environment based on national origin, the court ruled that Spun Steak's English-Only workplace policy did not necessarily have a discriminatory impact on employees whose primary language was not English.

As more immigrants enter the workforce, an increasing number of employers have instituted English-Only rules prohibiting languages other than English at work. The workplace has emerged as an important battleground of the Official English movement and the civil rights of language minorities. As of June 1994, there were approximately 120 active charges filed with the EEOC against sixty-seven different employers who had imposed English-Only laws. Some of the rules may be necessary to promote worker safety. Many are in response, however, to the xenophobia of the Official English movement and fear of employer sanctions under the Immigration Reform and Control Act (Adams, 1995). In order to carry out the intent of Title VII, courts should adopt the EEOC guidelines and recognize the close association between language and national origin. The long history of discrimination against members of language minority groups in the United States suggests that they, like persons whose race or religion differs from those of the majority, warrant protection under Title VII.

Major Federal Protection for Language Minorities

Current English-Only efforts are attempting to limit government services for language minorities. English-Only forces have particularly singled out bilingual education and bilingual ballots since they are perceived as disincentives to learning English. Bilingual education is said to provide a barrier rather than an important path for non-English-speaking students to learn English (Stefancic, 1997: 124), and bilingual ballots are claimed to send an erroneous message to non-English speakers that they can participate in the political system without learning English (Crawford, 1992: 192–193).

Four major statutes in addition to Title VII of the 1964 Civil Rights Act provide some protection for language minorities in the areas of education and voting. This section will briefly analyze the rights of language minorities under the Bilingual Education Act, the Equal Education Act, Title VI of the 1964 Civil Rights Act, and the federal Voting Rights Act.

Bilingual Education Act

The Bilingual Education Act was the first piece of federal legislation to recognize that minority-language children were not receiving an adequate education in schools that operated exclusively in English (McFadden, 1983). The new Title VII of the Elementary and Secondary Education Act, which became law in 1968, authorized resources to support educational programs, to train teachers and aides, and to develop appropriate instructional material. The focus of the law was children who were both poor and educationally disadvantaged because of their inability to speak English. Title VII was reauthorized under the Improving America's Schools Act in 1994.

Although there was optimism surrounding the Bilingual Education Act, which passed through Congress with remarkably little controversy, this optimism was short-lived. Under pressure from the White House, Congress failed to approve funding for the bill during 1968. In 1969, it appropriated $7.5 million, which was only able to serve twenty-seven thousand children and to finance seventy-six projects. By 1973, the act had benefited only 2 percent of the nation's bilingual schoolchildren. Since that time, the amount has increased to 163 million in 1995, peaking at almost 182 million in 1994 (Kindler, 1996). While more children have been served, the resources have been inadequate for the increased non-English-speaking population (Crawford, 1989; McFadden, 1983).[11]

The Bilingual Education Act did not provide a right to bilingual education; rather, it offered financial assistance for local bilingual programs designed to meet the needs of children with limited facility in English. When the act did not prove to be the panacea that many of its supporters had hoped it to be, parents of minority language children gradually turned to the federal courts to answer the question of whether there was a constitutional right to bilingual education.

Constitutional Issue Avoided: *Lau* and Title VI

In *Lau v. Nichols* (1974), the U.S. Supreme Court held that placing non-English-speaking students in a classroom with no special assistance and providing them with instruction that was not comprehensible to them violated Title VI of the federal Civil Rights Act of 1964. In *Lau*, a class of approximately eighteen hundred non-English-speaking Chinese students in the San Francisco schools raised an equal protection claim and a claim under Title VI. Title VI prohibits discrimination based on the grounds of race, color, or national origin in any program or activity receiving federal financial assistance.

In its analysis, the U.S. Supreme Court observed the importance of the English language in the California educational scheme. English fluency was a prerequisite for high school graduation. School attendance was compulsory. Furthermore, English as the basic language of instruction was mandated by the state. Given these state-imposed standards, "there is no equality of treatment merely by providing students with the same facilities, textbooks, teachers, and curriculum; for students who do not understand English are effectively foreclosed from any meaningful education" (*Lau v. Nichols* 1974: 566).

In reaching this conclusion, the *Lau* court relied, in addition to Title VI, on the guidelines promulgated by the Department of Health, Education and Welfare (HEW). The guidelines required that school districts take affirmative steps to address the language needs of minority language children. Failure to rectify language deficiencies constitutes discrimination on the basis of national origin, even if it is not deliberate. The Court did not resolve the question of whether the failure to provide educational assistance to non-English-speaking students violated the constitution. The *Lau* decision did not order a specific remedy, as none was requested by the plaintiffs, although it did identify bilingual education and English as a second language (ESL) instruction as options.

In *Serna v. Portales* (1974), the tenth circuit closely followed the reasoning in *Lau*, and also ruled on Title VI rather than constitutional grounds. The *Serna* court noted that the children were required to attend schools where classes were conducted in English. As it failed to provide remedial measures to meet the needs of Mexican American students, the Portales school curriculum was discriminatory and in violation of Title VI and the HEW regulations.

As the only recent U.S. Supreme Court case on the issue of the right of language minority children to an equal education, the *Lau* case established guidelines for similar cases. Courts tended to (1) avoid the constitutional issue, (2) rely on the discriminatory effect rationalization of Title VI, (3) choose a remedy on a case-by-case basis, and (4) take into account the number of students involved (McFadden, 1983). While there appears to be a limited right to rectify language deficiencies where school policies have had the effect of discriminating against national origin minorities under Title VI, there is not an absolute right to bilingual education. In school districts with both language and racial minorities, conflicting remedies present difficult problems. With the future of *Lau* remedies increasingly uncertain, there has been more reliance on the Equal Educational Opportunity Act of 1974. Shortly after the *Lau* decision, in effect, Congress codified the U.S. Supreme Court's holding.

Equal Educational Opportunities Act

Section 1703(f) of the Equal Educational Opportunities Act requires school districts to "take appropriate action to overcome language barriers that impede equal participation by its students in its instructional programs." For the first time, Congress recognized the right of language-minority students to seek redress for a school system's inequity, whether or not it received subsidies from the federal government. Soon after the passage of section 1703(f), the fifth circuit held that a violation of this act requires no discriminatory intent on the part of school authorities, simply a failure to take appropriate action (*Morales v. Shannon* 1975).

The courts have been split, however, on the form that this "appropriate" action must take. In 1978, the district court for the Eastern District of New York, in *Cintron v. Brentwood Union Free School District* (1978) held that where a bilingual program is implemented under section 1703(f), it must include instruction in the child's native language in most subjects. The ninth circuit, by contrast, in *Guadalupe Organization, Inc. v. Tempe Elementary School* (1978), concluded that appropriate action under 1703(f) need not be bilingual-bicultural education staffed with bilingual instructors. The ESL program proposed for the Arizona school district qualified as an appropriate program for English-deficient children.

The interpretation of 1703(f) was clarified in the 1981 fifth circuit case of *Castaneda v. Pickard* (1981). Agreeing with *Cintron*, the court held that it was not necessary for a school district to intentionally discriminate in order for 1703(f) to be invoked. It also determined that the type of appropriate compensatory languages programs should be left up to the state and local educational authorities. The Fifth Circuit Court of Appeals formulated a set of basic standards to determine a school district's compliance with the Equal Education Opportunity Act (EEOA). The *Castaneda* test included three major criteria: (1) the school must pursue a program based on an educational theory recognized as sound or, at least, as a legitimate experimental strategy; (2) the school must actually implement the program with instructional practices, resources, and personnel necessary to transfer theory into reality; and (3) the school must not persist in a program that fails to produce results. Therefore, the court specified that at a minimum schools must have a program predicated on and "reasonably calculated" to implement a "sound" educational theory and must be adequate in actually overcoming language barriers of the students (*Castaneda v. Pickard* 1981: 1019–1010).

The influence of *Castaneda* has extended beyond the fifth circuit, making it one of the most significant cases affecting language minority students after *Lau*. In *Keyes v. School District No. 1* (1983), a suit involving the desegregation of Denver's public schools, the three-part Castaneda analysis was used to determine whether the school system was meeting its obligations under the EEOA. It ruled that the Denver school district had failed to "take reasonable action to implement" its bilingual program—the second element of the Castaneda test. The Denver school system had failed to train its ESL teachers properly or to adopt adequate means to evaluate its limited English proficiency programs.

Although Section 1703(f) of the EEOA provides some protection for language minorities, there is not a right to bilingual-bicultural education. However, the EEOA did recognize a duty on behalf of educational agencies to ensure access to instructional programs for limited-English students. In addition, it provided aggrieved individuals with a private right of action to compel such relief, and it allowed the attorney general of the United States to sue on behalf of those individuals.

Although there is no duty to provide limited-English-proficient students educational programs in their mother tongue, bilingual and multicultural education is not inherently discriminatory. In *Carbajal v. Albuquerque Public School District* (1999), a federal judge in New Mexico ruled that the New Mexico Bilingual Multicultural Education Act does not discriminate against students, based on their national origin, by placing them in language-assistance classes. In March 1998, four-teen Albuquerque public school students and their parents sued the district. They demanded an end to bilingual education, claiming that the program failed to teach English effectively and, as a result, discriminated against the public school students based on national origin.

U.S. District Judge Vazquez held that "the mere fact that the statute uses a defi-nition which might be correlated with national origin does not itself establish a discriminatory classification. . . . On its face this statute does not divide the stu-dents but unites them: it specifically provides that bilingual educational programs in the state must accommodate everyone, children who speak 'minority' languages, Native American children, and all others who wish to participate in the program" (*Carbajal v. Albuquerque Public School District* 1999). The plaintiffs failed to state a claim for a facial constitutional or an EEOA violation because the APS statute did not impose a discriminatory classification.

Voting Rights Act

Another significant piece of legislation is the federal Voting Rights Act of 1965, as amended in 1970, 1975, and 1992. It is often assumed that any non-English speaker who is an American citizen is entitled to vote in his or her native tongue. The right to bilingual ballots is much more limited, however: it only applies to linguistic minorities who have historically faced discrimination at the polls—Hispanics, Asians, and Native Americans—and only in areas in which they meet strict re-quirements. The 1975 amendments required that state and local governments publish bilingual election materials when more than 5 percent of the voting-age residents were members of a single language minority and when the illiteracy rate in English of such groups was higher than the national average (Guerra, 1988).[12]

Furthermore, the 1965 Voting Rights Act and the 1970 amendment prohibited states from conditioning the right to vote of persons who attended school in Puerto Rico on their ability to read or understand English.[13] To limit the impor-tance of non-English speakers, advocates of Official English have attempted to use state laws to restrict the impact of the Voting Rights Act. In *Puerto Rican Organi-zation for Political Action v. Kusper* (1973), the board of election commissioners ap-pealed the authorized use of bilingual ballots, arguing that the amendment to the Voting Rights Act required the board to violate the state's Official English law. The court held the statute to be purely symbolic, observing that it "appears with oth-ers naming the state bird and the state song." It has "never been used to prevent publication of official materials in other languages" (*Puerto Rican Organization for Political Action v. Kusper* 1973: 577).

The 1975 amendments have significantly increased voter participation by non-English speakers. The General Accounting Office (GOA) published an extensive analysis of language-assistance provisions on the basis of the November 1984 elec-tions. The study showed that one in four Latino voters used Spanish assistance when available. Advocates of the English-Only movement criticize language assis-tance as expensive, yet the same report showed that the costs are nominal. The GOA concluded that of the 295 jurisdictions that responded, the average cost of providing written assistance was 7.6 percent of the total election expenditures, and an estimated eighteen states incurred no additional costs in providing assistance (MALDEF, n.d.).

Asians citizens also have gained increased access to the ballot box. According to exit polls in the November 1994 election, more than 31 percent of Chinese American voters used some form of bilingual assistance. In San Francisco, nearly 14 percent used bilingual ballots (Eljera, 1996).

English-Only proponents have proposed several federal constitutional amendments to limit access to linguistic minorities. Thus far, Official English proponents have failed to win congressional approval of federal laws restricting the use of non-English languages. The most recent attempt, H.R. 123, was passed in the U.S. House of Representatives in August 1996 by a largely partisan vote of 259 to 169, but it died in the U.S. Senate. Republicans have traditionally supported Official English laws to a greater extent than Democrats. The bill attempted to declare English the official language of the federal government. It would have outlawed most operations in other languages—from Social Security publications to consumer information services to bilingual voting. Although immigrants are the main political targets of this and similar federal legislation, it could affect many other populations, including Native Americans, whose languages are already endangered, and foreign visitors.

Summary

The English-Only movement, like the Americanization movement before it in the 1920s, has prompted a resurgence of antiforeigner sentiment. Fueled by high rates of immigration from Latin American and Asian countries, English-Only forces have attempted to limit bilingual services and encourage English-Only laws in the public and private sectors. They seek to limit bilingual education and bilingual ballots and to enforce English-Only rules in the workplace.

The legal effect of state Official English laws remains unclear. Many of the state laws are very broad. Thus far, courts—with a few exceptions—have ruled that they are of symbolic value. If enforced, they could deprive language minorities of important rights in the workplace, voting booth, and in the education arena. English-Only forces have been more successful in using the laws politically than in the courtroom. The passage of California's Proposition 63 in 1986 was employed by English-Only forces to pressure the governor into vetoing bilingual education legislation. Proposition 227, which was passed by a significant majority of California voters in 1998, restricted bilingual education classes in the state. By contrast, the attorney general in California rejected a demand by U.S. English to ban election materials published in Chinese and Spanish by courts in San Francisco and in other jurisdictions.

There remain many troubling aspects of the English-Only movement and the Official English laws. The laws have not increased the proficiency of individuals with a limited knowledge of English. Rather than promote national unity and tolerance of Hispanic and Asian newcomers, the laws have promoted an antiforeigner attitude among the population. Immigrants are perceived as refusing to assimilate and to learn the English language, even though studies show that most language minorities lose their mother tongues by the second or, at most, the third generation. There is a need to rethink to what extent one should have the "right to language" (Piatt, 1986), independent of the national origin label. Unless there are proper safeguards for language minorities, U.S. English and allied groups will be able to promote a hidden agenda that has little to do with language.

In the second half of the twentieth century, non-English-speaking immigrants did have more legal protections than those who entered the United States before them. There is not an entitlement to language rights, however, either under the U.S. Constitution or under the major federal statutes. The analysis has shown that courts have rejected challenges to language minorities unless they fall squarely within the scope of national origin discrimination. Statutes giving access to remedial education programs for those who lack proficiency in English have established a limited right for language minorities. These programs, however, are not required to use instruction in the mother tongue of limited-English-speaking students. The use of interpreters in courtrooms in an effort to protect citizens who are not fluent in English is required by 28 USC Section 1827(d). The Voting Rights Act has mandated bilingual voting assistance for non-English-speaking citizens, but many language minorities remain outside the requirements of this act. Even though federal laws, court decisions, and administrative regulations have given limited ability to use other languages in the public sphere, most citizens regard English as a symbol of American nationhood that must be defended. The next chapter will turn to the attitudes toward Official English of both majority and minority language communities.

5

ATTITUDES TOWARD LANGUAGE, NATIONAL IDENTITY, AND CULTURAL PLURALISM

"What do you call a person who speaks two languages?"
"Bilingual."
"And one who knows only one?"
"American."

(Portes and Rumbaut, 1996: 195)

Currently there is a political confrontation between "language rights" and "English-Only," which is connected to a deeper debate over the meaning of American identity and the means of preserving it. Is speaking English a condition for full membership in the American community? How do most Americans judge the need for a common language? To what degree are there differences in opinion among Americans and immigrants about the need for an official language, bilingual education, and the desirability of maintaining one's culture? How do different language and cultural groups see one another? To what degree are there major differences in the understanding of the American creed between Latinos, blacks, and whites? Do Latino citizens and those who have been naturalized share fundamentally similar orientations toward language and immigration issues with more recent immigrants? Are we on the way to a "Quebecification" in attitudes and behavior, as some English-Only proponents have suggested? These are important questions, which have received little analytical discussion in the academic and popular literature.

Many Americans assume that English is the official language of the United States. In a 1987 poll, two out of three Americans believed that English was already the official language of the United States (see Califa, 1989), despite the fact that the U.S. Constitution does not contain a provision giving official status to English. For many Americans, there is the belief that national identity and speaking accentless English are intertwined. Alejandro Portes and Rubén Rumbaut (1996: 196) observe "the remarkable rapidity and completeness of language transition in America is no mere happenstance, for it reflects the operation of strong social forces. In

a country lacking centuries-old traditions and culture and receiving simultaneously millions of foreigners from the most diverse lands, language homogeneity
came to be seen as the bedrock of nationhood and collective identity." In the
United States, immigrants and their children were compelled to speak accentless
English if they desired social acceptance and integration in their adopted country.

Enactments and Attitudes toward Making English
the Official Language

Legally, as outlined in the last chapter, there is still much uncertainty about the implications of state Official English measures. Whereas opponents can point to few
direct legal effects thus far, the political impact of the Official English movement
has been substantial. Opinion polls show between 50 to 90 percent approval of
making English the official language, depending on how the question is phrased
and to whom the question is asked. In general, the more specific the question, the
lower the rate of agreement. For example, when asked, "Would you favor or oppose
an amendment to the Constitution that requires federal, state, and local governments to conduct business in English and not use other languages, even in places
where many people don't speak English?," the population was evenly split between
those agreeing and disagreeing with this statement (asked in a *New York Times*/CBS
News poll of 1,618 adults, June 19–23, 1986). By contrast, a survey of 1,208 likely
voters polled August 2–6, 1995 by Luntz Research Companies for U.S. English
found overwhelming support for a much less specific question. When asked, "Do
you think English should be made the official language of the United States?" 86
percent of those questioned answered affirmatively as compared with 12 percent
negatively (polls cited in Crawford, 1997b).

A 1996 national poll that asked respondents on a seven-point scale how much
they opposed or favored "making English the official language of the United
States" found significant differences between ethnic and social groups (see Table
5.1). The Hispanic population had the most reservations about making English the
official language of the United States; they are almost split in half between those favoring and opposing making English the official language of the United States. The
highest support for making English the official language is among Republicans (84
percent) and citizens sixty-five years old or older (80 percent). Social class seems to
have some effect, with greater support among low- to middle-income laborers (77
percent) and managers and entrepreneurs (76 percent) than among poor laborers
(63 percent) and professionals (67 percent). Religion also exerts a significant effect,
with lower support for language legislation among orthodox Catholics (69 percent) and among secularists (64 percent) than among evangelical Christians (80
percent), mainline Protestants (76 percent), and progressive Catholics (74 percent). By contrast, sex, race, and region of the country show no major differences.

Although there is general support for Official English, this result does not explain why most states adopted legislation to establish English as their official language after 1980. Only three states had Official English laws prior to the recent

Table 5.1 Attitudes toward Making English the Official Language of the United States (%)

	Strongly oppose	(2)	(3)	Neutral	(5)	(6)	Strongly favor	Don't care
Total	5	2	3	12	7	11	55	4
Ethnicity								
African American	4	1	5	14	5	10	55	6
Hispanic	15	6	2	22	14	12	26	4
White (Non-Hispanic)	4	2	3	10	7	12	60	4
Gender								
Female	5	2	3	12	7	10	57	4
Male	5	3	3	11	8	13	54	4
Age								
18–34	7	3	4	12	10	13	48	4
35–49	5	3	2	13	6	13	55	4
50–64	4	2	4	11	7	9	60	4
65 or older	3	2	2	10	6	9	65	3
Region								
East	3	2	3	12	7	16	53	4
Midwest	4	2	2	11	7	13	57	5
South	6	2	4	12	8	11	54	4
West	9	4	1	12	9	7	57	2
Religion								
Evangelical Protestant	3	1	2	11	5	10	65	3
Mainline Protestant	4	2	5	9	9	12	55	3
Orthodox Catholic	7	4	1	16	5	9	55	4
Progressive Catholic	6	3	2	12	9	16	49	3
Secularist	9	5	2	13	4	13	47	6
Education								
Less than H.S.	5	3	2	17	7	8	53	5
High School Graduate	4	1	2	11	5	11	61	4
Some College or Tech.	6	1	3	11	7	11	58	3
College Graduate	6	4	2	10	12	15	47	4
Post-College Study	7	6	5	9	12	15	45	2
Social Class								
Poor Laborers	10	3	4	15	8	6	49	5
Lo-Mid Income Laborers	4	2	4	10	7	12	58	3
Managers and Entrepreneurs	7	2	1	8	4	16	56	6
Professionals	4	2	3	12	10	14	52	2
Social Elite	10	9	1	8	9	13	46	5
Political Party								
Democrat	6	3	3	12	7	13	53	3
Republican	4	2	2	6	6	9	69	2
Independent	6	3	3	12	9	13	51	4

Source: State of Disunion, Survey of American Political Culture (Ivy, VA: In Media, Res Educational Foundation, 1996), vol. 2, table 105. By permission of the Institute for Advanced Studies in Culture.

movement spearheaded by U.S. English. Two of the enactments were a backlash from World War I. In 1920, Nebraska passed a constitutional amendment to affirm English against the large German population. Three years later, Illinois passed a law making "American" its official language (this was amended in 1969, substituting "English" for "American"). The third law is of more recent vintage: in 1978, Hawaii codified English and Hawaiian as official languages. English still retains primacy, however, as public acts and transactions must only be published in Hawaiian as required by law.

Between 1981 and 1999, twenty-one states established Official English by statute and state constitutional amendment (see Table 3.2). The enactments in the fourteen post-1981 "statutory states" in which Official English laws were passed by state legislatures were essentially non-issues, passed by overwhelming legislative majorities. These states included Arkansas, Georgia, Indiana, Kentucky, Mississippi, Missouri, Montana, New Hampshire, North and South Carolina, South Dakota, Tennessee, Virginia, and Wyoming. In the 1990s, Alabama and Alaska voters by referendum passed constitutional amendments by large majorities. More contentious were referendums in California, Colorado, Arizona, and Florida. In the referendum states, U.S. English and its affiliates helped to collect signatures to place the constitutional amendment on the ballet. Using a multivariate analysis to predict the voting behavior and legislative sponsorship of Official English bills, Raymond Tatalovich (1997) concluded that among the statutory states the movement for Official English is driven by the elites. The push for Official English did not represent a groundswell from mass opinion. Attributes of the legislators (including party, race, and gender) were far more important than the characteristics of their home counties in explaining sponsorship and voting behavior among legislators. Tatalovich (1997) found that while patterns varied among states and across groups of states, the state legislators who were supportive of Official English were likely to be Republicans, whites (irrespective of their party affiliation), and men.[1]

Nativism—rather than large immigrant populations—seemed to be the driving force behind Official English laws in the statutory states. Although Asians are the target of language and racial discrimination in a few localities, the main focus of antiforeigner sentiment is Spanish speakers. In 1985, 7.3 percent of the United States was composed of Spanish speakers. The twelve states that adopted Official English statutes during the period between 1980 and 1996, however, had Hispanic populations of less than 2 percent. These states are conspicuous for having few linguistic minorities.

In contrast to the statutory states, the Latino population in the referendum states of California (22.1 percent), Arizona (16.8 percent), Colorado (11.9 percent), and Florida (9.8 percent) is much higher. Texas, with a 22.8 percent Hispanic population, does not have a popular referendum and was unable to muster the two-thirds vote required in the state House and Senate to approve a constitutional amendment. In the four states that passed Official English laws, U.S. English and allied groups failed to obtain enough support in the legislature and, therefore, had to resort to a popular initiative. In California and Florida, Democratic-controlled Houses refused to enact constitutional amendments requiring the use of English in state-sponsored activities. In Colorado, the Democratic governor, Roy Romer, withdrew a bill that appeared destined to be approved. The Republican-controlled Arizona legislature also backed down when faced with sustained pressure from Hispanic and Native American groups (Tatalovich, 1997).

In each of the six states that passed Official English constitutional amendments since 1986 direct and indirect support was received from U.S. English. Groups such as Arizonans for Official English, the California English Committee, the Colorado Official English Committee, and Florida English, and Alaskans for a Common Language spearheaded those campaigns. As discussed in chapter 4, except for the restrictive Arizona law, the constitutional amendments have probably had more political than legal significance. The debate over Official English or English-Only as opposed to "English Plus" (the phrase coined by those favoring English plus additional languages and a multicultural approach in American society) is largely a symbolic confrontation over a group's status and identity in American society.

An examination of the 1992 National Election Study by John Frendreis and Raymond Tatalovich (1997) also confirmed the relationship between identity and Official English laws. When asked, "Do you favor a law making English the official language of the United States, meaning government business would be conducted in English only, or do you oppose such a law?" 64.5 percent of the sample favored it. In their multivariate analysis, Frendreis and Tatalovich found that the strongest predictors for supporting the English-Only law among the non-Hispanic population were attitudes regarding national identity and cultural diversity. Three attitudinal variables that described qualities that make a "good American" (speaking English, treating people equally, and endorsement of the melting pot, as opposed to the maintenance of separate cultures) provided the strongest predictors for supporting the English-Only law. Thus widespread support for Official English laws is based on a particular conception of American identity and cultural pluralism at the end of the twentieth century. Only Hispanics consistently challenge this notion (Schmid 1991, 1992a). Only 39.3 percent of the Latino 1992 sample favored the Official English law, in contrast to a majority of all other racial, class, and political groups (Frendreis and Tatalovich, 1997).

Public Opinion and Attitudes toward Immigration

Immigrants have proved to be the perfect target in troubled and turbulent times. Like the Americanization movement before it, the late-twentieth-century confrontation has grown out of "a search for America in an age of social upheaval" (Bennett, 1988: 103). Many recent surveys and studies indicate the widespread misconceptions and negative attitudes toward immigrants. A public opinion poll conducted by Princeton Survey Research in 1997 (cited in National Immigration Forum 1999) found that 46 percent of respondents thought that immigration should be decreased or stopped. This represented a change from 1993, when 65 percent gave the same response to this question. In 1986, slightly under 50 percent believed immigration should be halted. In the vigorous economy of the late 1990s, anxiety over immigration and its effects seemed to have at least temporarily abated. By 1998, polls in California found that fewer than 10 percent of residents identified either legal or illegal immigration as a major concern. Surveys at the end of the millennium by the Public Policy Institute of California showed residents about evenly divided over whether immigrants are a benefit or a burden, with whites the most skeptical. Hispanics, on the other hand, expressed significantly more optimism about the future (Purdum, 2000). There appears to be a cyclical relationship between the economy and tolerance of immigration during the late 1980s and 1990s. A more robust economy and low unemployment rates are correlated with more tolerance for newcomers.

Many Americans believe—incorrectly—that more foreigners enter the country illegally than legally. A 1996 CBS News poll found this result cross-cut ethnicity and race with 73 percent of Hispanics, 69 percent of African Americans, and 62 percent of whites believing that most people in the previous 10 years had emigrated illegally (Public Agenda Online, 1999a). In reality, the vast majority of immigrants enter the United States legally. In 1996, the Immigration and Naturalization Service (INS) estimated that there were approximately five million undocumented immigrants in the United States, with an estimated 275,000 added between 1992 and 1996. Approximately 41 percent of the undocumented immigrants arrive in the United States legally—as students, visitors, and temporary workers—but overstay their visas. Most of the others cross into the United States illegally from Mexico, other Latin Mexican countries, and Canada. In 1996, Mexico was the source of 54 percent of the undocumented immigrants, followed by El Salvador (7 percent), Guatemala (3 percent), Canada (2 percent), Haiti (2 percent), and the Philippines (2 percent). Undocumented residents are disproportionately concentrated in a few states. California has the largest single number—two million, or 40 percent,[2]—followed by Texas with 14 percent, New York with approximately 11 percent, Florida with 7 percent, Illinois with about 6 percent, and New Jersey with 3 percent (U.S. Immigration and Naturalization Service, 1997). Perhaps it is not suprising than that many individuals in 1997 thought that reducing illegal immigration should be an important prioritiy in the United States—42 percent said it was a top priority, 47 percent said it should be given some priority, and only 11 percent believed it was not a priority or didn't know (Public Agenda Online, 1999b).

In 1996, in response to a growing popular resentment against illegal immigrants, President Bill Clinton signed a Republican-sponsored bill that cracked down on undocumented foreigners, in part by hiring more agents for the United States Border Patrol and stiffening requirements for sponsoring immigrants. The Immigration Act of 1990 raised the limit for legal immigration to seven hundred thousand people a year. During the latter half of the 1990s, dozens of immigration control measures were introduced in Congress to deal with legal immigrants, illegal aliens, refugees, and individuals seeking asylum. To date, the basic framework of the immigration system established by the 1990 law has survived these attacks; however, with the conservative mood of the country and a Republican-dominated Congress, it remains to be seen whether this situation will remain. As shown in chapter 3, it is already more financially difficult for immigrants to sponsor family members.

Another common misconception concerns the belief that American immigration is currently at its highest level ever. Between 1991 and 1998, the total foreign-

Table 5.2   Immigration and Proportion of Foreign Born in the United States, 1871–1998

Decade	No. of Immigrants	Foreign Born (%)
1871–80	2,812,191	13.3
1881–90	5,246,613	14.7
1891–00	3,687,564	13.6
1901–10	8,795,386	14.7
1911–20	5,735,811	13.2
1921–30	4,107,209	11.6
1931–40	528,431	8.6
1941–50	1,035,039	6.9
1951–60	2,515,479	5.4
1961–70	3,321,677	4.7
1971–80	4,493,314	6.2
1981–90	7,338,062	8.0
1991–98	7,605,068	9.8

Source: U.S. Immigration and Naturalization Service, Statistical Yearbook 1996 (Washington, D.C.: U.S. Government Printing Office, 1997), table 1 and Steven Camarota, "Immigrants in the United States—1998: A Snapshot of America's Foreign-born Population. Backgrounder. (Washington, D.C.: Center for Immigration Studies 1999), table 1.

born population made up nearly 10 percent of the population, less than the almost 15 percent recorded for the decades between 1881 and 1890 and 1901 and 1910 (see Table 5.2). Other misconceptions abound about the racial and ethnic composition of the United States. White Americans think that 14.7 percent of the United States population is Hispanic; in actuality, in the mid-1990s it was 9.5 percent. White Americans also overestimate the percentage that is Asian, believing that 10.8 percent is Asian; the true percentage is 3.1 percent. There is also a gross overestimation of African Americans—white Americans believe that 23.8 percent of the population in the United States is black, whereas the real percentage is 11.8 percent. It is little wonder then that white Americans underestimate their own number; they believe that only 49.9 percent of the population is white, whereas it is actually 74 percent (Labovitz 1996).

At best, the current mood of public opinion is very mixed toward the foreign born. While a significant majority believe that immigrants who moved to the United States in the previous ten to fifteen years are hard-working (67 percent), basically good and honest people (58 percent), and productive citizens once they get their feet on the ground (65 percent), 64 percent say that they take jobs away from Americans and add to the crime problem (59 percent) ("Not Quite So Welcome," 1993). A 1995 *Newsweek* poll found that 52 percent of blacks, 53 percent of whites, and 39 percent of Hispanics believed that "immigrants today are a burden on our country because they take our jobs, housing and health care" (Hancock, 1995: 31). Individuals from Latin America and the Caribbean (30 percent) and the Middle East (26 percent) are named as groups to which the respondents felt least favorable. Asians came in a distant third, with 11 percent of the sample saying they were the least favorable group ("Not Quite So Welcome," 1993). A poll issued in 1998 revealed that nearly 50 percent of the respondents thought that immigration weakens the American character, as new arrivals do not adopt the language and culture and put a strain on public services (Public Agenda Online, 1999c).

Powerful sets of legends provide support for the English-Only movement. The increase of immigration from Mexico and other Latin American countries has produced public outcries, even among some academics. Morris Janowitz, a well-known sociologist, laments the polarization that he sees as imminent from the Spanish-speaking immigrants south of the border:

> Mexicans, together with other Spanish-speaking populations, are creating a bifurcation in the social-political structure of the United States that approximates national-ity division. . . . The presence of Mexico at the border of the United States, plus the strength of Mexican cultural patterns, means that the "natural history" of Mexican immigrants has been and will be at variance with that of other immigrant groups. For sections of the Southwest, it is not premature to speak of a cultural and social ir-redenta—sectors of the United States which have in effect become Mexicanized and, therefore, under political dispute. (cited in Heer, 1996: 196)

One rationale for denying Latino population full integration in American soci-ety is the argument that Hispanics are incapable of internalizing American values. A 1990 poll conducted by the National Opinion Research Center found that when images of Jews, blacks, Asians, Hispanics, and Southern whites were compared with the general population with respect to six core characteristics, Latinos and blacks ranked last or next to last on all of the characteristics. The survey indicated that Latinos are perceived to be the least patriotic of the six groups. Similar senti-ments have been voiced by organizations such as U.S. English and by elected offi-cials. Some leaders have even suggested that Mexican-origin and other Latino se-cessionists threaten national security (de la Garza, Falcon, Garcia, and Garcia, 1994: 229). To what extent is this an accurate perception of the Latino population? The next section examines attitudes toward the "American creed," language loyalty, and Latino attitudes toward learning English. Speaking English appears to be one unwritten sacrament of the American creed.

Support for the American Creed among African Americans, Hispanics, and Whites

Identity Politics and the American Creed

At the core of American political culture is the American "creed." As a nation of im-migrants, the United States rests on a heterogeneous cultural foundation. No sin-gle cultural pattern defines who is an American. Unlike France, Germany, and Japan, a shared history and culture do not serve as the foundation of identity in the United States. Lacking that bond, American identity has been molded around an explicit—if imperfectly realized—commitment to liberal democratic principles that have been labeled the American "creed" (Huntington, 1981), a "civic culture" (Almond and Verba, 1963), and a "civil religion" (Fuchs, 1990).

Arthur Schlesinger (1992) suggests that the essential elements of the American creed include a commitment to liberty, equality, democracy, and the "melting pot" theory of national identity, according to which our previous national and ethnic identities are assimilated into a new American identity. Schlesinger contends that this American creed, which has contributed to our success, is being undermined by multiculturalism and bilingualism, "conducted in the interests of all non-English speakers but particularly a Hispanic-American project" (1992: 107). He maintains that today the idea of the melting pot is under attack, and a new orthodoxy describes America, past and present, as a nation of self-interested groups. The idea of assimilation into the mainstream is giving ground to the celebration of ethnicity. Jean Bethke Elshtain (1995) maintains that Americans inhabit their own little islands of bristling difference where they comport with those just like themselves. They live in a society where people increasingly are defined by their race, gender, and ethnicity.

Nowhere is the articulation of America's collective identity more controversial than in the schools. From the time of Plato, those political philosophers who stress the importance of habits, manner, and tastes as the foundation of a society have seen the paramount place of education in the political and social order. Writing around the turn of the twentieth century, Emile Durkheim emphasized that public schools must shape the national morality, instill the collective consciousness, and maintain national solidarity (1961: 8). Schools are given the task of imparting the basics of the social and moral order to the next generation.

The 1996 Survey of American Political Culture (1996)[3] asked African Americans, Hispanics, and whites to evaluate the relative importance of various themes of American history. Rather than specific historical events, the questions related to the framing narratives within which American history is taught. The survey posed broad questions about America's purpose and contribution to the world.

The survey data showed remarkably high levels of support for the American creed from all three racial and ethnic groups. Nearly nine out of ten respondents of the three groups agree it is important for children to learn that America from its beginning "has had a destiny to set an example for other nations." By similar margins, these individuals also agree that it is important to teach children that "our nation was founded on biblical principles." Only a slightly weaker majority agrees that it is important to teach children that "America has a special place in God's plan for history" (blacks—86 percent, Hispanics—79 percent, and whites—68 percent) (see Figure 5.1). The lower rate of agreement of whites on this question appears to be related to higher average educational attainment. In general, this sentiment toward America's special place decreases as education increases and as religious orthodoxy decreases (State of Disunion, 1996: vol. I, 5).

A central theme in American history, in the minds and imagination of most Americans, is the expansion of freedom. Over 90 percent of a representative sample of African Americans, Hispanics, and whites agreed that it is important to teach children that "America's contribution is one of expanding freedom for more and more people." By about the same margin, the three groups agreed that children should be taught that "our founders limited the power of government, so government would not intrude too much into the lives of citizens." Another aspect of the American legacy is the idea that "America is the world's great melting pot, in which

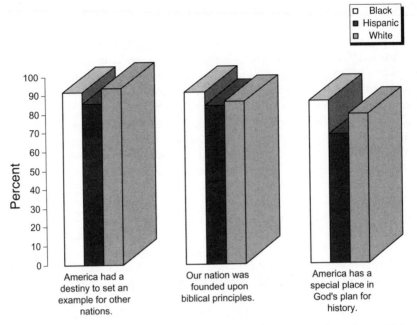

Figure 5.1   The American Creed—America's Destiny (percent agreeing). *Source*: State of Disunion, Survey of American Political Culture (Ivy, VA: In Media Res Educational Foundation, 1996), vol. 2, table 23, a, h, j. By permission of the Institute for Advanced Studies in Culture.

people from different countries are united into one nation" (see Figure 5.2). The high level of agreement among Hispanics toward the melting-pot ideology is particularly noteworthy. This is significant since a third (33 percent) of the Latino respondents were born outside the United States (in comparison to only 2 percent of African Americans and whites) (State of Disunion, 1996: table 58).

Americans realize that the ideal of the melting pot has been less than perfectly realized. More than eight out of ten (with slightly higher percentages for African Americans (89 percent), and Hispanics (87 percent), than whites (82 percent)—agree that it is important to teach children that "ours has been a history of war and aggression; our expansion occurred at the cost of much suffering." The majority of all groups agree that it is important to teach children that "our nation betrayed its principles by its cruel mistreatment of blacks and Indians." However, blacks (by 21 percent) and Hispanics (by 17 percent) express much higher levels of agreement with this statement than do whites. Finally, the majority of Americans agree it is important to teach children that "our founders were part of a male-dominated culture that gave important roles to men while keeping women in the background" (see Figure 5.3). The teaching of gendered history, however, was felt to be less important than the role of race and the suffering, which accompanied our expansionist history.

The injustice of the American system is still felt in the lives of the respondents. Fifty-seven percent of African Americans, 49 percent of Hispanics, but only 35 percent of whites agreed that "people of other races can't really understand the way my race sees things." There was also a higher level of agreement among blacks (27 percent) and Hispanics (32 percent), than whites (18 percent) that "in political discussions, a person's ethnic or group identity is more important than the things they say." Finally, considerably more African Americans (46 percent) and Hispanics (37 percent) replied that they had been victims of racial discrimination than did whites (10 percent) (Figure 5.4).

Despite the failures to live up to the American principles of justice and fairness, Americans, whatever their racial or ethnic heritage, still overwhelmingly believe that children should be taught that "with hard work and perseverance, anyone can succeed in America." There is also widespread agreement with Alexis de Tocqueville's (1969) view that democracy is only as strong as the virtues of its citizens (see Figure 5.5).

This agreement on the American creed plays out in attitudes toward the American political system, as well as in the realm of basic educational ideals. A majority of African Americans (63 percent), Hispanics (58 percent), and whites (54 percent) indicated that they had "respect for the political institutions in America" and pride in "living under our system of government" (73, 71, and 76 percent, respectively). All three groups—blacks (78 percent), Hispanics (71 percent), and whites (81 percent)—also expressed a high degree of "support for our system of government." Finally, a majority (63, 62, and 70 percent of blacks, Latinos, and whites, re-

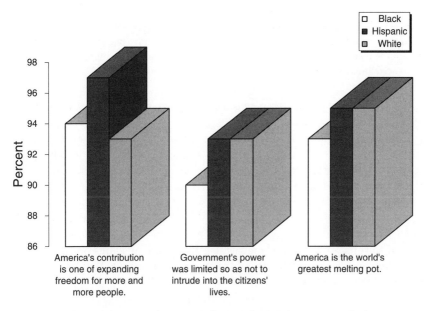

Figure 5.2 The American Creed—America's Contribution (percent agreeing).
Source: State of Disunion, Survey of American Political Culture (Ivy, VA: In Media Res Educational Foundation, 1996), vol. 2, table 23, c, g, k. By permission of the Institute for Advanced Studies in Culture.

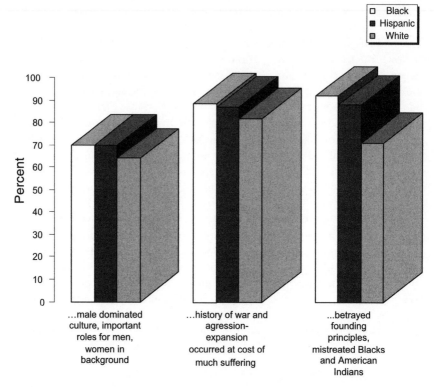

Figure 5.3 The American Creed—America's Weaknesses (percent agreeing).
Source: State of Disunion, Survey of American Political Culture (Ivy, VA: In Media Res Educational Foundation, 1996), vol. 2, table 23, d, f, i. By permission of the Institute for Advanced Studies in Culture.

spectively) felt that our government is the best system possible" (State of Disunion, 1996: table 12 a, b, c, d).

In sum, Hispanics, both citizens and newer immigrants, show strong support for the American creed. Arthur Schlesinger's concerns—and those of other social scientists—that we are presently witnessing the tribalization of American life and the celebration of ethnicity is not supported by current survey data. Opinion polls, of course, cannot capture the battles being waged over educational policy.

Current findings on the American creed do not mean that there is consensus on all social issues among Hispanic and Anglo Americans. Language loyalty, attitudes toward learning English, and language sensitivity among Latinos continue to be important and misunderstood issues among many Americans. These issues are the subject of the next section.

Latino Language Loyalty and Attitudes toward Learning English

Two major conclusions according to Alejandro Portes and Rubén Rumbaut (1996: 210) can be derived from data on language loyalty of Latino and other immigrant

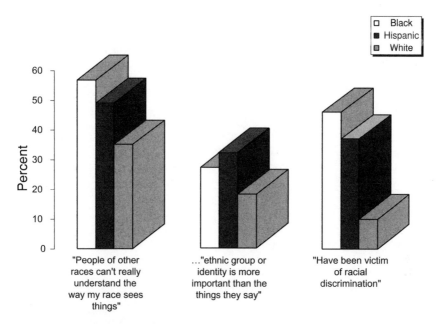

Figure 5.4 The Politics of Difference (percent agreeing). *Source*: State of Disunion, Survey of American Political Culture (Ivy, VA: In Media Res Educational Foundation, 1996), vol. 2, table 41, b, f, 83b. By permission of the Institute for Advanced Studies in Culture.

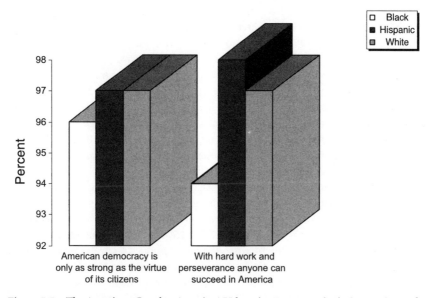

Figure 5.5 The American Creed—American Values (percent agreeing). *Source*: State of Disunion, Survey of American Political Culture (Ivy, VA: In Media Res Educational Foundation, 1996), vol. 2, table 23, b, e. By permission of the Institute for Advanced Studies in Culture.

Table 5.3   Spanish-Speaking and Asian Immigrants' Ability to Speak English "Very Well," by Year of Immigration

Country of Birth	Speaks English "Very Well"			
	Immigrants 5 Years Old and Over	Immigrated 1980–1990	Immigrated Pre-1980	Total
Colombia	268,980	28	44	35.7
Japan	237,171	26	44	33.2
Korea	520,003	25	44	33.2
Nicaragua	158,610	26	49	31.8
Vietnam	521,207	24	45	31.6
Dominican Republic	328,320	23	35	28.5
Guatamala	214,550	21	39	26.9
Mexico	4,032,703	19	34	26.5
Laos	164,150	23	38	26.3
Cambodia	113,720	24	37	25.8
El Salvador	445,144	23	34	25.5
China	506,653	20	31	25.1

Source: U.S. Bureau of the Census. The Foreign-Born Population of the United States. CP-3-1 (Washington, D.C.: U.S. Government Printing Office, 1993), table 3.

groups. First, newly arrived immigrants tend to remain loyal to their native tongues, regardless of age and education. Second, there is a strong eroding effect of native language retention over time. Table 5.3 shows that these two trends hold true for immigrant groups from the two largest recent groups: newcomers from Spanish-speaking and Asian countries. There is also some evidence, according to Portes and Rumbaut (1996), that nationalities with higher proportions of college graduates and professionals shift toward English more rapidly than do less educated groups. This trend is confirmed in Table 5.3. Asian immigrants—on average, better educated than Latino groups—are gaining English competency more rapidly than their Hispanic counterparts. However, there is considerable variation among nationality groups, from both Asia and Spanish-speaking countries. Immigrants of Mexican origin have most often been singled out for their inability to speak English; however, the 1990 census data shows that by the second generation, over 50 percent speak English very well (Lopez, 1996: 151).

There is some evidence that language learning is proceeding more rapidly today than in the late nineteenth and early part of the twentieth century. In 1990, only 3 percent reported speaking English less than "well" or "very well." In all, only eight-tenths of 1 percent spoke no English at all. The 1890 census, on the other hand, reported 4.5 times as many inhabitants who were unable to speak any English. A large single ethnic-language group is not new in the American experience. In 1790, when the first census was taken, German-Americans accounted for 8.6 percent of the population. This percentage is comparable to that of Hispanic Americans, who comprised 9.0 percent of the population in the 1990 census (Crawford, 1997a).

U.S. English and proponents of making English the official language of the United States have ignored the above facts and the importance placed on learning

English by the non-Anglo population. Several polls have shown that, for Hispanics, learning English figures prominently as an obligation that a citizen owes to the country. A 1984 national sample found that 61 percent of Hispanics and 84 percent of non-Hispanics believed that it is a very important obligation of citizenship to speak and understand English (Public Opinion, 1985). Moreover, 66 percent of Hispanics and 77 percent of Anglos in a 1988 California poll conducted by the Field Institute said that speaking English was very important in making one an American (Citrin, Reingold, Walters, and Green, 1990). In the Latino National Political Survey conducted in 1989–90, over 90 percent of Mexican, Puerto Rican, and Cuban Americans agreed or strongly agreed that citizens and residents should learn English (de la Garza, DeSipio, Garcia, Garcia, and Falcon, 1992: 98).[4] A 1998 survey found that only 32 percent of Hispanic parents with children in public schools would encourage the United States to become a bilingual country, with Spanish as its second language, in comparison to 29 percent of African American parents, 16 percent of foreign-born parents, and 12 percent of white parents (Public Agenda Online, 1999d). In the same study, a majority of all groups believed that if a person didn't try to learn English they would consider them a "bad citizen" (65 percent of foreign-born parents, 63 percent of white parents, 56 percent of African American parents, and 53 percent of Hispanic parents) (Public Agenda Online, 1999e).

Further evidence of the desire of Hispanics to learn English comes from a Florida poll. A 1985 Miami survey found that 98 percent of the Hispanic respondents said it was "essential for children to read and write English perfectly," as compared with 94 percent of Anglo respondents (Crawford, 1989: 30). Alejandro Portes and Richard Schauffler (1994), in a study of language adaptation of second-generation children in south Florida, confirm these results. They found that knowledge of English was nearly universal, with preference for English nearly as high, even among children educated in immigrant sponsored bilingual schools.

The strong desire to learn English is also evident on Spanish-language television.[5] Commercials can be instructive in this regard. One of the most common kind of commercial on Spanish-language stations advertises the multitude of schools and home-study programs that teach English. These advertisements stress that the key to advancement in the United States is a command of the nation's dominant language. In one typical ad, a husband sorrowfully informs his wife he has been passed over for a better job because his English just isn't good enough. About six months later, after taking an *Inglés sin Barreras* (English without Barriers) course, he is able to tell his family over dinner that he has obtained a promotion to manager because he is now fully bilingual. "Gimme five," one of his children says to him, in English. "Way to go, Dad," another proudly proclaims (Rohter, 1996: sec. 4, 6).

One should not, however, underestimate the language sensitivity within the Latino community (see Table 5.4). The results of a 1991 Gallup poll—sponsored by U.S. English—of 995 likely voters illustrate that the Latin community is far more likely to believe that making English the official language may discriminate against one's family. Only 3 percent of the non-Hispanic likely voters—but 31 percent of their Hispanic counterparts—believe that making English the official lan-

Table 5.4 Attitudes toward Bilingual Education among Hispanics and Non-Hispanics, 1991 (%)

Attitudes toward Bilingualism	Hispanic	Non-Hispanic
In favor of making English the official language of U.S government	42	78
In favor of bilingual education only until a child learns English	34	54
In favor of continuing bilingual education to maintain native language	64	37
Believe that making English the official language discriminates against one's family	31	3
Believe that public schools should be responsible for maintaining the languages and cultures that people bring with them to the United States	38	23
Believe that maintaining the languages and cultures that people bring with them to the United States should be a private concern	45	71

Source: Data from U.S. English / Gallup Public Opinion Poll. A Gallup Study of Attitudes toward English as the Official Language of the U.S. Government. 1991

guage promotes this type of discrimination. Hispanics are also much more likely to believe that bilingual education should be continued in the schools in order to maintain the native language. Sixty-four percent of Hispanics gave this response as opposed to 37 percent of the non-Hispanic sample (U.S. English/Gallup Opinion Poll, 1991).[6]

As the composition of the public schools changes, and Hispanics and blacks represent a majority of the school population in many districts, confrontations and power struggles over the curriculum and the role of language are likely to emerge. It is significant that blacks also place more importance on the role of the school in maintaining language training and minority cultures. Some 58 percent of blacks believe that the schools should continue bilingual education to maintain the native language, and 49 percent believe that public schools should be responsible for maintaining the languages and cultures that people bring with them to the United States (U.S. English/Gallup Opinion Poll, 1991).

One of the difficulties of the U.S. English/Gallup Opinion Poll discussed here, and many other studies analyzing Hispanic groups, are small sample sizes. This makes it very difficult to analyze potential differences between citizens (individuals born in the United States or naturalized in the United States) and more recent noncitizen residents. Do citizens and noncitizens in the United States hold similar attitudes toward language, immigration, and other social issues? Are there differences between individuals residing in different parts of the country? To what degree are language and immigration important variables in Latinos' understanding of cultural pluralism in the United States? These are essential and largely unexplored areas in the study of intergroup relations in the United States. Two recent national surveys of attitudes of Latino citizens and noncitizens will help us answer these questions, as well as paint a more dynamic picture of language, national and subnational identity, and cultural pluralism in the United States.

The data come primarily from the Latino Issues Survey (LIS), which was administered in the spring and summer of 1996 to 2,285 Latino respondents in California, Texas, New York, Illinois, Arizona, Colorado, New Mexico, and Florida by

Table 5.5   Selected Characteristics of Hispanic Origin Population, 1996

Variable	Mexico	Puerto Rico	Cuba	Central/South America
		Origin		
Number (in thousands)	18,039	3,123	1,127	4,060
Hispanic Population (%)	64	11	4	14
Female-Headed Population (%)	21	42	19	29
Under-18 Population (%)	39	38	19	31
High School Graduate or Higher (%)	47	60	64	61
B.A./B.S. Degree or Higher	7	11	19	14
Professional, Administrative, Sales (%)				
Men	23	37	44	29
Women	55	64	72	48
Service, Skilled, Unskilled Labor (%)				
Men	77	63	56	71
Women	45	36	28	52
Family Income (1995) (%)				
$25,000 or more	47	45	62	54
$50,000 or more	17	20	31	21
Percentage of All Families Below				
Poverty Level (%)	28	36	16	22
U.S.-Born of U.S. Parents (%)	29	N/A	2	3
First or Second Generation	63	N/A	31	32
Growth of Hispanic Origin Population				
(1990–1996) (%)	34	15	8	21
Fertility Rate (1995) (%)	3.3	2.2	1.7	2.8

Source: Jorge del Pinal and Audrey Singer, "Generation of Diversity: Latinos in the United States," Population Bulletin 52 (October 1997), tables 1, 3, 5, 6, 7, 9 and figures 7, 12.

the Southwest Voter Research Institute (1996).[7] The Southwest Voter Research Institute study will be supplemented by the Latino National Political Survey (LNPS), which was conducted between 1989 and 1990 (de la Garza et al., 1992). Unless otherwise stated, this section will rely on the 1996 Latino Issue Study, which has not been previously analyzed in the social science literature.

The investigation will be primarily concerned with the process of acculturation between Latino citizens and more recent arrivals. Neither of the two large Latino studies includes a comparative representative national Anglo sample, so the analysis will focus exclusively on the Hispanic population. Some social scientists question whether one can speak of a Hispanic or Latino category in the politics of the United States. Jorge Domínguez (1995) concludes that while there are several differences between Mexicans, Puerto Ricans, and Cubans (including lack of a panethnic identification), there are also many similarities, particularly in relationship to language policy and government spending and problem solving. Current stereotypes of Latinos also tend to lump the different Spanish-speaking nationalities together, even though various Latino groups show large differences between nationality groups (see Table 5.5). Most surveys, because of their small sample sizes, aggregate the various Hispanic groups together. The Latino Issues Study, which will be analyzed in the next section, also follows this procedure.

Latino Citizen and Noncitizen Attitudes toward Language, Immigration, and Social Issues

Table 5.6, from the Latino Issues Study (LIS), shows that sensitivity toward language issues crosscuts Hispanic groups, whether they are American or foreign-born. As one might expect, noncitizens are somewhat less likely to agree that English should be made the official language of the United States. A majority of citizen and noncitizen Latino national groups disagreed with the proposition that English should be the official language of the United States.[8] There was also a strong feeling by citizen and noncitizen Latino groups that bilingual education and bilingual ballots should not be eliminated.

Use of the Spanish media declines over time. The results of the LIS study show significant differences between citizens and noncitizens. The percentage of individuals who plan to use a Spanish ballot decreases from almost 36 percent among noncitizens to 9 percent for citizens. The decline in Spanish usage is also evident for various forms of the media among American Latinos. One notable exception is the continued popularity of Spanish-language television, which is watched by

Table 5.6 Hispanic Attitudes toward Language (%)

Attitude	Citizens	Noncitizens
Would you support a law that would do the following?		
A. Make English the official language of the United States		
Yes	37.1	23.2
No	59.8	74.5
Don't know / No answer	3.0	2.3
B. Eliminate bilingual education		
Yes	12.2	7.5
No	85.9	91.6
Don't know / No answer	1.9	1.0
C. Eliminate ballots in Spanish		
Yes	10.1	9.2
No	88.0	90.2
Don't know / No answer	2.9	0.6
D. Eliminate the use of Spanish in Government (for example interpreters in court, case workers)		
Yes	8.7	5.4
No	90.0	93.9
Don't know / No answer	1.3	0.8
E. Will you use a ballot in English or Spanish?		
English	83.5	54.7
Spanish	8.9	9.5
Don't know / No answer	7.6	9.5

Source: Southwest Voter Research Institute, "Latino Issues Survey." 1996. Author's calculations.

Table 5.7   Hispanic Attitudes toward Media Use (%)

Attitude	Citizens	Noncitizens
How often do you use the following media as a source of information about politics and community issues?		
A. English-Language TV		
2–7 times a week	77.7	61.0
Once a week or less	21.3	37.9
Don't know / No answer	1.1	1.2
B. English Radio		
2–7 times a week	63.6	42.4
Once a week or less	35.2	56.5
Don't know / No answer	1.2	1.2
C. English-Language Newspaper		
2–7 times a week	62.1	33.6
Once a week or less	36.7	64.5
Don't know / No answer	1.2	2.0
D. Spanish-Language TV		
2–7 times a week	41.2	80.1
Once a week or less	57.9	19.1
Don't know / No answer	0.8	1.0
E. Spanish-Language Radio		
2–7 times a week	36.3	62.0
Once a week or less	63.1	37.3
Don't know / No answer	0.7	0.8
F. Spanish-Language Newspaper		
2–7 times a week	16.2	37.2
Once a week or less	83.0	62.2
Don't know / No answer	0.8	0.6

Source: Southwest Voter Research Institute, "Latino Issues Survey" 1996. Author's calculations.

slightly over 40 percent of Latino citizens. English-language television is also a popular medium for both Latino citizens and for noncitizens (see Table 5.7).

Immigration is another source of considerable concern to Latino residents. Whereas noncitizens overwhelmingly oppose legislation that would significantly lower the number of legal immigrants allowed into the country, Hispanic citizens are almost evenly divided between those who support and those who oppose more restrictive immigration legislation. Both groups are concerned with the denial of citizenship, healthcare, and education to the children of undocumented workers. Predictably, there are higher levels of sensitivity among newcomers than among citizens. The Mexican origin population, which in 1996 encompassed about 64 percent of the Latino population (Pinal and Singer, 1997), is particularly aware of anti-immigrant sentiment toward newcomers from south of the border.

The immigration of Mexican Americans has long reflected the immediate labor needs of the U.S. economy (Barrera, 1979; Hansen, 1988; Moore and Pachon, 1985). During the 1930s, state and local government forcibly sent hundreds of thousands of Mexican immigrants back to Mexico, but when the United States experienced a labor shortage in World War II, immigration was once again encouraged. The policy of encouraging immigration from Latin America continued until after the war under the *bracero* program, which enabled four million Mexicans to work as temporary farm laborers in the United States, often under extremely harsh conditions. Following the repeal of the *bracero* program in 1964, Mexican immigration was once again discouraged but, by the 1980s, immigration was again on the upsurge. Millions of Mexicans tried to flee poverty by crossing the border. Subsequent efforts to halt immigration have thus far proved difficult. Against this backdrop, it is understandable that Latino citizens and noncitizens feel much of the anti-immigrant sentiment and immigrant bashing unfairly focuses on Mexican immigrants. In California, where the sample is overwhelming made up Latinos of Mexican background, over three-fourths of the citizens felt that their group was singled out for unequal treatment.

Both the collective national sample and individual state samples show that citizens and noncitizens of Latino background are sympathetic toward individual rights for children of undocumented workers, provision of social services to newcomers, and the positive role of immigrants in the United States (see Table 5.8). In general, these are issues that unite all Latinos despite diverse backgrounds, although there is more sensitivity expressed by newer Hispanic residents.

The Cuban American experience is significantly different from that of Mexican Americans. After Fidel Castro came to power in 1959, Cubans who opposed his regime sought to immigrate to the United States. These included both political opponents and a large number of middle-class Cubans whose standard of living had declined as a result of Castro's programs and the U.S. embargo. Unlike most other immigrants who entered the United States in the second half of the twentieth century, for the most part Cubans initially were welcomed by the United States government since they were regarded as refugees from communism. About three-quarters of all Cubans arriving before 1974 received some form of government relief, the highest of any minority community. The Cuban community in Miami is the most successful Latino immigrant group, with considerable economic and political power (Stepick and Grenier, 1993, Wilson and Portes, 1980). The Cuban community encompassed approximately 4 percent of the Hispanic origin population in 1996 (Pinal and Singer, 1997).

Puerto Ricans are the second largest Latino group, comprising about 11 percent of the Hispanic origin population in 1996 (Pinal and Singer, 1997). Since becoming a U.S. protectorate in 1917, more than two million Puerto Ricans have migrated to the United States. Over half of the Puerto Ricans in the mainland United States currently live in and around New York City. In terms of education, employment, and income, Puerto Ricans share with African Americans and Mexican Americans the problems of lower educational attainment, higher concentration in lower level jobs, lower income, and higher rates of poverty. They also must adjust in school and work to a foreign language (Portes and Rumbaut, 1996).

Table 5.8   Hispanic Attitudes toward Immigration Issues (%)

Immigration Issue	Citizens	Noncitizens
1. Congress is proposing legislation that would greatly lower the number of immigrants legally allowed into the country. Do you support or oppose these efforts?		
Support	48.7	24.0
Oppose	44.7	70.1
Don't know / No answer	6.7	5.9
2. Do you believe that children of undocumented immigrants should be denied citizenship, health care, and education?		
Yes	20.0	8.3
No	75.7	90.4
Don't know / No answer	4.3	1.4
3. Immigrants whether legal or illegal are a necessary evil, they fill jobs Americans don't want.		
Agree	47.0	65.4
Disagree	45.9	31.0
Don't know / No answer	7.1	3.6
4. America was built by immigrants and the energy they bring is a tremendous plus both emonomically and culturally, they are being wrongly scapegoated for American economic problems.		
Agree	60.1	54.1
Disagree	30.5	39.0
Don't know / No answer	4.5	3.7

Source: Southwest Voter Research Institute, "Latino Issues Survey" 1996. Author's calculations

In spite of the very diverse experiences of the different Latino groups, they all adhere to the American creed and express strong love and pride in the United States. The LNPS study (de la Garza et al., 1992: 80) found that 84 percent of Mexican Americans, 69 percent of Puerto Rican Americans, and 88 percent of Cuban Americans expressed very strong or extremely strong love for the United States. Pride in the United States was even stronger, with 91 percent of Mexican Americans, 83 percent of Puerto Rican Americans, and 92 percent of Cuban Americans answering that they were either very proud or extremely proud of America.[9]

Education, which is the subject of Table 5.9, continues to elicit strong reactions from the Latino community. We have seen previously that Hispanics have a much stronger belief than the white non-Latino population that bilingual education should be continued in the schools. Two other questions relating to education were included in the LIS study. When asked about the quality of the public schools, approximately one-third of both the citizen and the noncitizen Latino population said that the quality of the public schools had decreased in the previous four years. Hispanics were particularly concerned about the high dropout rate. Three-fourths of the citizens and 80 percent of noncitizens stated that the lack of high school completion is a problem. The large number of Latinos who drop out of high school is a cause for alarm. The 1990 census found that one in ten Americans be-

Table 5.9   Hispanic Attitudes toward Education (%)

Education Issue	Citizens	Noncitizens
A. In the past four years, do you think the quality of public schools and education has		
Increased	32.8	28.0
Decreased	36.4	30.9
Don't know / No answer	5.3	6.9
B. In your community, do you think the Latino high school dropout rate is		
A problem	74.6	79.7
Not a problem	18.1	15.0
Don't know / No answer	7.2	5.4
C. Do you support bilingual education		
Yes	86.9	91.0
No	18.1	15.0
Don't know / No answer	2.2	1.2

Source: Southwest Voter Research Institute, "Latino Issues Survey" 1996. Author's calculations.

tween the ages of sixteen and nineteen was neither a high school graduate nor enrolled in school. The proportion was highest among Hispanic teenagers (22 percent) than among African Americans (14 percent), whites (10 percent), and Asian-Americans (5 percent). Hispanic and black students fall behind white students early and stay behind. Among whites, 5 percent more are below their expected grade in the nine- to eleven-year-old group than in the six- to eight-year-old group. Among Hispanics and blacks, the gap between students who have fallen behind grows to 14 percent and 11 percent, respectively. By the time students were between the ages of fifteen and seventeen, 32 percent of whites were behind, compared with 48 percent of the African American and Latino students (Roberts, 1995: 239–240).

Limited language skills and poverty are two major factors that contribute to the high dropout rate of Hispanic students. Almost 57 percent of persons who spoke Spanish at home lived in families who earned less than $20,000 in 1989 ("Immigration and Limited English," 1995). A national study found that 54 percent of the limited-English-proficient students in the first and third grades came from families with incomes under $15,000—twice the rate for all public school students (Crawford, 1997a).

The Politics of Language: Advantage or Disadvantage and for Whom?

Coupled with other factors, language influences the low educational attainment of many limited-English-proficient students. Rather than closely examining the educational environment for many limited-English-proficient students, it is too easy to blame victims for their inability to speak English. This unfortunately has been the strategy of U.S. English and even some well-meaning politicians and social scientists. Racial and ethnic segregation, along with poor and underfunded urban schools, rather than a lack of desire to learn English, are the major factors responsible for insufficient English communication skills and low educational attainment.

James Crawford (1997a: 9) summarizes the difficult odds that recent immigrant students and children of limited-English-proficient immigrant children must overcome. Hispanic students are currently more segregated than any other ethnic or racial group, including African American students. In 1991–92, 73 percent of Hispanic children attended elementary and secondary schools with predominantly minority enrollments, an increase from 55 percent in 1968-69. Over a third of Latinos went to schools where more than nine out of ten students were minorities, up from 23 percent a generation earlier. LEP children, on average, are even more segregated. In 1991–92, 55 percent of Hispanic students attended schools with 91 to 100 percent minority enrollment, as compared with 19 percent of other language minorities and 5 percent of native English speakers. During the same academic year, about half of LEP Hispanic first-grade students were in high-poverty schools, in comparison to 8 percent of Asian first graders (see also Bennici and Strang, 1995; Orfield, Schley, Glass, and Reardon, 1993).

Another problem that many language minority students face is overrepresentation in special education classrooms. Teachers and administrators often confuse the consequences of lack of English proficiency with underachievement, learning difficulties, lack of attention in class, and language disorders. Hispanic students who, according to one recent study, were labeled "language disabled," actually lost ground in IQ tests and other achievement tests after three years in special education classes (Crawford, 1997a; Ortiz, 1992).

LEP students who need help learning English are often handicapped by the lack of qualified teachers. Between 22 and 30 percent of LEP children do not receive any language assistance whatsoever. Many classroom teachers are inadequately prepared to teach LEP students. According to the 1995 National Education Goals Panel, 40 percent of American teachers had LEP students in their classrooms in 1994, but only 29 percent had received any training in serving limited-English-proficient students. The inadequate supply of bilingual and English as second language teachers has forced many schools to rely on aides whose only qualification is the ability to speak a language other than English. Almost 60 percent of LEP children in high-poverty schools nationwide during the 1991-92 academic year were taught English reading by such paraprofessionals, most of whom had no education past high school (Crawford 1997a, Moss and Puma 1995). More than half of minority-language speakers and more than a third of those who report some difficulty in English were born in the United States (Fix and Passel, 1994). Unless more resources and effort are spent on LEP students, the United States may face a new minority crisis in the twenty-first century. According to a recent report cited by the National Center on Bilingual Education, the number of Hispanic elementary and high school students with limited English proficiency is expected to double to more than five million by the year 2020 (Stewart 1998: A48).

Summary: National Identity and the Ambivalent Role of Language and Immigrants

Alejandro Portes and Rubén Rumbaut (1996: 194) observe that "Language shift and language acquisition parallel in many ways the story of immigrant adaptation to American culture, polity, and economy." Language is more than just a purely instrumental means of communication: "In the United States the acquisition of nonaccented English and the dropping of foreign languages represents the litmus test of Americanization."

This chapter has explored many of the misconceptions about language, immigrant status, and attitudes toward the American creed. Contrary to the belief of over two-thirds of Americans, the United States does not have an official language. For many Americans, there is a conviction that national identity and speaking accentless English are inseparable. Lacking a unified culture, many Americans believe that English is one of the few values that holds Americans together. Large-scale immigration from Spanish-speaking and Asian countries has hardened this attitude in the last two decades of the twentieth century. Legislators have taken advantage of this symbolic issue, even in states with few language minorities. In states with large Hispanic-origin populations, referendums initiated by U.S. English and similar groups have won constitutional amendments in California, Florida, Colorado, and Arizona. Opinion polls show between 50 and 90 percent approval rate for making English the official language of the United States, with highest rates among conservative whites and lowest approval rates among Hispanics.

Among the American populace, there is a general feeling that immigrants, especially Spanish speakers, do not want to learn English. In fact, this is a fallacy. Every major poll or survey taken during the last decade and a half of the twentieth century has shown that the majority of immigrants believe it is very important to learn the English language. The United States has probably incorporated more bilingual people over the last two centuries than has any other country in the world. In no other country (see, for example, a thirty-five-nation study by Lieberson, Dalto and Johnson [1975]) did the mother tongue shift toward monolingualism approach the speed found in the United States. It is largely poor and recent LEP students and their families, who are segregated in poverty-stricken schools where English proficiency falls behind. These neighborhoods have few resources, and certified ESL and bilingual teachers. This situation is not by choice but reflects the vast inequality of opportunity in the American school and class system.

Many recent surveys and studies illustrate widespread misconceptions about immigrants and their numbers, and legal as opposed to illegal status. In general, white Americans overestimate the number of minorities in the United States and believe that most immigrants enter the country illegally, which is incorrect. Also, there is a general conviction that immigration has never been higher. In actuality, as a percentage of the American population, foreign-born residents were a larger proportion of the United States at the beginning of the twentieth century. The most negative sentiment toward immigrants is directed toward Latinos, especially

Mexicans, perhaps because of the large size of the immigration wave and the relatively high number of undocumented workers. Few surveys deal with the employers who are responsible for employing these illegal workers.

Despite a recent outcry about identity politics and the tribalization of American society, there is a surprising agreement among African Americans, Hispanics, and whites about the American creed. A strong majority of all three groups thinks students should be taught that the United States "should set an example for other nations," that "America's major contribution is one of expanding freedom for more and more people, and that "America is the world's great melting pot, in which people from different countries are united into one country." By contrast, African Americans and Hispanics are more sensitive to the injustices of American history.

Language maintenance in the schools and public sector bilingual services are issues that draw all Latinos together, independent of their national origins and citizen/noncitizen status. The desire to maintain bilingualism and their culture in the school milieu, and the provision of bilingual ballots and government services, exists contemporaneously with language loss for most individuals by the third generation. The dominant trend in the United States is to see assimilation as a zero-sum process. Acculturation involves shedding the mother tongue and learning English. Most programs in the United States are based on subtractive linguistic acculturation—not English, but "English-Only"—with no attempt to maintain the mother tongue.

There is an irony in this approach. Several studies have shown *additive bilingualism*—supporting LEP children's native language while they learn English—to have proven to be superior to *subtractive* approaches in cognitive-academic benefits and the ability to understand another culture (Lambert, 1984; Portes and Hao, 1998; Ramírez, Yuen, Ramey, Pasta, and Billings, 1991). Elizabeth Peal and Wallace Lambert (1962) in their Canadian study found that there were significant advantages to learning a second language fluently. Knowledge of more than one language provides a resource in terms of expanding intellectual horizons, as well as of facilitating communication across cultures. The associated advantages that fluent bilingualism permits, however, all too often have been seen as a serious threat to native monolinguals, both in terms of labor force competition and the understanding of American national identity.

The United States spends thousands of dollars and hundred of hours of effort to teach college students a second language. Over one-quarter of American colleges and universities require a foreign language for admission (Dutcher, 1995). Over the last thirty years, however, the portion of American college students studying a foreign language has dropped by half, to 7.9 percent in 1998 (Modern Language Association, quoted in Brooke, 1999b). Increasingly, businesses are looking for employees who know more than one language. Therefore, there are very contradictory goals in the United States—English monolingualism for the immigrant masses and bilingualism or multilingualism for domestic elites. These antithetical goals shed light on the complexity of linguistic nativism at the end of the twentieth century (Portes and Rumbaut, 1996).

Before returning to questions of language policy and cultural pluralism at the end of the twentieth century, it is important to anchor recent linguistic politics in the experience of other countries. U.S. English and other groups have continually warned that we are heading on a path of Quebecification of American society. Yet most Americans are unfamiliar with the background of Canada and the Quebec situation. The next chapter examines language policy in Canada.

6

LANGUAGE AND IDENTITY POLITICS IN CANADA

"While the threat of official bilingualism poses may not seem grave today, just consider whether, 21 years ago, anyone would have predicted that the Canadian government would now be at the point of disintegrating because of language!"

(de la Peña, 1991: 64)

"Whether a united Canada will survive into the twenty-first century is a question too close to call. Much of the anxiety about language in the United States is probably funneled by the 'Quebec problem.'" (King 1997: 60)

"One of the most fascinating political developments in North America, and one of the least understood by the vast majority of North Americans, concerns the evolution of Quebec— a thoroughly modern, Westernized society whose majority population remains defiantly proud of its French language and culture." (Lemco, 1992: 423)

"The vibrancy of contemporary Québec stands out as the most remarkable difference between the Canadian and the American experience." (Thompson and Randall, 1994: 303)

This chapter analyzes the politics of identity and language relations between Quebec and the rest of Canada. Is the United States likely to face the same problems as Canada? Does accommodation to languages other than English mean that separatist demands are likely, as the representative of U.S. English insinuates? Or do many Americans, as well as the members of U.S. English, misunderstand the Quebec case, as Lemco indicates? Seymour Martin Lipset (1990), in *Continental Divide*, argues that national behaviors—including language relations—can only be understood comparatively, for those who know only one country, know neither well. In order to understand language relations in the United States, it is important to discover the differences and occasional similarities between Canada and the United States.

In analyzing the relations between Quebec and Anglo Canada, four major areas are examined here. First, I discuss the historical setting out of which bilingualism emerged. It also includes a brief demographic overview of the major language groups and population changes that have occurred among francophones, anglophones, and allophones (non-English, non-French speakers). Second, I emphasize the consistently different approach to individual and group rights, as well as education in languages other than English in Canada and the United States. Third, I concentrate on the role of mass attitudes in preserving ethnic and national identity, and analyze the degree to which majority and minority language groups adhere to the same or different core values. Finally, I conclude by reviewing some of the major differences between the American and Canadian cases.

An Overview of Language History in Canada

In this section, I shall briefly outline the chief social forces that gave rise to multilingualism in Canada. Very different factors have influenced the uneasy official recognition of French in Canada and the persistent preeminence of the English language in the United States.

Historical Factors Explaining Quebec Nationalism

The sixty thousand or so French who were abandoned to the English by the Treaty of Paris in 1763 outnumbered the English speakers in what was eventually to become Canada. It was not until the mid-1800s that French speakers became a minority and not until the 1871 census that they comprised only 31.1 percent of the total population (Wardhaugh, 1983). Although the French in Canada initially outnumbered the English, the French found themselves a minority in North America and faced the prospects of dispersal or absorption. The twin pillars of their survival were their religion and their language.

The chief forces explaining the persistence of the English language in the United States, as compared to Canada, are related to the number of speakers and the resulting political strength of the British settlers. In 1790, the white population of the United States was 76 percent English-speaking. Even as late as 1860, 53 percent of the foreign-born residents in the United States came from the British Isles (Conklin and Lourie, 1983).

Territorial concentration, relatively large numbers of French speakers, parallel development of the two societies, and the absence of a central government that could dictate terms of inclusion produced a reluctant official bilingualism in Canada. French Canadian history began with defeat for the French on the Plains of Abraham and continued through the Constitutional Act of 1791. The Act of 1791, while confirming the Quebec Act of 1774 and therefore the rights of the French to much of their distinctive way of life, nevertheless subordinated the French legislature of Lower Canada (Quebec) to an English executive and established a separate Upper Canada (Ontario) for the English. The common experience of facing the hardships of life in the colony and physical isolation from France led the population to develop a certain sense of identity (McRoberts, 1988).

The status of the French in Canada was influenced by three major factors (Brooks, 1996: 301-304), which allowed French in Canada to survive—unlike francophones in Louisiana, who succumbed to assimilationist pressures, after the territory passed from French to American control. One of the most important factors explaining the different fates of the French language and culture in Quebec compared to Louisiana is demography. French speakers comprised a large share of Canada's population, one that remained remarkably stable in view of the lack of any significant French-speaking immigration after 1759 and a large exodus of French Canadians to the New England states during the second half of the nineteenth century. By confederation, individuals of French background made up about one-third of the Canadian population, but French speakers made up about three-quarters of the population of Quebec. The high fertility rate allowed French Canadians to retain this percentage of the Canadian population between confederation and the 1950s. In contrast, French-speakers in the south of the United States were very quickly swamped by a rapidly growing Anglophone population, and a stronger central government that did little to protect the French language and culture.

A second factor involved the policies of the British colonial authorities in New France. By the terms of the Quebec Act of 1774, they granted formal protection to the status of the Catholic religion and the *code civil*, which was the basis of the civil law in New France. The British faced rebellion in the Thirteen Colonies, who in 1776 declared their independence from the mother country. The recognition of rights for the French Canadian population was probably motivated by the desire to ensure the allegiance of the clerical and civil leaders of that population (Brooks, 1996).

The case of New Mexico, as was discussed in chapter 2, seems to contain many historical similarities to Quebec. Spanish speakers were a majority in the territory, with almost seven out of ten schools administered entirely in Spanish in 1874 (Conklin and Lourie, 1983). Unlike Canada, however, the United States refused to officially recognize the Spanish-speaking majority and did not grant statehood to New Mexico until 1912, when Anglos finally outnumbered Hispanics. This put an end to any challenge of Spanish to the preeminence of English in American life and to the possibility of official bilingualism at the state level. William Mackey (1983) observes that two different strategies were employed to dilute the importance of Spanish. First, state boundaries were drawn to ensure an English-speaking majority. Second, the U.S. Congress waited until a majority was created before it would grant the territory statehood. Consequently, different parts of the Spanish territory became states at different times, depending when an English majority was achieved. California became a state in 1850; Nevada in 1864; Colorado in 1876; and Utah in 1896.

French Canadian nationalism is a third factor that explains the ability of French Canada to resist the pressures of assimilation. French Canada met the challenge of anglophone domination in business and politics by remaining loyal to its traditional values and institutions. "Traditional French-Canadian nationalism was guided by the idea of *la survivance*-survival, against the pressures of a dominant culture that was Anglicizing, Protestant, materialistic, liberal-democratic, and business-oriented" (Brooks, 1996: 302). French Canada during this period thought of itself as a distinct nation, whose Catholic religion and French language were inseparable.

The lack of receptiveness of the other provinces toward granting language rights to French speakers promoted a defensive French Canadian nationalism. For example, a 1890 provincial statute abrogated early guarantees for the French language in Manitoba. Therefore, French speakers remained largely concentrated in Quebec. Finally, francophones were excluded from Canada's economic elite. Even in Quebec, the English dominated the economic life of the province. Fueling the struggle was a conflict of economic interests between the anglophone colonial bourgeoisie and the predominantly agrarian *Canadiens*. The struggle was due also to periodic attempts by the anglophone leaders to assimilate French speakers in Lower Canada by eliminating their schools or reuniting Upper and Lower Canada (McRoberts, 1997). The Rebellion of 1837 was a French protest against the ways of the mercantilist minority who controlled them and threatened to subvert their culture, religion, and language.

The British joined Lower Canada to Upper Canada in the Act of Union of 1840. Further changes became necessary in the 1860s, both for economic development and to protect the north from a post–Civil War United States (Wardhaugh, 1983). The British North America (BNA) Act of 1867 officially recognized the bilingual character of Canada. Article 133 of the British North America Act declared that both English and French were the official languages of the national parliament and of Quebec's provincial assembly. Under its provisions, an individual had the right to use either French or English before the Canadian Parliament or any court created by Parliament and federal courts. There was no nationally recognized right to be educated in one's own mother tongue. Section 93 of the BNA Act placed culturally sensitive policy areas such as education and social services under the control of the provinces. While there was some recognition of the French fact, at the national level the lingua franca of the state was clearly English.

Before the early decades of the twentieth century, the traditional society of francophone Canada—with its high birthrate and extended families, its rural, agricultural base, and its common religious faith—had few points of sustained contact with Anglo-Canadian society (Gill, 1980). By the 1930s, there was evidence of profound changes in French Canadian society, although the extent of the change to "traditional" Québécois society was not widely perceived until the 1950s. Where before French Canada had been a rural, agricultural society, by the 1930s a steady migration to the cities was taking place, and by 1961 most French Canadians lived in urban areas and worked in industrial settings. By the early twentieth century, the typical Québécois lived in a city or town, worked in the nonagricultural sector, primarily manufacturing, and had family members who had left the province, looking for job opportunities in other provinces or the United States. With the passing of traditional Quebec society, the French Canadian extended family structure lost its reason for being and the birthrate began to decline. Finally, the breakup of traditional society also signaled a weakening in the position of the Roman Catholic Church in Quebec.

The first hints of nationalism in Quebec came in reaction to the quickening pace of economic development. In the 1930s, with the onset of the depression, this reaction took the form of antimodernism and a cultural critique of capitalism. The Union Nationale, formed in 1936, reaffirmed traditional social structures and authority patterns. Under its best-known political figure, Maurice Duplessis, the Union Nationale sought to revert Quebec to its preindustrial, habitant past. During his leadership of the province, between 1936 and 1939 and again between 1944 until his death in 1959, Duplessis was an avid defender of provincial rights and the farming interests. By contrast, he never challenged the unity of Canada and had no objection to extensive economic development. As a consequence of his profarmer and probusiness policies, as well as the corrupt and authoritarian style of his rule, nationalism began to develop in new directions.

Nationalism is based on some concept of the nation, including who belongs to it and who is excluded. The traditional nationalism did not identify *la nation canadienne-française* exclusively with the province of Quebec. The boundaries of *la nation* extended beyond Quebec to embrace French Canadians throughout Canada. There were two important reasons for this more comprehensive notion of the nation. First, Catholicism and the role of the church were important elements of the traditional nationalism. Second, the antistatist Catholic tradition in Canada prevented the traditional nationalism from associating the French Canadian nation with the Quebec state (Brooks, 1996: 305). This notion of nationalism changed significantly with the advent of the Quiet Revolution in Quebec.

Quebec Nationalism and the Quiet Revolution

The frustration of French Canadian nationalists at the inferior position of French-speaking Quebecers and their language and culture in the Quebec economy led to a widespread determination to use Quebec's provincial government to build a modern, French-speaking Quebec (Gill, 1980). Many observers view the Quiet Revolution of the early 1960s as the single most important turning point in Quebec's recent history (Gingras and Nevitte, 1983; McRoberts, 1988).

Two major themes in relation to language policy and practice surfaced during the Quiet Revolution. The first was the use of French as a language of work in the modern sector of the economy, including commercial, financial, and industrial enterprises. In 1961, the Quebec economy was characterized by ethnic and linguistic stratification that weighed heavily against French-speaking Quebecers. Average yearly incomes during this year stood at $5,502 for unilingual anglophones, $4,772 for bilingual individuals (most of whom were French Canadians), and $3,099 for unilingual francophones (Government of Quebec, 1972).

The second theme was the growing fear of French as an "endangered" language both within North America and the province of Quebec (Esman, 1985). Immigrants to the province overwhelmingly adopted the English language. In addition, with industrialization and urbanization, the fertility rate declined from 4,348 children ever born per 1,000 married women in 1941 to 2,632 in 1981. The comparable rates for Canada as a whole were 3,341 in 1941 and 2,493 in 1981 (Census of

Canada, 1983: Tables 1 and 4). At the end of the twentieth century, Quebec's birthrate was the lowest of all the Canadian provinces (Joy, 1992). For the period from 1986 to 1991, the Quebec fertility rate was only 1.5 (Données démolinguistiques, 1997: table 1.6). These trends, along with evidence that francophones were excluded from much of the province's economic structure, formed the basis for the policy recommendations of the Quebec Royal Commission of Inquiry on the Position of the French Language on language rights in Quebec.

The Quiet Revolution also brought in its wake an increasingly critical examination of the Canadian constitutional system and the extent to which it acted as a barrier to the realization of French Canadian demands for national determination. The ensuing changes in Quebec under Liberal leader Jean Lesage (1960-1966) included provincial control of education and welfare institutions away from the church, increased industrialization, and saw the provincial government—rather than the English-speaking business class—as a primary engine of development. During Lesage's administration, the provincial government sought to increase its powers, either through a general evolution of powers to the provinces or through granting a "special status" to Quebec (Weaver, 1992: 23).

In 1967, René Lévesque left the Liberals to establish a new political movement dedicated to the sovereignty of Quebec. In 1976, after almost a decade of grass roots organizing, the Parti Québécois (PQ) was capitulated into power. The PQ was committed to achieve a sovereign state in a step-by-step strategy through a "ballot box revolution." The PQ lost the referendum for sovereignty-association in 1980 by a three to two margin. Despite the failed sovereignty referendum, it had an important influence on both Quebec and Canadian politics. According to McRae, "the nine years period from 1976 to 1985, during which Quebec was governed by a legally elected regime actively committed to Quebec independence, constituted the most fundamental challenge to the federal system in this century" (1990: 205). The 1980 referendum failed at least in part because then-prime federal minister Pierre Trudeau offered Quebecers a "renewed federalism" that seemed to promise to satisfy national aspirations within the framework of a revised Canadian constitution. Although a new Canadian constitution became a reality in 1982, the PQ government refused to endorse it (Clarke and Kornberg, 1996; Russell, 1992).

As the challenge of Quebec nationalism emerged on the political scene, Ottawa lacked anything that could be called a language policy (Brooks, 1993). The origins of current language policy in Canada lie in developments in Quebec during this period. The federal government, observed Eric Waddell, "was facing a legitimacy crisis in the 1960s and 1970s and had the immediate task of proposing a Canadian alternative to Quebec nationalism" (1986: 97). As a response to the initiative of the Quiet Revolution, the Royal Commission on Bilingualism and Biculturalism (B and B Commission) was set up in 1963. It was a first step toward adoption by Ottawa of a policy of official bilingualism. This policy was intended to defuse the indépendantiste sentiment building in Quebec.

Through Trudeau's efforts, the B and B Commission put into motion both symbolic and statutory changes in Canadian language policy. Since the 1960s, there has been significant alterations in what Raymond Breton (1984, 1986) calls the "Canadian symbolic order." These include a new flag, national anthem, the renaming of Dominion Day to Canada Day, and new stamps and coins. A deliberate effort was made to create symbols that did not alienate French Canadians. Another important change involved the passage of the Official Language Act in 1969, which gave statutory expression to the policy of bilingualism. Furthermore, the act attempted to equalize the status of French and English at the federal level by giving the right of the public to be served in either French or English, providing for the equitable representation of francophones and anglophones in the federal service, and allowing public servants of both languages to work in the language of their choice (Brooks, 1993).

The independence movement in Quebec was the most important catalyst for change in language and ethnic policies in Canada after World War II. The immediate threat of Quebec nationalism led to the adoption of a federal language policy. The B and B Commission had to choose between two competing principles, the principle of territoriality, and the principle of personality.

According to the territorial principle, language rights are based on the region in which one lives. In Switzerland, for example, the four national languages are not only guaranteed public usage but, additionally, each language territory has the right to protect and defend its own linguistic character and to insure its survival. The canton in accordance with this principle determines the official cantonal language (or, in a few cases, languages). The cantonal language is the medium of instruction in the public schools and the operation of the cantonal government (Schmid, 1981). This principle is in contrast to the personality principle, in which language rights are the same throughout the country. Each of the principles has its advantages and disadvantages, and its advocates, and detractors.

> The personality principle attached uniform rights to citizenship and facilitates movement across a country. It favors geographically dispersed linguistic groups: however few in numbers the members of a language group may be in any locality they possess the full set of language rights. The territorial principle, on the other hand, offers language groups the security that comes from effective dominance over certain regions. In effect, a language group trades minority rights in one region for majority rights in another. (McRoberts, 1997: 89)

The B and B Commission made a conscious decision to reject the territorial principle, in favor of the personality principle. It argued that the Canadian population was too mobile for language rights to be concentrated in a few areas. Ironically, the B and B "commissioners came down in favor of integral coast-to-coast bilingualism at the very time when Quebec was abandoning such an option" (Waddell, 1986: 90). An important goal of Premier Trudeau's (1968–1983) language reform was to place French on an equal footing with English in the federal government. Trudeau's vision for language reform, however, went far beyond bilingualism in Ottawa. The ultimate goal was to let Canadians, whether French or English, deal with the federal government in their own language. Trudeau selected the principle of personality over the territorial principle as the ruling principle for Canada.

McRoberts observes that Trudeau was vehemently opposed to any enhanced recognition of Quebec as the primary base of francophones: "In effect, Trudeau was attempting to redefine Canadian dualism, drastically reducing its meaning. Rather than a dualism of collectivities, it was one of individuals who happen to speak one of two different languages. Nor was this dualism touted in geography. It was to extend throughout Canada as a whole once language rights were recognized" (McRoberts, 1997: 65).

A second component of the Trudeau strategy was based on multiculturalism, which he proclaimed in 1971. By this he meant support of all cultures, however "weak and small." Trudeau rejected the B and B Commission's conception of biculturalism, built upon the two charter groups, which was the French Canadian understanding of Canada. By rejecting biculturalism, Trudeau was attempting to reduce the Canadian dualism to language alone. Rather than two cultures, Canada was seen as composed simply of individuals, some of whom spoke French and others English. By trying to link multiculturalism and bilingualism, the Trudeau government created an obvious contradiction, one that has dominated the last decade and a half of Canadian political life (McRoberts, 1997).

Trudeau's vision of Quebec and Canada was not shared by most Quebec francophones. The 1960s onward was characterized by a reformation of ethnic identity among Québécois from religion to language, and to the province of Quebec from the federal nation-state. The adoption of the self-referential "Quebécois" in place of the former "Canadien" is indicative. Instead of defining *la nation* in terms of religion, in which the boundaries extended beyond Quebec to embrace French Canadians throughout Canada, the new nationalism of the 1960s developed an understanding that defined the nation in terms of the Quebec state and the French language. This understanding was translated into law in the passage of Bill 101 under the PQ in 1977, which made French the sole official language in Quebec. Three of its most important provisions established (1) French as the exclusive official language for proceedings of the provincial legislature and the courts and the main language for pubic administration;[1] (2) the requirement that businesses with fifty or more employees receive a "francisation" certificate as a condition of doing business in the province; and (3) children with few exceptions were required to attend French-language schools in Quebec.[2]

The 1960s and 1970s were characterized by the reformulation of ethnic identity among French Canadians. The primordial attachment was to be to language rather than religion and to the province rather than the continent. "In Quebec the state was to incarnate the nation, but it was the *État du Québec* rather than Canada" (Waddell, 1986: 86). This new understanding was in direct conflict with Trudeau's interpretation of language as an individual characteristic and culture as separable (Driedger, 1996; McRoberts, 1997). Evidence of the increasing identification of French-speaking Quebecers toward the province and away from the Canadian state and a pan-French Canadian identity is shown in Table 6.1. This trend that has escalated since the 1970s has been instrumental in the redefinition of nationalism.

Table 6.1   Self-Identification of Québec Francophones, 1970–1990 (%)

Year	French Canadian	Québécois	Canadian	Others or Not Stated
1970	44	21	34	1
1977	51	31	18	—a
1984	48	37	13	1
1988	39	49	11	1
1990	28	59	9	2

a. Excluded from tabulation.

Source: Kenneth McRoberts, Misconceiving Canada: The Struggle for National Unity (Toronto: Oxford University Press, 1997), table 4. © Kenneth McRoberts. Reprinted by permission of Oxford University Press Canada.

Current Sources of Quebec Nationalism

The resurgence of Quebec nationalism in the late 1980s can be traced to three major factors. First is the continued fear of assimilation. One of the main reasons that nationalist sentiment has refueled a powerful secessionist movement in Quebec is the fragility of the French language in North America. The entire history of Quebec from the Quiet Revolution onward is haunted by the fear of anglicization. From a high of 29 percent in the 1940s, the proportion of the French-speaking population has steadily declined to slightly less than 24 percent.

Even in Quebec most immigrants prefered the utility of English to the French language in 1996. Despite efforts to encourage immigrants to shift to French, English is dominant between allophones (who speak neither English nor French) who do shift to one of the country's official languages. In 1996 in Quebec, 39 percent moved to French and 61 percent to English as their mother tongue. The proportion of Canadians who are francophone has slipped to the lowest level ever. The 1996 census showed that even though the percentage of francophones is decreasing, the actual number rose 2 percent from 1991 to 1996. That was less than half the rate of growth for the anglophone population—4.7 percent—and a smaller fraction growth for the allophone population—15.1 percent. The trend is even more significant when one looks at a longer time frame. Between 1971 and 1996, the anglophone population grew by about 33 percent, compared with only 16 percent for the francophone population (Mitchell, 1997: A1).

In 1986, Canada's 25 million people included 5.3 million French speakers in Quebec and nearly .5 million in northern New Brunswick and the north and east of Ontario, regions that are adjacent to Quebec. Less than 4 percent of Canada's francophones were scattered in the vast expanse that includes southern Ontario, the four western provinces, the northern territories, and most of the Atlantic region (Joy, 1992: 8, 124–125). Quebec is increasingly French and the rest of Canada is increasingly English. As political power in Ottawa is related to population, Quebec fears the loss of political clout and leverage within the federation. This demolinguistic situation has exacerbated linguistic tension within Quebec. Table 6.2 shows that French has decreased in all provinces except Quebec. The reality of linguistic assimilation of French Canadians outside of Quebec was one important

Table 6.2   French as Home Language

Province	1971		1991		1996	
	Number	%	Number	%	Number	%
Total Canada	5,546,025	25.7	6,288,430	23.3	6,359,505	22.3
Newfoundland	2,295	0.4	1,340	2.0	880	1.6
Prince Edward Island	4,405	3.9	3,050	2.4	2,915	2.1
Nova Scotia	27,220	3.5	22,260	2.5	19,970	2.2
New Brunswick	199,080	31.4	223,265	31.2	219,390	30.1
Quebec	4,870,105	80.8	5,651,795	83.0	5,770,920	81.9
Ontario	352,465	4.6	318,705	3.2	287,190	2.7
Manitoba	39,600	4.0	25,405	2.3	22,015	2.0
Saskatchewan	15,930	1.7	7,155	0.7	5,386	0.6
Alberta	22,700	1.4	20,180	0.8	15,730	0.6
British Columbia	11,505	0.5	14,555	0.4	14,085	0.4

Source: McRoberts, 1997: 105; Census of Canada, 1996a. Kenneth McRoberts, Misconceiving Canada: The Struggle for National Unity (Toronto: Oxford University Press, 1997), table 2 and Census of Canada. Population by Home Language (Ottawa: Statistics Canada), table

factor that promoted the shift in allegiance from French Canada and the dream of an *Amérique française* to the concrete reality of Quebec. The Quebec nationalism of the 1980s confirmed the divorce between the *Québécois* and the francophones of the diaspora (Waddell, 1986).

The need to learn two languages falls disproportionately on those of French mother tongue. Across the country, 41 percent of francophones were bilingual in 1996, almost five times higher than the proportion of anglophones (9 percent). The rate of bilingualism of francophones living outside Quebec was even higher, with 84 percent of all francophones bilingual compared with 7 percent for anglophones. Only in Quebec are anglophones twice as likely to be bilingual as are francophones (62 percent compared to 34 percent). Most Canadians continue to be unilingual. The 1981 census showed that 15.3 percent of Canadians were able to carry on a conversation in both French and English, compared with 16.3 percent in 1996. In 1996 the number of bilingual Canadians living outside of Quebec was only 12 percent, compared with 38 percent in Quebec (Census of Canada, 1996a, 1996b).

The second factor, related to the resurgence of Quebec nationalism, is connected to optimism in the profitability of sovereignty. This feeling is inspired by a "self-confidence rooted in the economic progress of francophones, the development of provincial institutions, and their condition relative to the federal one" (Dion, 1992:117). Québécois increasingly believe that the help of the federal government is not essential. In a 1991 poll, 26 percent of Quebecers said that Quebec had gained from its relationship with the rest of Canada, 38 percent believed the relationship had been detrimental, and 36 percent answered it has made no difference (Blais and Nadeau, 1992: 90).

Finally, there is a feeling of rejection born from the constitutional crisis. The 1982 Constitution passed without the consent of Quebec. The crowning element of the Constitution Act of 1982 was the Charter of Rights and Freedoms, which was driven by the goal of pan-Canadian bilingualism. In the charter, language rights were framed in terms of the needs of individuals rather than collectivities. This individualistic notion of language conflicted with the territorial conception espoused in Quebec. Quebec abandoned linguistic equality and adopted French as its official language in 1977 with the passage of Bill 101. In order to normalize Quebec's place in Canada two more attempts were made—the Meech Lake Accord in 1990 and the Charlottetown Referendum in 1992, both of which failed to endorse a special status for the province of Quebec.

The PQ defeat in the 1985 provincial election paved the way for the Meech Lake Accord, which was formulated by Prime Minister Brian Mulroney and the ten provincial premiers. In addition to other revisions, the accord recognized Quebec as a "distinct society" within Canada. Its failure to secure ratification within the proscribed three-year period by all ten provinces, however, sparked another constitutional crisis and revived separatist's sentiments in Quebec. Raymond Breton (1992: 34) observed:

> The Meech Lake episode offered a great opportunity for the PQ to reorganize itself, to promote its cause, and to bolster its support among the electorate. It could mobilize its members and gain additional support among those who sympathized with the sovereignty-association cause. It should be noted that as long as there was consensus on the accord, many pro-independence Quebecers opposed it, as recorded in newspaper accounts. But when opposition to it grew in English-speaking Canada, they changed their position. As a Quebec commentator observed, the reaction was: "If English-speaking Canadians are opposed to it, than it must contain something valuable for us."

A 1991 poll, taken after the failure of Meech Lake, indicated that 70 percent of Canadians outside of Quebec would not endorse further concessions to Quebec, even if it meant that the province would separate (Dion, 1992:113–114). This reality has spurred the federal electoral victories of the Reform Party in the west of Canada and the Bloc Québécois in the province of Quebec. Lucien Bouchard, a cabinet minister in the Mulroney government, resigned after the failure of Meech Lake and formed a new party—the Bloc Québécois, dedicated to Quebec sovereignty in the federal political arena. The failure of Meech Lake and the revival of separatism also set another constitutional attempt in motion. The result was the Charlottetown Accord, which was designed to satisfy everyone. Prime Minister Brian Mulroney had committed himself to ending the constitutional deadlock in Quebec's favor. Quebec was to be recognized as a distinct society and would receive a guaranteed 25 percent of House of Commons seats, and the Western provinces could get a revised Senate. The problem with the Charlottetown Accord was that it dissatisfied everyone and was badly defeated in a national referendum in October 1992 (Clarke and Kornberg, 1996).

Despite the uneasy movement to a bilingual country, there remains a significant tension between Quebec and the rest of Canada. Language policy in Quebec has been shaped with the idea that French Canada is coextensive with the boundaries of Quebec and therefore occupies a unique or "distinct society." This interpretation continues to be a source of unresolved conflict between Quebec and Anglo

Canada. Recent failures at constitutional change that would have recognized Quebec's special status, by reducing the Quebec question to "one among many others" has given a strong impetus to Quebec nationalist and separatist sentiment.

The 1995 Quebec Sovereignty Referendum: Unresolved Nationalism

In September 1994, the PQ, led by Jacques Parizeau, was again victorious. A referendum on sovereignty became the PQ's first order of business. On December 6, 1994, the PQ released the draft of a bill to be placed before the Quebec assembly. The draft began with the declaration that "Quebec is a sovereign people" and went on to define sovereignty as the exclusive power to pass laws, collect taxes, and sign agreements with other states. Furthermore, the December bill authorized the government of Quebec to conclude, "with the government of Canada, an agreement the purpose of which is to maintain an economic association between Quebec and Canada." The bill did not give any indication of the terms of the agreement so it could be interpreted in many different ways (McRoberts, 1997).

Early into its second administration, the PQ began to lay the political groundwork for a second sovereignty referendum. The PQ tried to convince voters that sovereignty would not cost them the programs and economic benefits tied to the Canadian safety net such as universal healthcare, pensions, and social security and other programs, which are more extensive than those in the United States. Despite these efforts, most public opinion polls failed to show a majority for the sovereignty option. The weakness of this option in opinion polls led the federal government to maintain a "strict silence strategy." In June of 1995, the PQ moved to bolster public support by announcing an agreement with the Bloc Québécois and the small Action Démocratique, to conduct a united campaign for sovereignty. This paved the way for Bloc leader Lucien Bouchard to assume a leading role in the campaign. Unlike Parizeau, Bouchard was a very popular leader among French Quebecers (Clarke and Kornberg, 1996).

In September 1995, a modified version was presented to the national assembly. The wording was again ambiguous, implying that a sovereign Quebec might be able to maintain economic and political ties with Canada. The referendum question asked, "Do you agree that Quebec should become sovereign, after having made a formal offer to Canada for a new Economic and Political Partnership, within the scope of the Bill respecting the Future of Quebec and the agreement signed on June 12, 1995?" The bill was to be adopted if the "Yes" forces prevailed in the referendum. The October 1995 referendum came within a hair of passing— 49.4 percent voted "Yes" and 50.6 percent voted "No." The turnout was exceptionally high, with over 93 percent of the qualified voters in Quebec casting a ballot. The split was clearly along language lines, with almost 60 percent of francophones voting "Yes," while about 95 percent of nonfrancophones voted "No" (Clarke and Kornberg, 1996; McRoberts, 1997).

The 1995 referendum is poignant evidence of the split between the two language groups. This split was reaffirmed in the December 1998 Quebec provincial election. Although the separatist PQ was returned to power, they did not muster a plurality of the popular vote. The PQ won 76 national assembly votes to the 48 won by the Liberals—almost the same proportion as in 1994. In the popular vote, which is seen as an indication of probable strength for sovereignty, the separatists received 42.7 percent of the vote, while the Liberals won 43.7 percent. A clear majority would be needed for a referendum to pass. This means that PQ Premier Lucien Bouchard will probably not call another referendum on breaking away from Canada unless he believes that the referendum would win a solid majority. The issue, however, has not been put to rest (Bauch, 1998; DePalma, 1998). According to a Sondagem poll conducted in September 1999 for *Le Devoir*, a separatist daily in Montreal, about 70 percent of Quebec voters do not want another referendum. Austerity policies adopted by the PQ government seem to have contributed to a fall in separatist support, which at the end of 1999 is around 40 percent in opinion polls (Brooke, 1999a).

Canada continues to be evidenced by two solitudes—a significant split between Quebec and the rest of Canada. For much of Canadian history, there were two separate societies kept together by a centralized government framework. Quebec, from the times of its inclusion in the Canadian federation, has contained key elements of a submerged nation including differences based on language, religion, and history (Schmid, 1990) that has "gravitated between a concern for cultural survival and a messianic sense of *mission providentielle*" (Waddell, 1986: 73). The appeal of Quebec sovereignty lies primarily in the affirmation of collective identity. The growth in the support of sovereignty is linked to the failure of the Canadian political institutions over the last three decades to recognize and accommodate this identity (McRoberts, 1997).[3]

The establishment of two enduring language communities is the major factor that distinguishes Canada from the United States:

> In some almost perverse way Canada's greatest weakness, her ethnic composition, is also her greatest strength. Perhaps the only real distinction between Canada and the United States is that Canada is bilingual and either a bicultural or multicultural country whereas the United States is neither. In this view, that difference alone accounts for Canada's claim to a separate identity and protects the country from becoming, even more than it is at present, just another satellite or appendage of the United States. (Wardhaugh, 1983: 77)

Individual and Group Rights in Canada and the United States

Group rights, including special rights and entitlements, has a long history in Canada (Paltiel, 1987). "Although Canada is a country where the protection of individual rights is considered mandatory, collective rights are regarded as almost as important in both English-Canadian and French-Canadian political cultures" (Lemco, 1991: 429). The difference of the two countries may be seen by comparing the Charter of Rights that became part of the Canadian Constitution in 1982 and the Bill of Rights of the U.S. Constitution. In addition to individual rights such as freedom of conscience, religion, expression and association, other charter sessions entrench "group rights." These stand in contrast to the exclusive concern with the rights of the individual as set forth in the U.S. Bill of Rights. The charter recognizes rights that "implicitly or explicitly" accrue to linguistic minorities (francophones in English Canada and anglophones in Quebec), native peoples, women, and multicultural groups, as well as the old and disabled (Stark, 1992). Consequently, the charter has created an "an environment in which (Canadians) are highly conscious of their identity as members of particular groups and are encouraged to organize and lobby for their (constitutional) interests" (Williams, 1985: 125).

Seymour Martin Lipset, in the *Continental Divide* (1990), fails to mention the pervasive difference based on two separate national communities, which differentiates Canada from the United States. The Canadian mosaic and American melting pot are linked to imagined and grounded patterns of interethnic and linguistic relations in the two countries. Since 1971, Canada has had an official policy of "multiculturalism." Prime Minister Trudeau announced this policy on October 8, 1971. In his address, he proclaimed that "there are no official cultures in Canada." He committed the government to acting in four different areas, however: (1) permitting the government to assist all Canadian cultural groups that have "demonstrated a capacity to grow and contribute to Canada"; (2) assisting members of all cultural groups to overcome barriers to full participation in Canadian society; (3) promoting creative encounters and interchange among Canadian cultural groups in the interest of national unity; and (4) assisting immigrants acquiring at least one of Canada's official languages (McRoberts, 1997: 125).

Despite differences its official policy toward multiculturalism, Jeffrey Reitz and Raymond Breton (1994) concluded that the Canadian cultural mosaic was actually not very different from the American melting pot, with respect to the integration of recent immigrant groups. While there are differences of tone in race and ethnic relations in Canada and the United States, they found that on a number of indicators, including promoting cultural maintenance of immigrant groups, linguistic retention in Anglo Canada and the United States and overall economic opportunity the differences between the two countries were not overwhelming; at least "they do not appear to be large enough to justify the distinction implied by the choice of metaphors" (Reitz and Breton, 1994: 125).[4]

The major difference between Canada and the United States relates to the incorporation and conflict between the two enduring language communities. Group rights are ingrained in the Canadian experience, unlike the almost exclusive American emphasis on individualism and protection from government. The way in which the two countries treat non-English-speaking students in the public schools illustrates the different notions of group as opposed to individual rights. Equal rights in Canada and the United States have almost diametrically opposite meanings. Equal rights in Canada means the establishment of "separate but equal" facilities, not their abolition. In this case, it led to the establishment of separate facilities on a linguistic basis, to protect French speakers both inside and outside of Quebec (Tetley, 1982). Bilingual schools, in which students would have a choice between English and French as a language of instruction, were resisted. In the United States, the first goal of civil rights was the desegregation of the school system, so that schools would not draw their population by race or national origin.

In recent decades, bilingual education has been one of the most controversial and misunderstood issues in American educational policy. On the whole, bilingual education in the United States is a transitional compensatory measure aimed at a disadvantaged segment of the school population (Fishman, 1981). Federal law and court precedent, as we have seen in chapter 4, established the right of children in the United States to equal educational opportunity—but that opportunity is essentially one within an anglophone society. Dennis Baron has aptly summarized the existing attitude toward languages other than English in the United States:

> With or without intent and the passage of official language laws, English will still be first in the United States. . . . Moreover, regardless of the law and regardless of how desirable it may be, the language situation in the United States is not likely to change radically from what it has been in the past or what it is right now. Nonanglophones will continue to meet with resentment from many English speakers. . . . Some of them will fight these laws, and in some cases they will have limited success. . . . But in most cases, nonanglophones will continue to learn English, sometimes imperfectly, at least for early generations or for those otherwise isolated from the standard English mainstream. (Baron, 1990: 199)

The approach of the United States is not completely different from that of Canada toward non-English and non-French speaking minorities. Canadian "heritage language" programs have some of the same characteristics as bilingual programs in the United States. One obvious contrast between the situation in the United States and Canada is that, whereas the government of the United States has poured significant amounts of money into its programs for non-English speakers, the Canadian government has been primarily concerned with promoting French as a second language through immersion classes in the public schools and French classes for adults, especially for those in the federal bureaucracy.

The United States acknowledges only one language; in contrast, Canada accepts two. Canada's position on the issue of linguistic minority educational rights reveals the competing pressures of two deeply rooted languages. In the United States, the preeminence of English in American education is now a reality, despite the fact that English is not now nor has it ever been the only language in the United States.

Another important factor differentiating Canada and the United States had to do with the public school curriculum and organization. The schools played a very different role in the two societies, in supporting either assimilation into a melting pot or preservation of subgroup loyalties. When the great immigrations of the 1840s and 1850s took place, Calvin Stowe and William McGuffey in the United States argued that the public schools held out the best hope of turning foreign children into Americans. The education had to be uniform and systematic. Stowe, McGuffey, Horace Mann, and many likeminded educators strongly believed that the schools must find ways of inculcating patriotism and republicanism in the young (Stamp, 1977; Tyack, 1967). There was no similar feeling of national patriotism among educators in British North America during the 1840s and 1850s, when public control of education was expanded in Canada.

This clearly was seen in the writings and policies of Egerton Ryerson, superintendent of education for Upper Canada from 1844 to 1876. While his American counterpart, Horace Mann saw public schools producing "good little Americans." Ryerson never saw the production of "good little Canadians" as a central reason for advocating for publicly supported schools. Ryerson did see political value in free schooling; but it lay in inculcating loyalty to Britain and to British institutions in the face of persistent republican threats from the south. (Stamp, 1977: 31)

The Canadian educational system was and continues to be very decentralized and fragmented. In the years after 1867, each of the provinces continued to develop its own school system or systems. State-supported Protestant and Catholic divisions meant that some provinces—in particular, Quebec—developed dual school systems that lacked coordination. In addition, provincial loyalties remained strong. French- and English-speaking leaders emphasized different concepts of the relationship between schooling and patriotism (Jain, 1977; Stamp, 1977). Thus, "American universalism—the desire to incorporate diverse groups into a culturally unified whole" and "Canadian particularism—the preservation of subnational group loyalty" (Lipset, 1990: 172) was fostered in the respective school systems in the United States and Canada.

Despite the threat of separatism, French occupies a much higher status in Canada than Spanish does in the United States. French has gained increased importance in politics in the last thirty years.[5] According to Lysiane Gagnon (1993), a political columnist for *La Presse*, being able to communicate in French has become a political necessity born of the need to address the sensitivity of the huge pool of Quebec voters. Québécois will not cast a ballot for someone unable to talk to them in their own language. The movement for bilingualism came from the elite, but it cut deep into the Canadian psyche. Academics, the literati, and Canadian nationalists were quick to realize that bilingualism was one of the few features that distinguished Canada from the United States, its powerful neighbor to the south. Education, in particular, responded to the desire of parents who wanted their children to be bilingual in order to qualify for better jobs.

Federal spending on language programs for 1989 totaled over $589 million in Canada in comparison to $180 million for bilingual programs in the United States, with ten times the population. Nearly 2.5 million elementary and secondary pupils received second language instruction in either French or English in Canada in comparison to 240,000 students in the United States in 1989 (Fleras and Elliott, 1992: 161). Immersion programs in English-speaking Canada have spread rapidly. The number of elementary and secondary schools offering French immersion programs increased from 237 in 1977–78, with 37,881 student enrolled, to 1,592 schools and 288,050 students in 1990–91 (Brooks, 1993: 248). The new bilinguals in English Canada who have attended immersion programs have a strong ethnic class component. In cities where a great number of school children were born in third world countries and do not speak English at home, immersion classes are a heaven for the middle- and upper-middle-class, an elite form of education functioning within the public system. "For this 'new' class, the bilingualism that mastery of the French language confers constitutes something profoundly Canadian in the sense of being sophisticated and more 'European.' Hence it serves increasingly to demarcate this class from other social classes and, strikingly, from our southern neighbors" (Waddell, 1986: 97).

Attitudes toward Identity, Diversity, and Multilingualism

Quebecers of French origin continue to be ambivalent about their identity. Quebec and the rest of Canada are putting forth different models of identity. Anglo Canada insists on multiculturalism and individual rights as embodied in the Charter of Rights, while Quebec is proposing integration into a common French political culture that takes into account the plurality of cultures (Labelle, F. Rocher, and G. Rocher, 1995). These two diverse models of integration and identity have left Canada devoid of a common set of core values that holds the United States and Switzerland together. Attitudes between Quebec and the rest of Canada toward identity, constitutional change, core values, and mass attitudes are the subject of the next section.

Canadian Multiple Identities

A sense of linguistic identity, which for most French Québécois is synonymous with the province of Quebec, is much more strongly felt among French than the rest of English Canada. This attachment to a territorial submerged nation is absent among Spanish speakers in the United States, who do not comprise a majority in any state, and are much more heterogeneous in their attitudes than the Québécois. Table 6.3 shows that less than a third of Quebecers in 1991 had a deep attachment to Canada, and slightly less than a half in 1994 were saddened by the thought of leaving Canada. In 1991, there were also almost 30 percent more individuals outside of Quebec than inside Quebec who showed strong agreement (6 or 7 on a

Table 6.3   Canadian Multiple Loyalties (%)

Canadian Identity	Province of Respondents	
	Quebec	Rest of Canada
Proud to be Canadian[a]	58	87
Canadian primary identity (compared to national average)[b]	45	72
Province primary identity (compared to national average)[b]	49	22
Satisfied with life in Canada (% agreeing)[b]	63	62
Deep emotional attachment to Canada (% agreeing)[b]	30	68
Canada is the world's best country to live in (% agreeing)[c]	90	96
All of Canada is the best (not just area where one lives) (% agreeing)[c]	83	77
The thought of Quebec leaving makes me sad/heartbroken (% agreeing)[c]	48	64

Source: a. Multiculturalism and Canadians: Attitude Study, Angus Reid Group (Ottawa: Multiculturalism and Citizenship Canada, 1991), author's calculations. Maclean's/CTV Poll. Maclean's. 107(January 3 1994), p. 11. c. Maclean's/Decima Poll, "In Search of Unity." Maclean's 107(July 1, 1994), p. 17.

Table 6.4   Self-Identification of Québec Francophones, 1995

Self-Identification	Percentage
Québécois only	29.0
Québécois first, but also Canadian	29.1
Québécois and Canadian equally	28.1
Canadian first, but also Québécois	6.7
Canadian only	5.4
None of these	1.2
Don't know / Refuse to answer	0.5

Source: Kenneth McRoberts, Misconceiving Canada: The Struggle for National Unity (Toronto: Oxford University Press, 1997), table 5. © Kenneth McRoberts. Reprinted by permission of Oxford University Press Canada.

7-point scale) to the statement "I am proud to be a Canadian citizen." By contrast, both language groups agree that Canada is the best country to live in.

Attitudes toward separatism are closely related to language and feelings of attachment toward Quebec rather than the Canadian state. André Blais and Richard Nadeau (1992), in an analysis of a 1991 survey, found that francophone Quebecers are 40 percent more strongly attached to Quebec than to Canada, and the great majority of them are sovereignists. One-third of the Quebecers had divided loyalties between Quebec and Canada, and were strongly supportive of federalism. Finally, there remained a group, representing more than a quarter of the sample, slightly more attached to Quebec and equally divided between sovereignists and federalists. The ebb and flow of support for sovereignty is also related to highly symbolic events such as Meech Lake and the Charlottetown referendum, which are interpreted as a rejection of Quebec's distinct society, and reinforce a closer attachment to Quebec and consequently support for independence.

Quebecers also have an attachment to Canada[6] through Quebec, although too often provincial and national loyalties are seen in conflict, rather than complementary, with one another. In Canada, there is a lack of official support for simultaneous attachment to ones province and the nation. Often questions are asked in a format that makes the informant choose between loyalty to one's province or Canada. When presented with several levels of loyalties, strong identification with Quebec does not exclude identification with Canada as well. Table 6.4 shows the results of a survey taken during the last week of the 1995 referendum campaign. Although 29 percent of the sample defined themselves as "Quebecer only," the majority shared an allegiance between Quebec and Canada.

Political Issues and Core Values

Perhaps what is most striking in Table 6.5 is the degree of disagreement on the importance of separatism and bilingualism between Quebecers and the national average. Almost four in ten Quebecers put bilingualism and language at the top of their list of "the things that most divide us," as compared to less than a quarter nationally.[7] Further examination of Table 6.6 shows that Quebec separatism elicits a much

Table 6.5   Political Issues and Core Values in Canada (%)

Issue	Province of Respondents	
	Quebec	Rest of Canada
Quebec separatism is the thing that most divides Canadians (compared to national average)[a]	10	26
Bilingualism/language is the thing that most divides Canadians (compared to national average)[a]	39	23
Things that most tie Canadians together as a nation (% agreeing)[a]		
a) health care system	70	75
b) hockey	62	70
c) national culture	49	58
d) bilingualism	40	28
The Constitution of Canada should recognize that Quebec, although equal to other provinces, is different, notably because of its language, culture and law (% agreeing)[b]	87	62
Quebec should have the constitutional means to foster and protect its language and culture (% agreeing)[b]	88	59
Quebec should be recognized as a distinct society in the constitution (% agreeing)[b]	73	38

Source:

a. Maclean's/Decima Poll, "In Search of Unity." Mclean's 107(July 1, 1994), p. 17–19.

b. Rethinking Government. Final Report (Toronto: Ekos Research Associates, 1995), pp. 95–96.

greater response nationally than in Quebec—with Quebecers seeing it as significantly less important (26 percent nationally versus 10 percent in Quebec). The poll was taken over a year before the 1995 referendum, which may understate the results. While English Canada expresses very little support for a special status for Quebec, both language groups give significant support to decentralization of powers to all provinces or offering all provinces the same deal as Quebec (77 percent in Quebec and 64 percent in the rest of Canada) (Maclean's/Decima Poll, 1994: 17–19). The majority of Canadians, both inside and outside of Quebec, would prefer a Swiss solution with extensive provincial autonomy within a federal framework.[8]

Language policy in Canada is fraught with ambiguity and ambivalence. Nearly two-thirds of the respondents in Quebec and the rest of Canada rejected the notion of "territorial bilingualism" with a unilingual French Quebec and English as the official language in the rest of Canada. A significant majority (90 percent) of francophones, however, believed that there should be special measures taken to ensure the survival of French, in contrast to only 37 percent of those outside Quebec. There also was a consensus that there should be services in both French and English; however, francophones were much more likely to endorse this position (90 percent) than anglophones (56 percent). Neither French- nor English-speaking Canadians believed official language minorities received adequate protection of their language rights (Fleras and Elliott, 1992: 160–161).

Roughly three-fourths of Canadians outside of Quebec and 54 percent within

Table 6.6   Politics and Separatism in Canada

	Province of Respondents	
Issue	Quebec	Rest of Canada
Quebec politicians are currently raising the issue of Quebec's place in Canada[a]	33	57
Quebec's future is still unsolved because of the failure of politicians[a]	41	38
Quebec's future is still unsolved because of the public's lack of faith in solutions offered by politicians[a]	32	25
Political officials don't care what we think (agreement—5, 6, or 7 on a scale of 7)[b]	57	58
Politics and government are too complicated (agreement—5, 6, or 7 on a scale of 7)[b]	4	43

Source:
a. Maclean's/Decima Poll, "In Search of Unity." Mclean's 107(July 1, 1994), p. 17.
b. Multiculturalism and Canadians: Attitude Study, Angus Reid Group (Ottawa: Multiculturalism and Citizenship Canada, 1991), author's calculations.

Quebec blame politicians for pushing the divisive issue of Quebec into the limelight (see Table 6.6). There is considerable agreement (about two-thirds outside Quebec, and almost three-fourths inside Quebec) that it is the ineptitude of politicians, or the public's lack of faith in them, that stands in the way of a resolution to Quebec's place in Canada. In this sense the political elite is out of step with the mass of Canadian citizens. Kenneth McRae (1990: 7) argues that "one special problem in the functioning of the Canadian system . . . is a chronic lack of cohesion between political elites and their mass support." This gulf between provincial and federal politicians and the citizenry of both language groups is a source of continued tension in Canada.

An examination of qualities that tie Canadians together point to the difficulty of establishing a unique Canadian identity that cross-cuts language barriers (see Table 6.5). The healthcare system and hockey came out much higher than the two political responses: a national culture and bilingualism. English Canada rated bilingualism much lower than Quebec. This result is in contrast to the American situation, where common political values hold the diverse ethnic and racial groups together. Nevertheless, there is a language sensitivity, particularly among Latinos, that should not be underestimated.

Summary: Language Politics in Canada and the United States

Grappling with questions of language diversity but lacking much tradition in language politics, Americans are prone to draw superficial parallels with Canada. U.S. English, an organization that has promoted a restrictive and at times xenophobic approach to immigrants and non-English speakers, has exploited this ignorance of the Canadian language situation. For example, U.S. English loyalists have described bilingual ballots in the United States as "the opening Quebec gambit" and proposed English-Only legislation to prevent the "kind of split we see in Canada or Belgium". U.S. English has even subsidized the Alliance for the Preservation of English in Canada, a militant anglophone group (Crawford, 1992: 232–235). Without understanding the Canadian situation, it is easy to equate language diversity with conflict and language homogeneity (even if it is in part coerced) with domestic peace. The example of racial inequality in the United States should put this simplistic argument to rest.

In Canada, defeat, religion, language, and isolation formed a common identity among Quebecers. Economic subservience, fear of assimilation, and the fragility of the French language in North America have shaped the current tensions between Quebec and English-speaking Canada. Canada and the United States differ significantly in language relations. As Canada developed from colony to state, the French language became entrenched in the new state, even though English maintained a dominant position. The United States was home to many languages, but English became the undisputed national language, making it unofficially a unilingual state. The chief social forces explaining the preeminence of the English language in the United States as compared with Canada are related to three main factors. First, the number of British settlers was initially much greater as a proportion of the population in the American colonies. In Canada, French initially outnumbered the British and remained approximately one-third of the population until the end of the nineteenth century. A second factor was the greater concentration of French speakers in Canada than German or Spanish speakers in the United States. Finally, the political dominance of the British colonists was greater in the United States than in Canada. Therefore, they were better able to dictate the conditions of admission to the new federation of states.

In Canada, the distinctiveness of the two language groups was institutionalized by the British North America Act of 1867, which set up a federal government system. The origins of present-day language policy in Canada lie in the developments in Quebec during the 1960s. The "Quiet Revolution" set the stage for a number of institutional reforms. "The fact that it was the provincial state to which the new nationalism of the Quiet Revolution turned—the state in which French-speaking Quebecers were unquestionably in the majority—reinforced the identification of French Canada with the territory of Quebec" (Brooks, 1993: 242). In the area of language and ethnic relations, the bilingual and bicultural nature of the Canadian state is the most important single factor differentiating it from the United States.

While comparisons are frequently drawn between the large Spanish-speaking populations in the United States and the French speakers in Canada, these comparisons fail to consider the different positions of the minority languages in the two countries. This is perhaps most apparent in the area of education. In the United States, the Bilingual Education Act is basically not an act for bilingualism but rather an effort to anglify America's language minorities. As Joshua Fishman (1981: 517) observes

> The greatest linguistic investment by far has been in the Anglification of its millions of immigrants and indigenous speakers of other languages. Without either constitu-

tional or subsequent legal declaration or requirement that English is the official language, a complex web of customs, institutions, and programs has long fostered well-nigh exclusive reliance on English in public life.

Thus, bilingualism has a very different meaning in Canada and the United States. Equal education in the United States means equal opportunity to be schooled in English rather than to maintain one's language. In Canada, the question is not if French will be recognized but rather the symbolic, political' and economic importance of the two languages in relationship to one another, especially in Quebec.

In contrast to Canada, Switzerland has been referred to as "the most successful multilingual state in modern history" and a "persistent counterexample" to the instability of many plural societies (McRae, 1983: 229). Does Switzerland have lessons for the United States, or is it a *Sonderfall*, their *cas unique*, a special case? We shall turn to the Swiss case in the next chapter.

7

IDENTITY AND SOCIAL INCORPORATION IN MULTILINGUAL SWITZERLAND

[In Switzerland] the basic idea of creating this nation was
not that there was one language common to all citizens, but
rather that there existed the political will to create one national
community in spite of differing cultural origins and traditions
(Camartin, 1996: 284).

This chapter examines identity and social incorporation in Switzerland. As the United States embarks upon the twenty-first century, it must look to other models of integrating linguistic and ethnic minorities into the American polity. We have seen in previous chapters that America's ability to reconcile political unity and cultural diversity has been challenged in the last third of the twentieth century. A massive wave of immigration from Latin America and Asia has transformed the character of many local communities, fueling demands for bilingual services in the public and private sectors. The specter of linguistic diversity has, in turn, sparked insecurity about national cohesion and fostered a movement to designate English as the official language of the United States.

In contrast to Canada, Switzerland has adopted a territorial approach to dealing with its four language groups. Each language group, with the exception of Romansch, is a majority and the dominant language within its own territory or canton (state). While this policy is certainly not likely to be adopted in the United States, it may provide a possible model for Puerto Rico, should it obtain statehood. Unlike the rest of the United States, Puerto Rico has maintained a Spanish-speaking majority for over a hundred years. This situation has persisted in spite of the fact that many attempts have been made to change the dominant language to English.

The first part of this chapter discusses the historical setting out of which multilingualism emerged in Switzerland. It also includes a brief demographic overview of the major language groups. The second section concentrates on the role of mass attitudes in preserving ethnic and national identity, and analyzes the degree to which majority and minority language groups adhere to the same core values. Finally, the chapter concludes by reviewing the various explanations advanced to explain the relative social and political stability in Switzerland.

Overview of Language History and Demography in Switzerland

In this section, I briefly outline the chief social forces that gave rise to multilingualism in Switzerland. Very different factors have influenced the uneasy official recognition of French in Canada and the late emergence of a plurilingual society in Switzerland.

The Swiss Enigma

Cultural and linguistic diversity is a relatively recent phenomenon in Switzerland. In the five centuries following the birth of the Swiss state, it remained primarily a loose confederation of German-speaking cantons. The original defensive alliance —formed in 1291 of the three mountain cantons of Uri, Schwyz, and Underwalden —gradually increased to thirteen by 1513. Only Fribourg, which was admitted in 1481, had a significant French-speaking population, and the urban aristocracy that ruled it attempted to Germanize the entire population. The confederation of thirteen cantons was bound together mainly as a system of military alliances. Effective central institutions did not develop. The major cleavages arose between rural and urban cantons, and after the Reformation between Catholic and Protestant cantons. There is no history of organized conflict between language groups before the nineteenth century, although German remained the only official language of the Confederation until 1798 (Haas, 1982: 62; Weibel, 1986).

The population of the confederation became affiliated with French, Italian, and Romansch speakers from the sixteenth century onward. The League of Grisons, Valais, Neuchâtel, and the ecclesiastical principality of Basel (which became the Jura district of Bern) were associated as allies of the confederates. Ticino and Vaud, as well as part of present-day Switzerland (including the present day canton of Thurgau and much of Aargau), were ruled as subject territories by one or several cantons. These allies and subject territories did not obtain equality with the thirteen cantons of the Old Regime until much later. A strong heritage of communal independence, which can be traced back to the beginnings of Switzerland, however, helped mediate a tendency to dominate the minority language groups by the ruling cantons (Mayer, 1952: 358–360). This respect for local autonomy and linguistic diversity was an important factor in attracting the allegiance of the subordinate areas—areas which, when they had the option, decided to remain with their overseers and protectors (McRae, 1983).

Minority Recognition and Outside Intervention

Invasion by the French army in 1798 spelled an end to the ancient confederation of thirteen cantons. This network of feudal obligations and aristocratic privileges could not be maintained under the impact of the ideas of the French Revolution. It was replaced by the Helvetic Republic, whose constitution was based on the conceptions of the Enlightenment and the rights of man. Embodying the French tradition of centralization and authoritarian executive power, the new regime found support only in a few areas, such as Vaud and Aargau, which were enjoying their newly acquired independence. Despite opposition, centralization transformed Switzerland almost overnight into a modern state. The 1798 constitution abolished all privileges and established the equality of individuals and territories (Bonjour, 1952). As Edgar Bonjour (1952: 230) notes: "By raising the French and Italian districts to the status of cantons with equal rights the Helvetic Republic founded a multilingual Switzerland. In this way it checked the growth of different languages for rulers and ruled wherever there were signs of it." This experience sharply contrasts with the Canadian historical experience, in which the French language minority suffered a humiliating defeat, and language rights had to be battled for in the political and social arenas.

Despite its benefits to the linguistic minorities, the Helvetic Republic conflicted too strongly with the entrenched sentiments of local autonomy and of traditional diversity. The citizenry revolted against uniformity and widespread unrest rendered the constitution unworkable. In 1803, Napoleon intervened and imposed his Mediation, which restored to each canton its own government. The new constitution of 1803, which was intended to keep Switzerland in a state of weakness and dependence on France, however, was more in harmony with the country's mood than that of the Helvetic Republic (Bohnenblust, 1974). It maintained the chief gains of the Helvetic period: Old subject districts and the tangled network of ancient privileges were abolished and international or foreign alliances were prohibited. The linguistic equality of 1789 also was maintained, with the inclusion of the cantons of Ticino and Vaud. The other subject German-speaking territories of Aargau and Thurgau and the associated lands of Grisons and St. Gallen were admitted as cantons with equal rights, bringing the total of sovereign cantons to nineteen. Despite the harsh demands of Swiss troops in Napoleonic service, the Mediation period secured ten years of well-being and order for the nation at a time when most European lands suffered from wars and revolutions. The 1803 constitution remained a source of inspiration for the Swiss liberals in the troubled decades ahead (Schmid, 1981).

After Napoleon's downfall, the cantons resumed most of their old authority; of aristocracy, privilege and decentralization and reverted to German as the official language. Under the new Federal Pact of 1815, Switzerland became a confederation of sovereign states. One important achievement of the Revolutionary period was the addition of three French-speaking cantons—Geneva, Neuchâtel, and Valais—and the continued independence of the six newly incorporated cantons (McRae, 1983). After considerable squabbling, the Congress of Vienna finally awarded the Jura district to Bern as compensation for Bernese territorial losses in Vaud and Aargau. With the addition of these territories, Switzerland assumed the basic boundaries it has today, with the exception of the separation of the Jura into its own canton in 1979.

In Switzerland, conflict contributed to the process of nation formation. Resistance to foreign powers creates nations by transforming a vague sense of ethnic difference into a crystallized sense of national identity. Loring Danforth (1995: 18) observes that wars accomplish the most dubious of tasks by focusing attention on territorial boundaries and creating national communities in opposition to "enemies of the nation." It was Switzerland's good fortune that it not only endured Napoleon's conquest but also attained the national boundaries that form modern Switzerland. Ironically, a foreign power was instrumental in producing a multilingual Switzerland with secured boundaries and a sense of identity separate from its invader. This was particularly important in the new French-speaking cantons.

Religious and Linguistic Conflict

Through the extension of civil rights initiated by the revolutions, language differences gained in importance in Switzerland. This was especially the case when the followers of the progressive and conservative parties did not belong to the same language group. In the canton of Bern, the French and Catholic districts of the Jura attempted to break away from the old German-speaking Protestant canton. Unlike other plurilingual cantons, which developed linguistic pluralism within more organically integrated communities, the new canton of Bern was formed from the addition of the Jura territory, as decreed by the Congress of Vienna. This involuntary arrangement proved to be a source of future conflicts (McRae, 1964, 1983). There also were conflicts in the bilingual cantons; in Fribourg, the German and Protestant district of Murten defended itself against the French and Catholic majority of the canton, in Catholic Valais, a civil war broke out between the German-speaking groups of the upper Valais and the more liberal French-speaking groups in lower Valais (Weilenmann, 1925).

The Reformation split Switzerland into two opposing camps. From the first religious battle in 1529 until the nineteenth century, the division between the two was clear and remained unchanged. The present-day cantons of Uri, Schwyz, Unterwalden (both halves), Lucerne, Zug, Fribourg, Ticino, and Valais, as well as Appenzell Inner Rhoden, and Jura, remained Catholic, while Zürich, Bern, both Basels, Schaffhausen, Appenzell Outer Rhoden, Vaud, Neuchâtel, and Geneva adhered predominantly to the Protestant faith. In Glarus, Grisons, Aargau, Solothurn, and Thurgau the two faiths coexisted.

Religious bitterness, which had temporarily died down, reappeared in 1815. This discord rose with the revival of the spirit of the French Revolution in the Switzerland of the 1830s and in 1832 the seven leading "regenerated" cantons— Zürich, Bern, Lucerne, Solothurn, St. Gallen, Aargau, and Thurgau—united to protect their new constitutions and to press for a revision of the 1815 pact along more liberal lines. Spearheaded by the decision of the confederation not to enforce Article 12 of the Federal Pact (which guaranteed the maintenance of religious orders in the cantons), seven Catholic cantons—Lucerne, Uri, Schwyz, Unterwalden, Zug, Fribourg, and Valais—formed the Sonderbund (or separatist confederation) in 1845. Religious and economic differences as well as memories of former religious battles aggravated this conflict. The cantons of the Sonderbund were Catholic, rural, and conservative. They feared the prevailing liberalism of the Protestant cantons and the drive toward Swiss unification, which they saw as a threat to their religious and political traditions.

By 1847, the Free Democrats had a majority in the Diet and demanded that the Sonderbund be dissolved as being irreconcilable with the Federal Treaty. When the Catholic cantons refused, the Diet ordered the dissolution by force of arms (Remak, 1992). The war was short-lived. The Catholic cantons were defeated in twenty-five days, with a total loss of only 128 men on both sides. The division between Catholic and Reformed has been a moving force in Swiss history since the Reformation. Religious differences, even in those instances where religious and linguistic boundaries reinforced each other, have almost always been more salient than linguistic ones in Switzerland (Linder, 1994).

Modern Switzerland

The victors in the Swiss civil war were free to lay the foundation for the new nation. Although it was in their power to impose upon Switzerland a centralized authority, disregarding the needs of the religious and linguistic minorities, they chose instead to compromise between the excessive federalism of the old regime and the complete unity advocated by the more extreme Free Democrats. Although it underwent a thorough revision in 1874, the 1848 constitution in its basic aspects remains the constitution of Switzerland today. Both the 1848 and 1874 constitutions guaranteed the complete equality of languages by declaring that German, French, and Italian were the national languages of Switzerland. The constitution established a Council of States on the model of the old Diet, with each canton represented by two deputies. This council allowed the linguistic and religious minorities — taken together — to have a blocking role in federal legislation. In the National Council, the second chamber, each canton is represented by delegates in proportion to its population.

Respect of the language territories, which have stayed constant for several centuries, has prevented a unified Romand nationalism in Switzerland. This is reinforced by a more than equitable representation of linguistic minorities in the organs of the state and military and self-rule by ones linguistic group in the communities and cantons (Donneur, 1984). Although French Switzerland has tended to show lower rates of fertility than German Switzerland, this gap has been partially overcome by two important trends, in contrast to Canada. First, there has been a relatively greater immigration to French Switzerland from German Switzerland and abroad than to the territory of the majority language group, and, second, there have been more language transfers to French in French Switzerland than to German in German Switzerland (McRae, 1983).

The provisions of the 1848 constitution failed to put an end to religious and linguistic tensions. Religion again became a vital point of contention during the time of the *Kulturkampf*. The struggle between Liberals and Conservatives broke out in Europe following the declaration of papal infallibility in 1870. Free Democrats and Catholics in Switzerland were drawn into this struggle, which rekindled old animosities of the Sonderbund War. The revision of the Federal Constitution in 1873–74 was influenced by the *Kulturkampf*. The constitution of 1874 attempted to fully secularize the state by prohibiting Jesuit activities, banning the founding and restoring of new monasteries (both eliminated from the constitution by popular vote in 1973), requiring the cantons to establish confessionally neutral schools under the direction of the state and allowing complete freedom of religion without privilege of one of the Christian faiths (Linder, 1994).

The most critical period for Swiss linguistic unity came during the early years of the twentieth century. With the outbreak of World War I, both French and German Swiss felt the pull of conflicting nationalisms toward their respective cultural kin. A deep fissure, which came to be known as the trench (*Graben* or *fossé*), opened between French and German Switzerland and threatened to destroy the moral unity of the country. The *Deutschschweizerischer Sprachverein* founded in 1904, and the *Union Romande* that was founded three years later, were organized explicitly to defend the interests of German and French Swiss in the face of perceived threats from the other group (Stevenson, 1990: 230). For the German Swiss, this included the linguistic assimilation of German Swiss migrants to French Switzerland, especially in the Bernese Jura, where it sought German schooling in traditionally francophone territory (McRae, 1983).

The Swiss Federal Council found it necessary in an appeal on October 1, 1914 to reassert "the ideal of our country as a cultural community and as a political ideal above the diversity of race and language" (Kohn, 1956: 128). Carl Spitteler, a famous Swiss poet, reechoed this sentiment in 1914 in a famous address before the New Helvetic Society, entitled "Unser Schweizer Standpunkt." As the war dragged on, relations between French and German Switzerland became entangled with the issue of neutrality. General Ulrich Wille came under suspicion for his prior-German bias. In a letter addressed to the Federal Council on July 20, 1915, he suggested that Switzerland join Germany in the war. Arthur Hoffman, the federal councilor who headed the Political (foreign) Office, was forced to resign for his breach of neutrality. In the end, by deliberate effort and self-control, neutrality was precariously held together. The enormous cost related to mobilization and inflation precipitated a militant general strike in November 1918 that shifted attention away form the language *Graben* to the class division, which cross-cut linguistic and cantonal borders (Jost, 1983).

Twenty years later, as the start of World War II approached, Switzerland found herself in a strategically more precarious but intellectually more secure position than in 1914. The rise of European dictatorships led to a reinforcement of national unity. Italian and German Switzerland recoiled from the savage nationalism propagated in Italy and Germany. Even the ties between French Switzerland and France cooled down after the establishment of the Vichy regime.

In one recent case, linguistic cooperation failed in Switzerland. The Jura region, once the northern district of Switzerland's second-largest canton, Bern, engaged in riots and violence for more than forty years. The Jura region contained a double minority—French-speakers practicing the Catholic religion in a Protestant canton populated by German-speakers. At the outbreak of the crisis, Bern was 85 percent German-speaking and 15 percent French-speaking (Steiner, 1990: 112). Despite the fact that there were long-standing grievances, with the exception of the short-lived period from 1867 to 1878, separatist sentiments only surfaced after World

War II (Jenkins, 1986; Linder, 1994). The separatist movement was triggered by the Moeckli affair in September 1947, in which members of the legislature of the canton of Bern rejected the Bernese government's nomination of French-speaking Georges Moeckli for Director of Public Works, on the grounds that the office was too important to be filled by a francophone member of the cabinet.

The Moeckli affair ignited old hostilities and long-term claims of economic and political neglect in the Jura region. The overlap between separatist grievances and language was not equally distributed throughout the region. The southern Jura was economically better off and had a Protestant majority. The pro and antiseparatist movements and later votes to create a new canton, closely paralleled language and religious divisions. John Jenkins (1986), in his analysis of Jura separatism, found that the presence of both the French language and the Catholic religion were necessary for a commune to vote separatist in 1974.

On January 1, 1979, after a long struggle—which included several referenda by the communes involved, the canton of Bern, and a national vote—the three predominantly Catholic, French-speaking districts of the Jura were able to form their own canton. In a typical Swiss solution, a number of refendums were held to decide the fate of the Jura. First the populace of the entire Bern canton accepted a constitutional amendment that allowed the question of Jura separation to be put to a refendum in the Jura districts. In a second step, the Jura region decided by a slim majority for separation. In a third referendum, the districts of the Jura bordering Bern decided to stay with the canton. A fourth referendum allowed individual communities along the new frontier between canton Bern and the new Jura canton to decide whether they wanted to opt for the new canton of Jura or stay with the canton of Bern. Finally there was a nationwide referendum, which accepted the Jura as a new canton (Steiner, 1999). The creation of the new canton was praised as an innovative solution to moderate linguistic conflict. French Swiss elites exerted restraint and did not get involved in the Jura conflict. Even in the canton of Bern, none of the political parties had been wholly identified as for or against the separation of the Jura. In contrast to Canada, "Swiss political history is noteworthy and unique for the fact that no significant or political movements have ever emerged to promote the interests of any language group or language region as such in the Confederation" (McRae, 1983: 111).

The French-speaking Swiss are a slightly smaller percentage of the Swiss population and are more heterogeneous in terms of rural and urban residence than their counterpart in Canada. In 1990, the almost 6.9 million Swiss inhabitants (including 1.25 foreigners) spoke four languages, as well as several dialects. French speakers were 20.5 percent of Swiss citizens (19.2 percent of the resident population), 73.4 were German-speaking citizens (63.9 percent of the resident population), 4.1 were Italian-speaking Swiss (7.6 percent of the resident population), and .7 percent spoke Romansch, a minor Swiss language spoken in a few Alpine valleys in the Grisons. Since the Reformation, the Swiss citizenry has been fairly evenly divided along religious lines. The French, German, and Romansch Swiss populations find adherents among both Protestants and Catholics. Only the small Italian-speaking population is almost exclusively of the Catholic faith (Annuaire statistique de la Suisse, 1994: 252–253; Bickel, 1994: 46).

The relationship between the language groups is further complicated by the fact that in German-speaking Switzerland the colloquial language is Swiss German, which consists of a large number of dialects differing considerably from High German (Hochdeutsch) or Schriftdeutsch (written German). In contrast to Swiss German, the orginal dialects of western Switzerland, home of most French-speaking Swiss are considered insignificant today. The scope of the Ticino dialects is limited to familiar and intimate circles. A supraregional Lombardian dialect, very similar to its Italian neighbor, is used for communication. The official written language is the same in the Ticino and the rest of Italy. French- and Italian-speaking Swiss frequently complain about the widespread reluctance of German-speaking Swiss to speak High German. Understandably, they dislike the idea of having to learn Swiss German, which is understood only in German-speaking Switzerland and is used solely for oral communication, and see it as an unreasonable imposition (Wyler, 1990).

While Switzerland, unlike Canada, is not facing a separatist challenge, the decades after World War II have brought some critics to question whether the same commonality of outlook still prevails between Swiss linguistic groups. Some social observers maintain that there is currently a general "Helvetic malaise" in Switzerland (Imboden, 1964). This "crisis of identity" has been exacerbated with the denial and reluctant coming to terms with Swiss wartime dealings with the Nazis (Elon, 1998). Newspaper accounts from the later 1990s are filled with the renewed opening of a *Graben* or *fossé* between French and German Swiss. The trench widened at the end of the 1980s, when several decisions split the two major language groups. This has been particularly important in the area of foreign policy.

The December 1992 referendum on membership in the European Economic Area split the population. The larger question of possible membership in the European Union (EU) loomed conspicuously in the background of the referendum. In an unusual show of interest, 78.3 percent of Swiss citizens turned out at the polls. The treaty was defeated, narrowly missing a popular majority with 49.7 percent voting in favor. For a referendum to pass, it must gain a majority of the cantons in addition to a majority of the citizens. Only seven cantons voted for the measure. All the German-speaking cantons—with the exception of Basel Stadt and Basel Land—rejected the treaty with majorities of up to 74 percent, as did the Italian-speaking canton of Ticino. In contrast, all the French-speaking cantons voted to join the European Economic Area, with majorities of up to 80 percent (Linder, 1994:175). Because the German Swiss occupy a large majority of the population and cantons, the measure failed. The linguistic cleavage that has played an occasional role in Swiss politics since the end of the Sonderbund War seemed to have returned. In this case, suspicion of German dominance of the European Community and regional insularity pushed German-speaking Switzerland to reject the treaty, while French-speaking Switzerland showed more internationalism and fewer inhibitions regarding partnership with the rest of Europe (Kobach, 1994: 135).[1]

Support for Romansch and Weaker Language Communities

In spite of recent antagonism, particularly on the foreign policy front, Swiss language relations, with the exception of the Jura problem, have been characterized by an organic historical evolution of different language minorities (Linder, 1994; McRae, 1983; Schmid, 1991; Steiner, 1974, 1990). Recognition of weaker regions of Switzerland was recently given support through a constitutional amendment. In the March 1996 referendum, Swiss voters approved a new language article for the Swiss constitution, which went beyond recognition of the country's four national languages (German, French, Italian, and Rhaeto-Romansch). The new amendment calls for measures to protect and promote the language communities. According to the Federal Council (the executive branch of Switzerland), the modifications in the language article are aimed at three goals. First, the confederation and the cantons are made formally responsible for fostering mutual understanding and exchange between the language communities. Second, the cantons of Grisons and Ticino are to receive special support from the confederation. In Grisons, Romansch has suffered a dramatic decrease in recent years, and in some valleys Italian is under pressure. Finally, Romansch will receive added importance, as the Romansch-speaking population will be able to communicate with the federal government in their mother tongue (Volkabstimmung von 10. März, 1996).

Over three-fourths (76.2 percent) of the population and all of the cantons accepted the new article. The vote was clearly meant as an expression of support for Romansch and a strong indication that Swiss citizens are "unwilling to let a national myth die" (Swiss Review of World Affairs, 1996: 31). In 1938, Article 116 of the constitution was amended to include Romansch as the fourth national language in Switzerland. This was the result of a request of the executive of the Grisons in 1935 to aid Romansch "in its uphill struggle for survival against the inroads of modern communication and tourism" and to counter the irredentism of Fascist Italy that claimed Romansch dialects as forms of Italian (McRae, 1983: 120). At that time a distinction was made between national and official languages. The Romansch language, which is only spoken by approximately fifty thousand inhabitants, was not included as one of the three official languages of the confederation. Most texts and federal laws are only translated into German, French, and Italian. The main purpose of the new revised language article is to give explicit recognition to the country's endangered languages.

In March 1996, Swiss voters amended the language article. In the same referendum, they gave overwhelming (over 90 percent) approval to the transfer of the small community of Vellerat from the canton of Bern to the canton of Jura (Swiss Review of World Affairs, 1996). There was no controversy about this move, which had been requested by the people of Vellerat.

The new federal constitution, which was accepted by a majority of Swiss citizens and the cantons on April 18, 1999, incorporated the new language article.[2] While individual voters approved the new constitution solidly by 59.2 percent, the vote among the cantons was much closer, with twelve whole and two half votes in favor versus eight whole cantons and four half votes opposed. The strongest approval for the revised constitution came from francophone Switzerland and the big cities.

With the exception of Valais, the French-speaking voters were strongly behind the proposed revision. Opposition came mainly from the small central rural cantons, which made up the original nucleus of Switzerland (Vanoni, 1999: A1). In recent years, as their authority and identity have been threatened, these cantons have increasingly voted against referendums they perceive as centralizing power in the federal government or giving up power to international bodies. Steiner (1999: 14) observed that there is a clash between two perceptions of the place of Switzerland in Europe. One viewpoint has stressed that Switzerland should take its place in the EU like other small countries. The other point of view has been built on the historical myth of Switzerland as a special case, a small Alpine nation that has constantly been endangered and that must continue to be vigilant against potential threats to neutrality, direct democracy and independence of the small and affluent nation-state.

Group perceptions and attitudes play an important role in democratic stability in multilingual and multicultural societies. Even in countries with relatively peaceful relationships between linguistic groups, differences in culture, group perceptions and power arrangements often shape conflicting identities. The next section examines attitudes toward identity and cultural pluralism in Switzerland.

Attitudes toward Identity, Diversity, and Multilingualism

Pollsters in Switzerland have measured the strength of multiple loyalties by inquiring about three major areas of majority-minority language attitudes: (1) the degree to which national and subnational identities are an important aspect of one's self-identification; (2) the extent of divergence and consensus on political issues and core values between language groups; and (3) the belief in diversity and multilingualism.

In Switzerland, several surveys have measured national versus cantonal identity, as well as the importance of ones community, language group and cultural/linguistic group in Europe. Table 7.1 shows that German Swiss are more likely to identify themselves as "Swiss" than the French-speaking minority. Specifically language identification, however, is weak among both groups. The 1972 sample, which only asked about cantonal, linguistic group, and Swiss identity, is not comparable with the 1990, 1994, and 1996 samples. Perhaps because of the perceived attack on Swiss identity—with respect to revelations of Nazi gold dealings—both language groups sought refuge in identities removed from the larger Swiss state. The trend toward weaker Swiss identity for the French Swiss, however, remained during the three time periods in the 1990s.

Multiple Loyalties in Switzerland

The attachment to a territorial subnation is not absent among French speakers in Switzerland, although it takes a quite different form. A different question given to all army recruits in a 1985 survey found somewhat different results.[3] Almost half of the French Swiss, but only slightly more than a third of the German Swiss, agreed

Table 7.1   Self-Identification of French- and German-Speaking Swiss, 1972–1996 (%)

Entity	1972[a]	1990[b]	1994[c]	1996[b]
French Swiss				
Community	—	14	16	31
Canton	30	18	14	16
Linguistic group	30	15	14	14
Switzerland	40	25	30	18
Europe	—	10	11	8
World	—	18	15	14
German Swiss				
Community	—	21	25	26
Canton	32	6	7	9
Linguistic group	16	11	6	8
Switzerland	52	43	44	34
Europe	—	9	8	8
World	—	9	10	15

Source:
a. Kenneth McRae, Conflict and Compromise in Multilingual Societies: Switzerland (Waterloo: Wilfried Laurier University Press, 1983), p. 109.
b. Mattias Brunner and Lea Sgier, "Crise de confiance dans les institutions politiques suisses? Quelques résultats d'une enquête d'opinion." Swiss Political Science Review 3, p. 110.
c. Hanspeter Kriesi, Boris Wernli, Pascal Sciarini, and Matter Gianni, Le clivage linguistique (Berne: Office fédéral de la statistique, 1996), p. 55.

that belonging to one's linguistic group was important, and almost twice as many Romands as Alemands agreed that belonging to one's linguistic/cultural group in Europe was important. A greater awareness of linguistic identity is consistent with French Swiss consciousness of minority status in the confederation. Given a choice of three responses, both French and German Swiss showed a strong identification with the nation in 1994[4] (see Table 7.2).

In contrast to Canada, both French and German Swiss are equally very proud to be Swiss (see Table 7.3). In answer to the question, "Are you a patriot?," 37 percent

Table 7.2   Self-Identification of French- and German-speaking Swiss, 1994 (three responses, %)

Entity	French	German
Community	37	53
Canton	50	40
Linguistic group	60	35
Switzerland	74	82
Europe	46	36
World	33	28

Source: Hanspeter Kriesi, Boris Wernli, Pascal Sciarini, and Matteo Gianni, Le clivage linguistique (Berne: Office fédéral de la statistique, 1996), figure 17.

Table 7.3   Divergence and Consensus on Political Issues and Core Values in Switzerland (%)

Question	French-speaking	German-speaking
Proud to be Swiss[a]	86	78
Believe the relationship between French- and German-Swiss is satisfactory or very good[b]	35	56
A trench (*Graben* or *fossé*) exists between French- and German-Switzerland[a]	51	36
Qualities that make one most proud to be Swiss[a]		
A neutral country	15	25
A very pretty country	22	18
A democratic country	24	23
Has a good quality of life	27	29
Tolerance as a value is important in raising children[c]	81	76

Source:

a. Anna Melich "Nationale Identität" In Die Werte der Schweizer, ed. Anna Melich (Berne: Peter Lang), p. 28, 33.

b. Bruno Pedretti, "Die Beziehungen zwischen den einzelnen Sprachregionen der Schweiz. In Mehrsprachigkeit-eine Herausforderund, ed. Hans Bickel and Robert Schläpfer (Basle: Helbing and Lichtenhahn), p. 110.

c. Guilhermina Marques, "Die Familie." In Die Werte der Schweizer, ed. Anna Melich (Berne: Peter Lang), p. 83.

of Swiss Germans and 57 percent of Romands answered "Yes" (Schwander, 1992: 769). Although being proud of being Swiss or a patriot may mean different things to the two linguistic groups. In an earlier study, Kerr concludes that, "the Swiss Alemands have a stronger sense of specifically Swiss identity than do Swiss Romands, who express a stronger sense of linguistic identification" (Kerr, 1974: 21–22). These findings do not necessarily imply that French Swiss feel less Swiss than their German-speaking compatriots. In fact, Hardi Fischer and Uri Trier concluded in a study of the stereotypes that the two groups hold of each other that, "Whereas a Swiss Alemand brings his Swissness into full harmony with his native attachments to the German-speaking part of Switzerland, the Romand feels, in a greater measure, a sense of belonging to the Swiss Romands and, *as such Swiss*" (Fischer and Trier, 1962: 18).

Lüthy goes even further in this comparison, noting:

> A Breton, Basque, or Alsatian nationalist is very likely to be a bad Frenchman, a Welshman in favor of self-government for Wales will be a doubtful Britisher; in other countries too, separatist movements endanger national unity. . . . But the believer in self-government for the cantons of Valais or Grisons or Appenzell is a model Swiss patriot, in fact the type of man to whom Switzerland owes her existence. . . . All modern states have come into being through struggling against the regionalism of their component parts; Switzerland, however, was a product of such regionalism and has been sustained in the often serious crisis of her history by the local patriotism of her "twenty-two peoples. . . . " (1962:18)[5]

In Switzerland, strong cantonal and federal identities are perceived to be fully compatible. Kenneth McRae observes that in Switzerland, among the elite and at the official level, there is a deliberate effort to "discourage and downplay identification in term of language and ethnicity as potentially dangerous for political equilibrium, and to emphasize the expressions of diversity in cantonal rather than linguistic terms" (McRae, 1983: 109). This task is made somewhat easier in Switzerland since there are significant differences between French cantons in terms of religion, socioeconomic status, and urban-rural setting. Most Romand social scientists observe that French Switzerland is not a unified block. Unlike the Romansch speakers who are geographically concentrated in part of one canton (the Grisons) or the Italian Swiss, 95 percent of whom live in the canton of Ticino, the French Swiss are distributed among many cantons[6] (Donneur, 1984; Pichard, 1975; Schwander, 1992;).

Political Issues and Core Values

We turn next to political attitudes toward language relations between French and German Switzerland. Of special interest in this section are the similarities and differences between attitudes of the French-speakers and dominant language group on core values and mass attitudes toward politics and politicians.

Table 7.3 shows that the Helvetic "solution" is not immune from a heightened minority feeling and alienation of the smaller linguistic groups. The French Swiss are much more likely than their German-speaking counterpart to believe that the relationship between Romand and Alemand is unsatisfactory (65 percent versus 44 percent) and to perceive that there is a trench between the two language groups (51 percent versus 36 percent).

With increased Europeanization and globalization, there are increased strains on the political order in Switzerland. The tradition of multilingualism and multiculturalism makes Switzerland particularly vulnerable to such strains. Jürg Steiner names four major reasons for the widening gap between German- and French-speaking Swiss. These include the decreased importance of religion, the decreased saliency of neutrality as a foreign policy device, the lessened importance of cantonal borders, and the increased importance of television for political discourse (Steiner, 1999: 10–11). As multiculturalism and multilingualism gain strength in other nation-states as well, including Canada and the United States, similar strains between language and ethnic groups occur. In order to counter these trends, a strong political culture built on democratic values is very important to promote social cohesion.[7]

An examination of qualities that make one proud to be Swiss elicit similar responses from French and German Swiss. Political qualities, neutrality and democracy, and the quality of life were named by two-thirds of the French Swiss and over three-fourths of the German Swiss. In contrast to Canada, in Switzerland there is a common culture that exerts a powerful effect in moderating social conflicts and promotes stability, particularly in times of conflict between linguistic, religious, and cultural groups.

In an earlier study (Schmid, 1981), I analyzed the contents of several history schoolbooks used in French and German Switzerland, in Catholic and Protestant cantons. There is a tendency to emphasize both sides of disputes. One particularly important theme was the need for mediation of differences. Toleration is a value that is very highly regarded by both French and German Swiss speakers in socializing their young (see Table 7.3). Attitudinal differences do not necessarily disappear between linguistic groups with low levels of intergroup tension in Switzerland. Linguistic boundaries do persist and may easily become sensitized on specific issues. Nevertheless, in comparison with other multilingual countries, Robert King observes that "Switzerland is politically almost hyperstable" (1997: 61). The difference between Canada and Switzerland, he observes, is that Switzerland has a strong national identity, what he calls a "unique otherness."

> The Swiss have what the political scientist Karl Deutsch called "learned habits, preferences, symbols, memories, and patterns of landholding": customs, cultural traditions, and political institutions that bind them closer to one another than to people of France, Germany or Italy living just across the border and speaking the same language. (King, 1997: 61, 64)

Multilingualism is such an accepted part of Swiss life that questions asking about official recognition of plurilingualism tend to be absent, even from works entirely devoted to language relations in Switzerland. Unlike the francophone minority in Canada, all of the linguistic groups except Romansch are contingent to countries in which they share a linguistic tradition.[8]

Despite a sensitivity of French Swiss to their minority status in the confederation, this is partially offset by the willingness of the German-speaking majority to converse in French and to assimilate to the Romand language and culture, when they move to French Switzerland. When Romand and Alemand come in contact with one another, German Swiss are more than twice as likely to speak French as the French Swiss are to speak German. This is in part due to the difficulties of mastering both high German, which is the written language of German Switzerland (and taught in the schools of French Switzerland) and dialect, which is the usual spoken language of German Switzerland (Schläpfer, Gutzwiller, and Schmid, 1991). German Swiss are far less likely to perceive language as a hindrance to living in French Switzerland than the reverse. In an earlier study of schoolchildren, I found that the preferred canton of future residence most favored by francophones were all Latin or mixed cantons, while the germanophone list included all the Latin and mixed cantons, as well as several German-speaking ones (Schmid, 1981: 101–102).

It can be concluded from these data that attitudinal differences between linguistic groups do not disappear, even in countries such as Switzerland with low levels of intergroup tension. We have identified a greater sensitivity among Romand, which is characterized by a stronger linguistic identity, a more critical view of language relations, and less sympathy toward the language majority than is characterized by German Swiss. Nevertheless, in Switzerland there are mitigating factors such as high levels of pride in the Swiss state by both French and German Swiss, a generally accommodating attitude of the majority language group to the Latin language minorities and a common civic culture. G. Heiman, in comparing the Swiss and Canadian situation, observed: "Whether he is of French Swiss, German Swiss, or Italian background, the citizens of that country subscribes to one common political tradition. Such is not the case in Canada" (1966: 338).

Several institutional adaptations deeply rooted in the political system assist in accommodating the diverse linguistic and cultural interests in Switzerland. The final section of this chapter reviews the most important explanations advanced to explain the relative social and political stability in Switzerland, and contrasts them with intergroup relations and social integration in Canada.

Demographic, Political, and Institutional Factors Promoting Social Integration

Several demographic, political, and institutional factors have helped neutralize conflicts among language groups in Switzerland. Four major explanations of accommodating conflict in multilingual and multiethnic countries are analyzed with respect to Canada and Switzerland. The first concentrates on crosscutting cleavages. The second looks at legal and informal rules for accommodating language diversity on the federal level. The third focuses on decentralized federalism and communal autonomy. Finally, the fourth analyzes political accommodation and power-sharing as a way to reduce conflict in multilingual societies.

The fact that religious and socioeconomic cleavages crosscut linguistic borders is often invoked as an explanation of the stability and cohesion of the Swiss polity (Linder 1994; Mayer 1968; McRae 1983; Steiner 1974, 1990). In Switzerland, linguistic and religious cleavages crosscut each other. There are French-speaking Catholics and French-speaking Protestants, German-speaking Catholics and German-speaking Protestants. Only the Italian speakers are nearly all Catholics. In addition, the relatively equal distribution of wealth between French and German Switzerland and individuals of the two major language groups has contributed to linguistic harmony.

In contrast to the crosscutting cleavages representative in Switzerland, Canada is currently characterized by two blocs in which Quebec is pitted against the rest of Canada. All the other provinces are predominantly English-speaking, while Quebec is predominantly French-speaking. While the majority anglophone provinces are either predominantly Protestant or fairly evenly balanced between Protestants and Catholics, Quebec is primarily Catholic. Quebec, therefore, exhibits overlapping and reinforcing cleavages. The demographic basis for identifying French Canada with Quebec has become stronger over time.[9]

Canada has experienced an escalation of segmentation coinciding with language, religion, and provincial boundaries. The changing hierarchy of cleavages in the two countries helps to explain minority attitudes and behavior in Canada and Switzerland. Although both countries have experienced minority linguistic discontent in the last two decades of the twentieth century,[10] only Quebec has elected a provincial government and a federal delegation committed to separation. While overlapping cleavages are important, an understanding of linguistic conflict and social incorporation in Switzerland and Canada is incomplete without an examination of constitutional and informal rules for accommodating language diversity.

The second explanation emphasizes the recognition of formal language equality and adequate political and social participation of linguistic minorities. Article 116, which appeared basically unchanged from the 1848 constitution to the revised constitution of 1874 and Article 70 of the 1999 constitution, proclaims German, French, and Italian as the official languages of Switzerland. Romansch is only an official language in communicating with persons of Romansch mother tongue. This simple provision has been construed to allow for the complete equality of German, French, and Italian. Members of both Swiss houses of parliament are free to speak in the language of their choice. The texts of federal laws are published in all three languages, and all three texts have equal status before the courts (Malinverni, 1986). Because Italian (which is spoken by only 4 percent of Swiss citizens) is the weakest of the three official languages, and is not understood by a majority of French- and German-speakers, it suffers practical disadvantages in both the public and governmental spheres (McRae, 1964, 1983).

Romansch—as opposed to German, French, and Italian—does not have official status in the parliamentary, administrative, and judicial spheres of the federal government. The new language amendment only makes it an official Federal language in any dealings with citizens for whom it is a mother tongue. The group, which campaigned for the recognition of Romansch as one of the national languages of Switzerland, was aware of the burden and expense of an additional administrative language (fewer than 1 percent of Swiss citizens speak Romansch).

The federal government authorizes yearly sums for the preservation and furtherance of the Ticino and the Italian and Romansch-speaking communities of the Grisons. In 1992, for example, Radio Television della Svizzera received 25 percent of the whole budget of public radio and television, about five times its proportional share (Linder, 1994: 24). Part of the success of multilingualism in Switzerland is attributable to public expenditure and fiscal distribution in favor of the linguistic minorities in explicit recognition of their otherwise disadvantaged status. Table 7.4 shows that the three major language groups are represented in almost direct proportion to their number in the population.

Although the informal policy of public expenditure for the language minority in Canada is less established than in Switzerland, formal equality and participation in the federal services have made significant strides since the passage of the Official Languages Act of 1969. To increase the bilingual bureaucracy, important actions have included the designation of an increasing share of positions as bilingual. As of 1990, about 36 percent of positions in the public service were designated French or bilingual. A clear majority of appointments to bilingual positions are filled by francophones (Brooks, 1993). In 1962, the Royal Commission on Government Organization noted that the number of francophone officials was "insignificant." In 1999 francophones constituted 27 percent of the management category and 30 percent of the public service proper (Annual Report on Official Languages 1999: 67, 68). This representation compares favorably with Switzerland, where 21 percent of senior staff and 19 percent of the top management are Romand.

While formal language equality had been achieved in Canada in the federal sector, its institutionalization was achieved a half century later than in Switzerland. Wolf Linder (1994: 24) observes that Canada—probably because it has a more se-

Table 7.4   Representation of Swiss Linguistic Groups (%)

Entity	German	French	Italian
Population (Swiss citizens)	74.5	20.1	4.0
Federal Administration			
All personnel	76.5	15.4	5.2
Senior staff	73.6	20.9	3.5
Top management	78.8	19.0	2.2
Expert committees	76.9	20.0	3.1
Presidents of committees of the National Council	76.0	20.0	3.1

Source: Wolf Linder. Swiss Democracy: Possible Solutions to Conflict in Multicultural Societies (New York: St. Martin's, 1994), table 1.2. © Wolf Linder. Reprinted with permission of St. Martin's Press, LLC.

rious problem with the linguistic minority—goes much further than Switzerland in requiring that every document be published in French and English. In contrast with the organic development of federal language parity in Switzerland, in Canada formal language equality on the federal level came only after a substantial threat to national unity.

Proportional representation at the federal level of French-speaking minorities has not solved the language problem in the two countries. In Canada, increased representation of francophones has not necessarily led to the equality of French and English as languages of work in the federal state. Outside of federal departments located in Quebec, the language of work remains predominantly English (Brooks, 1993). In Switzerland, where the capital is located in the Swiss German city of Bern, there are complaints by French Swiss of the public service being organized along Germanic norms and work habits in which their own different mentality and cultural perspective are not always appreciated. For this reason there is a general reluctance for Romands to live in Bern (McRae, 1983).

The third explanation of conflict management in Switzerland emphasizes decentralized federalism and cantonal autonomy. At the federal level, in general, linguistic minorities have veto power in matters of vital interest to them. Although this rule may be occasionally broken, it is upheld to a large extent. Debates occur sporadically among elites and the populace as to whether an issue is really of vital interest to a linguistic minority (Steiner, 1999).

Differences in linguistic policy between Switzerland and Canada are far more pervasive on the local level than on the federal level.[11] The federal principal and the geographical concentration of the languages in Switzerland have given rise to the principle of territoriality. The four national languages are not only guaranteed public usage, but, furthermore, each language territory has the right to protect and defend its own linguistic character and to ensure its survival (Linder, 1994; Schäppi, 1971). The principal of territoriality is not expressly guaranteed in the constitution. As the Swiss jurist Walter Burckhart has noted, however:

> It is now a tacitly recognized principle that each locality should be able to maintain its traditional language regardless of immigrants of other languages, and consequently that linguistic boundaries once settled should not be shifted, neither to the

detriment of the majority nor of minorities. It is trust in this tacit agreement that provides a foundation for peaceful relations among the language groups. Each group must be sure that the others do not wish to make conquests at its expense and diminish its territory, either officially or by private action. Adherence to this rule, as well as respect of each group for the individuality of the others, is an obligation of Swiss loyalty. It is not less sacred because it is not laid down in law; it is one of the foundations of our state itself. (quoted in McRae, 1983: 122)

Swiss authors refer to the ability of the canton to regulate all cantonal affairs involving language as *kantonale Sprachhoheit* or linguistic sovereignty. Thus the canton (in accordance with the principle of territoriality) determines the official cantonal language (or, in a few cases, languages). The cantonal language is the medium of instruction in the public schools. There is an obligation on the part of the citizen to enroll their children in the local schools and acquire a sufficient knowledge of the local language. Even in the bilingual cantons, the principle of territoriality finds further application in communal governments, services, and schools. In predominantly French-speaking Valais and Fribourg, which tend to see themselves as part of French Switzerland and are sensitive to their minority language position in the confederation, the minority-language function of local autonomy benefits the German-speakers, who constitute almost a third of the population in both cantons. Bilingual municipal administrations such as those of Biel and Fribourg are the exception; most communal administrations are unilingual. All cantonal laws and regulations are issued only in the official language(s). While compromises are made in practice, the cantons have no legal obligation to provide translations or deal with citizens in languages other than their own.

The consequence of the territorial solution is that linguistic autonomy is guaranteed. While restricting individual freedom of schooling and other services in ones mother tongue in the whole of Switzerland, the territorial solution has been instrumental in maintaining language stability and establishing French, German, and Italian (at least in the last decade or so) melting pots.[12] Only Romansch Switzerland has lost substantial mother-tongue speakers as some communities have chosen the utility of German over Romansch as the official language of the community (McRae, 1983; Schäppi, 1971; Schmid, 1981).

In contrast to the principle of territoriality—which operates on the cantonal level—the principle of personality (*Personalitätsprinzip*)—on the federal level—regulates relations between the individual and the federal government. According to the constitution, in direct dealings between the citizen and the confederation, and vice versa, the federal government must adapt to the language of the individual within the limits of the four national languages. Furthermore, there is an obligation of the federal authorities to deal with cantonal authorities in the official language or languages of the canton (McRae, 1983).

In Canada, the Royal Commission on Bilingualism and Biculturalism explicitly rejected the territorial solution, arguing that because French is a "pan-Canadian reality" "bilingualism therefore cannot have a local or regional character, as in Belgium or Switzerland" (Gagnon, 1989: 5). The principle of personality prevailed over the principle of territoriality. This conception of bilingualism, with the passage of the Charter of the French Language in 1977 by the Parti Québécois, has been firmly rejected by many French Quebecers whose linguistic laws have evolved progressively toward a territorial solution (Nelde, Labrie, and Williams, 1992). The 1982 Canadian Charter of Rights was widely seen by French Quebecers as an attempt to strike down Bill 101, Quebec's charter of the French language, and to reduce Quebec's power to legislate in the area of language within its borders. French Quebecers continue to be weary of assimilationist assumptions behind equal rights as "same treatment," which they believe erodes the position of French in Quebec.

The fourth explanation—neutralizing conflict between language, cultural, and religious groups in Switzerland—emphasizes political accommodation and power sharing. Informal traditions embedded in the Swiss political and civic culture are as important as formal constitutional arrangements. Jürg Steiner notes that "Executive power-sharing by language groups is a custom rather than a constitutionally or legally mandated rule. Therefore, the system can be practiced with some flexibility" (Steiner, 1990: 107). The federal council—the seven-member executive body of Switzerland—corresponds roughly to the population share of the three largest language groups and the four major parties. It is composed of two Free Democrats, two from the Christian Democratic Party, two Social Democrats, and one from the Swiss People's Party. This allocation of positions on the federal council has been called the Magic Formula.[13] A chairperson who rotates every year according to seniority leads the federal council. Each federal councilor heads a department, such as foreign affairs, defense, or interior.

The constitution provides that no two federal councilors may come from the same canton. But a complex network of rules has shaped the pattern of representation. Zürich, Bern, and Vaud have been almost continuously represented since 1848, with the Vaud seat assuring at least one French-speaking councilor. Generally there are two non-Germans, with a seat occasionally going to a Ticinese. Two seats are assured by the composition of the parties, the Christian Democratic Party members naturally choosing Catholics. The Free Democrats and the Swiss People's Party members select Protestants and Social Democrats choose a personality whose confessional loyalty is not too pronounced (Hughes, 1962; Linder, 1994). Thus, the collegial executive may be considered as an expression of the linguistic, religious, and regional differences within Swiss society.

Similar conventions for representation of the diversity of language and religion also apply to parliamentary committees, the judiciary, the public service, and federally supported institutions, including the military. At the highest level, the seven three-star generals are selected in such a way that there are usually four German-speakers, two French-speakers, and one Italian-speaker. If a French-speaking three-star general retires, the search for his replacement is practically limited to French-speakers. Jürg Steiner observes that Switzerland operates to a large extent by a quota system, which would be unconstitutional in the United States. "According to Swiss political thinking, not only individuals but also groups have rights" (Steiner, 1990: 109). A group's right of representation, however, cannot be enforced in court. Swiss power-sharing is part of the Swiss political culture rather than a legal right embodied in the constitution.

By sanctioning group rights outside the political sphere, Switzerland has been spared some of the current constitutional battles going on in Canada. Since 1982, with the inclusion of the Charter of Rights and Freedoms, the Canadian constitution has acquired considerable symbolic value. The Meech Lake and Charlottetown accords enlarged the symbolic component of the Canadian constitution and exacerbated conflict between Quebec and the rest of Canada without solving the tension between the three principles of equality: between individuals, between the provinces, and between the two main linguistic communities (Breton, 1992).

The Swiss have attempted to solve the Canadian problem of the tensions between the three equalities, at least in the constitutional amendment process, by acknowledging that cantons as well as individuals should have an equal existence in the political process. The Swiss system has been effective in "noncentralization," because it is able to prevent new powers from being assumed by the federal government, as all new constitutional amendments need a majority in both chambers of parliament, as well as a majority of the cantons and the people at a popular vote (Linder, 1994). Swiss democracy works slowly, because proposed amendments often fail several times before being accepted by both a majority of cantons and the popular vote.[14]

Under the Swiss system of direct democracy, the electorate has the last word in most important decisions. The popular referendum provides a substantial check on the federal parliament. At the demand of fifty thousand citizens, federal legislation must be submitted to the electorate for acceptance or rejection. The people also have a right of "initiative," which entitles any citizen or group of citizens who can obtain one hundred thousand signatures to propose constitutional amendments, which must be considered by parliament and be submitted to a referendum. Through the referendum process, the cantons of French, Italian, and Catholic Switzerland can combine to form a majority, thus enabling them to constitute a check on the powers of the majority. Linguistic groups are not formally recognized in the constitutional process. However, power-sharing between language groups and the recognition that groups not just individuals have rights is an enduring part of the Swiss political culture, and an important ingredient of social integration of the French- and Italian-speaking minorities in Switzerland.

Summary

Switzerland has been successful in accommodating linguistic, cultural, religious, and regional differences over a 150-year history. Contrary to the prevailing Anglo-Saxon model, it has rejected the notion that minority status is a temporary phenomenon and today's political minority will become a nucleus to build tomorrow's majority. In Switzerland, a strong emphasis on local particularism, linguistic equality imposed from the outside, and successful techniques for conflict moderation and resolution have promoted linguistic peace. The stability and relative equality of the language groups also proved important factors of linguistic accommodation with the advent of mass politics and the forces of nationalism, and centralization in the twentieth century. In contrast, in Canada, defeat, religion, and isolation formed a common identity among Quebecers. Economic subservience, fear of assimilation, and the fragility of the French language in North America have shaped the current tensions between Quebec and English-speaking Canada.

The examination of current attitudes toward diversity and multiculturalism has shown that attitudinal differences between linguistic groups do not disappear, even in countries such as Switzerland with low levels of intergroup tension. In both Canada and Switzerland, French-speaking minority groups have a stronger linguistic identity, a more critical view of language relations, and less sympathy toward the linguistic majority. There are more mediating factors in Switzerland than in Canada, however. The French- and German-speaking Swiss are united in a common political and civic culture and are equally proud to be Swiss. This is not the case in Canada, where there is a less developed common tie between language groups and where identity and allegiance continue to be strongly correlated with one's mother tongue and province of residence. Members of the linguistic majority in Switzerland are more likely to assimilate to the French language and culture and speak French when they encounter a minority speaker than is the case in Canada. In Switzerland, plurilingualism, fostered by the principle of territoriality, is an accepted part of everyday life.

The Helvetic strength lies in its solutions to the tensions in the three principles of equality: between individuals, between cantons, and between language groups. Social integration is fostered by language equality, decentralized democracy, communal autonomy, political accommodation, and power sharing among the linguistic groups. The Swiss civic and political culture recognizes individual, cantonal, and linguistic rights informally and on the constitutional level.

Can Switzerland offer any guidance to reconcile America's linguistic troubles, despite the striking difference between the two countries? The political, social, and legal aspects of multilingualism in the United States are connected to a number of issues, including racial politics and civil rights, immigration policy, ethnic diversity, cultural pluralism, and national identity, which are some of the most sensitive issues of our times. The penultimate chapter examines three important language debates that have erupted at the end of the twentieth century. All three will have lasting repercussions into the twenty-first century: the Ebonics controversy, the debate over Puerto Rican statehood, and the dispute over bilingual education in California.

8

THE POLITICS OF LANGUAGE IN THE
LATE TWENTIETH CENTURY

Public and educational policies have made a real mess of language policies. . . . Our national prejudice and ignorance about
language differences in ethnic or regional speech communities
is yet today a shared assumption that speakers in some communities and of certain ethnicities speak impoverished dialects
that reflect both an impoverished culture and impoverished
thinking. . . . The United States has made ethnicity a political
issue as much as it is a cultural identity.

(Holloway, 1995: 82, 85, 83)

Can [Puerto Rico], a state in which over three quarters of the
population speaks English with difficulty or not at all integrate
properly with a country in which ninety-seven percent of the
population speaks English? Would the United States need to
make special linguistic and cultural concessions to the new
state? And would a Spanish-speaking state, seeing its culture
gradually eroding under the influence of the overwhelming
numbers of the English-speaking majority, eventually turn to
the same separatist sentiments that have almost torn Quebec
from the rest of Canada? (U.S. English, 2000a: 2)

Proposition 227, which essentially limits help to non-native
speakers to a year of intensive English instruction, marks an
extraordinary intervention by voters in California into classrooms to mandate teaching methods, a sign of the growing importance of education in the nation's political debate.

(Bronner, 1998a)

Proposition 227 is a multi-layered debate. It's about politics.
It's about power. It's about disenfranchisement. And it's about
what is the purpose and responsibility of the school system.

(Bruni, 1998)

The Ebonics debate, the discussion about Puerto Rican statehood, and the bilingual controversy in California have challenged long-held beliefs about the melting

pot and symbolize the changing meaning of language and cultural pluralism in the United States. These three significant issues, often misunderstood, have served to polarize the American public. In the late 1990s, non-English and non-standard English become a substitute for a political agenda far beyond language itself. The English-Only movement gained widespread political momentum, often with racial overtones. An America Online poll about Ebonics drew thousands of responses ("Hooked on Ebonics," 1997). Many of the comments were racially motivated. Language differences became a new symbol for racial intolerance. U.S. English, the nation's largest English-Only lobby, testified before Congress on Puerto Rican statehood. The issue was whether an island where 98 percent of the population spoke Spanish should adopt English as their sole official language. Lack of speaking English, identification as "Puerto Ricans" rather than as "Americans," and possible conflict between Puerto Rican and U.S. culture were suddenly linked together (U.S. English, 2000a). In California, a June 1998 primary ballot measure that largely eliminated bilingual education in public schools received overwhelming support.

Is the nation's dominant language endangered by the encroachment of other tongues? Are we experiencing creeping bilingualism in the United States? This chapter will examine the politics and facts behind current debates on Ebonics, language issues, and Puerto Rico, and bilingual education in California that will have repercussions far into the twenty-first century.

Ebonics: An Impoverished Dialect?

In a decision that touched on educational, language, and racial issues, on December 18, 1996, the Oakland Unified School District in California approved a policy affirming Standard American English development for all students. In the resolution, the Oakland school board declared that many of its twenty-eight thousand black students did not speak standard English but a distinctive language referred to as Ebonics (literally "black sounds"), or "Pan-African Communication Behaviors," or "African Language Systems." The board resolution described black English as not merely a dialect of standard English, but an "African Language System (that is) genetically based and not a dialect of English" (Oakland Board of Education 1996).

After the resolution was made public in the mass media and on the Internet, it generated an explosion of misconceptions and negative press. The actions of the board of education were variously understood as attempts by the Oakland School District: (1) to teach Ebonics instead of English; (2) to classify Ebonics-speaking students as bilingual so it would be able to apply for more federal funds; (3) to create a system of incentives that would reward failure and lower standards; (4) to polarize an already divided school district; and (5) to support an approach that lacked educational research to improve student achievement (Oakland Board of Education, 1997b).

These misconceptions show how race, class, and language quickly become distorted in the public mind. The policy of the Oakland board of education was based on the work of a broad-based task force, convened six months earlier to review the districtwide achievement data, and to make recommendations concerning effective practices that would raise African American standards. The data showed disproportionately low levels of student performance among black students in the district. The Oakland Unified School District was 53 percent African American. However, 71 percent of the students enrolled in special education, 64 percent of students retained, 67 percent classified as truant, and 80 percent of those suspended —were African Americans (Applebome, 1997; Oakland Board of Education, 1997b). The recommendations in the original resolution sought to focus on the unique language stature of African American pupils and to address English-language proficiency and student achievement.

The intent of the Oakland board of education resolution was not to replace the teaching of Standard American English with Ebonics. Rather, its goal was to teach standard English and other academic subjects to black students by acknowledging the language spoken in many inner cities. Although there is an intense debate by linguists and educators over how to treat black English, no other school district had adopted such a measure acknowledging Ebonics as the language of many inner-city African American students. According to Sherri Willis, spokeswoman for the district, "The goal is to give African American students the ability to have standard English proficiency in reading, writing, and speaking. . . . To do that, we are recognizing that many students bring to the classroom a different language, Ebonics" (Applebome, 1996).

One of the problems of the resolution is the assumption that Ebonics is a "genetically based" language. Ebonics is used to suggest that there is a language, or features of language, common to all people of African ancestry, whether they live in Africa, Brazil, or the United States. Since the Oakland resolution, Ebonics has gone from a term most people had never heard of to a symbol for many of the most volatile issues in American education—a mixture of politics, pedagogy, and social issues. After a month of national debate and tense meetings, the Oakland schools task force that introduced the black English policy adopted a new resolution that called only for the recognition of language differences among black students in order to improve their proficiency in English. The amended plan, which eliminated the earlier proposal's description of black English as "genetically based," was approved by the Oakland board of education on January 15, 1997 (Golden, 1997; Oakland Board of Education, 1997a).

William Labov, a University of Pennsylvania linguistics professor, observes that Ebonics is not the term used by linguists who have studied the African American community. Instead, they refer to *African American Vernacular English* (AAVE), a dialect spoken by most residents of the inner cities. According to Labov (1972, 1997) and John Rickford (1999), AAVE shares most of its grammar and vocabulary with other dialects of English. It is more distinct, however, from standard English than other dialects spoken in continental North America. AAVE is not simply slang or a language of grammatical mistakes. It has a well-formed set of rules of pronunciation and grammar and is capable of conveying complex logic and reasoning.

Research in New York, Philadelphia, Washington, Florida, Chicago, Texas, Los Angeles, and San Francisco shows a remarkably uniform grammar spoken by African Americans who live and work primarily with other African Americans.

Repeated studies by teams of black and white researchers show that about 60 percent of the African American residents of the inner city speak this dialect in its purist form at home and with intimate friends. Passive exposure to standard English—through the mass media or in school—has little effect on the home language of children from highly segregated inner-city areas. Those African Americans, however, who have had extensive face-to-face dealings with speakers of other dialects show a marked modification of their grammar (Labov, 1972, 1997).

Some critics described the Ebonics policy as a way to get federal funds through bilingual programs rather than valid educational approaches. Oakland officials say the purpose of the decision was purely educational. They acknowledged, however, that the policy could allow the financially troubled Oakland district to apply for the same federal funds available for bilingual programs for Hispanic and Asian students (Applebome, 1996; Oakland Board of Education, 1997a). One problem of Oakland and other inner-city districts is that nationally 75 percent of all limited English proficient students attend high poverty schools (Crawford 1997). University of California professor of linguistics and African American studies John McWhorter observes, "They see it as a case where Latinos can get funds, but not black children" (Applebome, 1996). In 1996, the Clinton administration formally rejected the idea that Ebonics is a distinct language. The Department of Education, in response to the Oakland resolution, declared that programs based on Ebonics were ineligible for federal support as bilingual education (Bennet, 1996). The problems of poor urban school districts are exacerbated when limited English proficient speakers and African American students who speak AAVE are in the same schools and classrooms with limited resources. About one-third, or approximately eighteen thousand students in the Oakland school district are designated as LEP (Quan 1998).

The decision by the Oakland school board has been widely criticized for lowering standards for black children. Individuals such as liberal civil rights leader Rev. Jesse Jackson have lined up with conservatives like William Bennett, former secretary of education, against the Oakland resolution (Lewis, 1996). The strong social reaction against using the home language of African American children as the first steps to learning to read and write has meant there have been very few studies that have thoroughly tested this approach in the schools. Plans for programs to make the transition to standard English have been misunderstood as plans to teach the students to speak Ebonics, and to prevent them from learning standard English. Several efforts to incorporate black English into classroom instruction have been terminated because of protest from mainstream civil rights organizations and middle-class blacks who feel the effort stigmatizes black children by suggesting that they cannot learn using standard teaching methods (Holmes 1996; Labov 1997; Rickford 1997).[1] Therefore, because of the prevalence of dialect prejudice, sound educational studies have been displaced by racial and language politics.

At the heart of the Ebonics controversy are two opposite points of view taken by educators. One view is that any recognition of nonstandard language as a legitimate means of expression will only confuse children and reinforce their tendency to use AAVE instead of standard English. The other view is that children learn most rapidly in their home language and that they can benefit in achievement and motivation by learning to read and write in this way. This same debate is also evident in how best to teach limited proficient English students. For African American students, only the first approach has been tried. The essence of the Oakland school board resolution is that the first method, at least for poor inner-city students, has not succeeded and that the second approach deserves a trial (Labov, 1997). The goal of learning standard English is not disputed among black parents. In a survey conducted in March and April 1998, 86 percent of black parents considered it absolutely essential that all children speak and write standard English, with proper pronunciation and grammar ("Parents Value Standards," 1998).[2]

Ironically, few educators have looked to examples of how dialect speakers learn standard language outside the United States.[3] The next section will briefly examine the transition from Swiss German dialect to the reading and writing of standard German in the primary schools of Switzerland. Similar to the distance between AAVE and standard English, Swiss children also speak a dialect, which is distinct from High German.

Can Switzerland Provide an Example?

In Switzerland, which was examined in greater detail in chapter 7, dialect usage is prevalent in all parts of German Switzerland. The widely used term *Schwyzertüsch*, or Swiss German, represents not a single language but a wide range of local and regional dialects. Although quite different in the various German Swiss regions, most of the dialects are mutually comprehensible without difficulty (McRae, 1983: 68). The continuing existence of these dialects, and their resistance to standardization in an era of increasing mobility and mass communication, emphasizes the desire of Swiss Germans to maintain an identity distinct from Germany. One of the consequences of dialect usage is that it is viewed as less threatening in the eyes of the French and Italian language minorities; however, it also makes communication between language groups more difficult (Schmid, 1981). Unlike the Swiss German majority, French and Italian Swiss are not dialect-speakers.

In all areas of German Switzerland, regional dialects are the usual means of informal oral communication. Unlike AAVE, individuals without distinction to educational level or social class standing use dialect. In Switzerland, dialect usage has increased. In fact, many educators are concerned that it has extended its range in the twentieth century at the expense of oral High German, and is continuing to expand. High German is prominent in certain institutions and situations. Most notably, standard German is spoken in secondary and postsecondary education, the churches, the army, and—less rigorously—in public meetings, most legislative bodies, and on radio and television. Standard German is used almost exclusively as a written language. With the exception of a limited dialect literature, virtually all printed matter and correspondence is in the standard language or *Schriftdeutsch* (Rash, 1998; Schläpfer, Gutzwiller, and Schmid, 1991). Yet, even standard German in recent decades has been influenced by dialect borrowing and the influence of French and English words. This means that wires in German from international agencies must be modified for Swiss usage (McRae, 1983: 69–70).

Virtually all German Swiss children must learn High German in school, starting in the early primary grades. Most German Swiss become bilingual between dialect and standard German during the first few years of elementary schooling. School is the institution where more High German is spoken than anywhere else. It is the responsibility of the schools to teach High German to children who have only a very vague and passive knowledge of standard German when they start school.

According to Alfred Wyler, education in High German is a step-by-step process:

> During the first year at school, nothing but dialect is spoken. In the second year, the teacher changes gradually from High German for certain subjects, whereas the texts for reading are in High German from the very beginning. It has been said with some justification that this imposes high demands upon German-speaking Swiss children, for they have to learn to read, write and use a relatively unknown language all at once. Later on the language spoken during the actual lessons is mainly High German, although dialect is used for discussions with pupils after school, and remarks concerning organization before class. (Wyler, 1990: 20)

There is an unwritten norm with respect to the use of dialect and High German. Conversations between pupils, and one-to-one conversations between teachers and pupils, will generally take place in dialect. Instruction in the factual subjects (*Sachfächer*) is chiefly in High German, whereas art, crafts, music, sport, and religious studies tend to be taught in dialect. Code-switching frequently occurs when there has been a misunderstanding in a direction given in High German. Conscious code-switching back to High German often has to be prompted by the teacher (Rash, 1998: 55).

The use of dialect as opposed to the standard language has deep roots in Switzerland. How to best educate children in a form of the German language that they do not speak as their first language has been debated since the introduction of compulsory education in the early nineteenth century. Johann Caspar Mörikofer, following Pestalozzi's humanitarian approach to education, wrote in 1838 that the overemphasis on the use of High German can impede the imagination and free expression of the students, so that ultimately learning will suffer. This seems to be the current educational philosophy in Switzerland. Educators stress that the precondition for effective education in two codes is a positive attitude of the teacher. If children encounter the standard language in a negative way, this can have a lasting effect on their attitudes toward it (Rash, 1998).

The trend toward dialect in the schools of Switzerland is a continuing concern to linguists and language policy makers. They warn that if the spread of Swiss German in the schools continues, there is a danger that German-speaking Switzerland could become cut off and culturally isolated from the larger German-speaking areas of Europe. Furthermore, a lack of consideration for non-German-speaking Swiss could impede communication within Switzerland itself (Rash, 1998). In both German-speaking Switzerland and among AAVE speakers, language is used to reinforce a sense of community and as a marker of group identity. Thus, it very unlikely that dialect will decrease in usage. The lesson of German Switzerland is not that there is one solution to diglossia, the coexistence of two forms of the same language in a speech community. Rather, mastering the standard language is easier if the differences in the vernacular and standard language are made explicit rather than ignored. This lesson was at the heart of the Oakland school board's proposal. Their educational reform that attempted to use AAVE to teach standard English is supported by the Swiss German case.

Avoiding an American Quebec: Language Issues Concerning Puerto Rican Statehood

Language and identity politics are also important components of the debate over the future of Puerto Rico. On March 4, 1998, the U.S. House of Representatives approved historic legislation. By a vote of 209 to 208, the House approved the United States-Puerto Rico Political Status Act. The House bill would have set terms for a vote to seek a final status choice among commonwealth, statehood, independence, or "free association." The U.S. Senate, however, failed to take up this measure in the 105th Congress. Despite the ultimate outcome, the legislation marked the first time in history Congress approved a mechanism to clarify the status of Puerto Rico.

The major effort to kill the United States-Puerto Rico Political Status Act (H.R. 856) was made by English-Only proponents. An amendment was brought to the floor that would have required Puerto Rico, if it became a state, to make English the state government's sole official language and the language of instruction in the public schools. Led by Chairman Gerald Soloman of the House Rules Committee, English-Only advocates wanted to affect the plebiscite's outcome. Under the Territorial Clause, it would be possible to require the territory of Puerto Rico to have English as its only official language. The amendment was defeated with the help of powerful critics, who said the language amendment was an attempt to undermine the self-determination question ("The Young Bill," 1998). The House approved a compromise amendment to soften the English language requirement encouraging Puerto Rico to "promote the teaching of English" to "enable students . . . to achieve English language proficiency by the age of 10" in order to enhance the island's statehood prospects (Puerto Rican Political Status Act, 1998: sec. 3c).

This section will specifically look at language and identity questions for the United States with respect to Puerto Rican self-determination. As we have seen in the previous chapters, English is not threatened as the official language on the mainland. Puerto Rico, on the other hand, offers new challenges to the current language debate at the end of twentieth century. The first section reviews the status of Puerto Rico in a historical context, with special emphasis on language, culture, and identity issues. The second section briefly reviews the options open to Puerto Rico: continued commonwealth, statehood, or independence. Finally, similarities and differences between Puerto Rico and Quebec will be examined.

Language, Culture, and Identity in Puerto Rico

There are political and economic concerns for the United States if Puerto Ricans opt for statehood. Puerto Rico also confronts the United States with identity problems, because a fifty-first state would make the United States more ethnically and linguistically diverse. Already, by the end of the nineteenth century, Puerto Rico had a well-defined national identity and a strong sense of its own culture. Despite significant gaps in education and socioeconomic status, language bound the society together. Spanish, enriched with Indian and African contributions, had extraordinary vitality. A great sense of pride in the language also helped to bind Puerto Rico to the rest of the Spanish-speaking world, especially Latin America (Monge, 1997).

Spain ceded Puerto Rico to the United States in 1898 after the Spanish-American War. Congress granted statutory U.S. citizenship to Puerto Ricans in 1917 and made the island a commonwealth in 1952. Puerto Rico has its own laws, taxes, and government. Puerto Ricans who live on the island are subject to U.S. military service, but do not pay federal taxes, cannot vote for president or members of Congress, and are not entitled to most federal benefits. The centennial of the Spanish-American War was marked in 1998. Over one hundred years after Spain ceded Puerto Rico to the United States, Puerto Ricans have kept their distinct identity, language, and culture, despite the status as a U.S. territory.

Language and bilingualism have been objects of heated controversy ever since the United States occupied Puerto Rico in 1898. Policy swings with respect to language policy in the schools stirred an intense struggle between the Puerto Rican school administrators and American colonial policy makers. Attempts to Americanize Puerto Rico and change the language to English has met with little success. In the first four decades of U.S. direct rule of Puerto Rican affairs, colonial administrators went from regarding the Spanish that Puerto Ricans spoke as an inferior "patois" to recognizing the value of Spanish, "from using hastily translated textbooks to using Puerto Rican writers to generate culturally 'appropriate' ones, from imposing English as the medium of instruction in the first grade to making English a special subject" (Negrón-Muntaner, 1997: 257).

Spanish remains the native tongue of the vast majority of Puerto Ricans. Although English is taught in the island's schools, less than a quarter of its residents (24 percent) speak English fluently, according to the 1990 census. Another quarter of the Puerto Rican population speaks English with difficulty (24 percent). Half of the population is unable to speak English at all (52 percent) (U.S. Census, 1993b).

Monge observes that "Puerto Ricans of all persuasions are principally cultural nationalists" (1997: 183). In a survey of six hundred Puerto Rican residents by American Viewpoint conducted from June 9–11, 1997, 65 percent of the sample said they considered themselves Puerto Ricans, 16 percent answered American, and 18 percent replied "both" (U.S. English, 2000: 15a). The vast majority of islanders want to continue to be Puerto Ricans. They do not view American citizenship, which they hold in high regard, as requiring them to cease feeling this way. In this respect, they resemble the Quebecois, who are fiercely proud of their French language and distinct culture. A 1996 poll showed that only 25 percent of the people of Puerto Rico consider the United States to be their nation; for three-fourths of the population, their nation is Puerto Rico. When asked which citizenship they would prefer if forced to choose, however, 54 percent said American, not Puerto

Rican. After four centuries of Spanish rule, Puerto Ricans do not want to be part of Spain, inspite of their common language. By contrast, they continue to be ambiguous about being a part of the United States. The retention of Spanish as the primary language of Puerto Rico, with English as a second official language, for most Puerto Ricans is a precondition to statehood (Monge, 1997: 185; Navarro, 1998). Of all the various cultural traits, language plays a paramount role (Barreto, 1998).

The American record on the entry of states with significant non-English-speaking populations is, at best, mixed. When Louisiana was admitted as the eighteenth state in 1812, a large part of the population still spoke French or Spanish. The enabling act required that judicial and legislative proceedings be conducted in English. In Arizona and New Mexico, with their large Spanish-speaking populations, Congress insisted that school instruction be in English. Furthermore, all state officials and members of the legislature were required to "read, write, speak and understand the English language sufficiently well to conduct the duties of their office without the aid of an interpreter." Finally, Oklahoma—which was admitted into statehood in 1906—with its large Native American population, had a similar condition imposed on it. There was a requirement that instruction in the public schools "shall always be conducted in English" (Kloss, 1977; Monge, 1997: 185).

Language dynamics in Puerto Rico are complicated by the paradoxes of language nationalism after 1898. At the time of the U.S. invasion, the creole elites in Puerto Rico were increasingly obtaining power over local affairs. With American domination over the island, the native elites loss substantial power. Segments of these groups upheld their Hispanic heritage as a way to symbolically express their opposition to the English-speaking Anglos. Puerto Rican nationalism finds its strongest support from intellectuals. Many of the poorest Puerto Ricans support the status quo. An even larger percentage of poor islanders uphold the statehood option (Barreto, 1998).

The seizing of language as a metaphor of a suddenly disempowered elite did not mean that they did not recognize the pragmatic need and desirability of learning English. In fact, proautonomist and *independistista* politicians and intellectuals are bilingual, at the same time defending a Puerto Rican monolingual "essence." In contrast the masses tend to "support the coexistence of both languages as the 'ideal' state of affairs while using Spanish as the undisputed vernacular. . . . At the heart of both proposals is a seemingly opposed project with a substantial investment in language as a metaphor for imagining political arrangements and power alliances" (Negrón-Muntaner, 1997: 257).

Commonwealth, Statehood, Independence: Choosing a New Future?

Three parties in Puerto Rico correspond roughly with three different "imagined" futures and status options. The New Progressive Party supports statehood, the Puerto Rican Independence Party supports independence, and the Popular Democratic Party supports enhanced commonwealth. The independence movement, while very active in the 1950s and 1960s, has never gained more than minimal support. By the 1960s, statehood advocates and supporters of continued commonwealth status held power alternately, while advocates of independence eschewed the electoral process.

In a 1967 plebiscite, the Puerto Rican populace reaffirmed their support for commonwealth status, with 60 percent voting for the status quo, although the statehood option received 39 percent. Proindependence factions boycotted the vote, and received less than 1 percent of the vote. The value of commonwealth status lies in its flexibility and its appeal to a broad spectrum of opinion in Puerto Rico. It has elements that make it resemble both statehood and nationhood. Puerto Ricans possess citizenship, but with limited voting rights and welfare state benefits, similar to statehood. Federal courts and agencies operate in Puerto Rico in the same manner as in the fifty states. Islanders are a self-governing territory under the U.S. Constitution and are able to choose their own local representatives, which is closer to nationhood. Since 1948, Puerto Rico has participated in the Olympics and other international athletic events and in beauty pageants under its own flag (Monge, 1997). Although the Commonwealth of Puerto Rico was given a considerable amount of political autonomy, the island is still under the direct authority of the U.S. Congress. The U.S. Constitution provides that "the Congress shall have Power to dispose and make all needful Rules and Regulations respecting the Territory or other Property belonging to the United States" (Art. IV, Sec. 3, Cl. 2).

Perhaps because it occupies a middle ground between the extremes of total separation and complete integration, commonwealth status has proved to be the most popular alternative. In 1993, the statehood forces launched a nonbinding plebiscite, which they lost by just 2 percent. Commonwealth won 48 percent; statehood, 46 percent; and independence, 4 percent. Despite the minority status of the language nationalists, in the same year one hundred thousand Puerto Ricans marched in defense of the vernacular, and the Movimiento Afirmacíon Puertorriqueña conducted a vigil in defense of Spanish (Negrón-Muntaner, 1997:279).

Former U.S. Attorney General Richard Thornburgh argues that as long as inequality exists through commonwealth status, "there will be pressure to establish special rights and a separate political order to 'compensate' Puerto Rico for the current lack of equal rights." For example, in 1987 Puerto Rico's commonwealth party Governor tried to conduct a separatist foreign policy including entering into treaties with other countries (Statement of Richard Thornburgh, 1998). In 1991, the legislature—with a Popular Democratic majority—voted to repeal Puerto Rico's official bilingualism and replace it with Spanish as the sole official language. The new law was not intended to discriminate against English speakers, whose language rights were largely protected. One of the relevant contexts for signing the legislation was the aborted 1989 plebiscite bill (Negrón-Muntaner, 1997: 264–265). In 1993, when the statehood party regained power, Puerto Rico's legislature reinstated the policy of official bilingualism.

Both Congress and the Puerto Rican population are sharply divided over the island's fate. For the first time in Puerto Rico, however, the major parties agree that the status quo is no longer acceptable. Puerto Rico occupies a unique relationship in American history that has no parallel. The other major territories either gained separate nationhood (e.g., the Philippines) or full integration (e.g., Hawaii and

Alaska). After the U.S. House passed a bill authorizing a Puerto Rico statehood referendum (by a one-vote margin) and the U.S. Senate failed to move on the legislation, Governor Pedro Rossello went ahead with his own plebiscite. On December 13, 1998, 46.5 percent supported statehood, but a majority 50.2 cast ballots for a "none of the above" option. The rest, 0.1 percent, voted for the territorial commonwealth status quo, while 2.8 percent voted for independence or free association.

On May 6, 1999, in a packed hearing of the Senate Energy Committee, each Puerto Rican party tried to put forth its own interpretation of the 1998 plebiscite. The only clear message from the plebiscite in Puerto Rico is that the question of the island's future remains deeply divisive. Congress's failure to define alternatives in consultation with the parties and sponsor orderly balloting has exacerbated the conflict. Much of the debate has focused on what is posssible under commonwealth and how this option is defined.

The independence option would allow the Puerto Rican people to maintain their language and culture and rule themselves. Although there have been periods in the twentieth century when the independence parties (the Union and Liberal parties) commanded a majority, less than 5 percent voted for this option in the 1967, 1993, and 1998 plebiscites. After four hundred years as a possession of Spain and one hundred years as a territory of the United States, this option still has appeal, especially to some elites; however, it is not likely to garner a majority of Puerto Rican voters. This probably would mean that Puerto Ricans would have to give up statutory American citizenship, which they hold in high regard.

Statehood has increased in popularity between 1967 and 1993 and maintained its hold in 1998. In the 1967 plebiscite, only 39 percent of the Puerto Rican population voted for statehood. Twenty-six years later, in 1993, statehood had narrowed the gap to 2 percent (48.6 percent for commonwealth and 46.3 percent for statehood). The island elections so far have been cyclical, alternating between procommonwealth and prostatehood parties. In the course of the twentieth century, the Progressive Democratic Party has not held power for more than eight consecutive years. So it remains to be seen if it can maintain the absolute majority it gained in the 1996 Puerto Rican island elections. If the statehood option were selected, many significant changes would take place. Puerto Rico would become a part of the permanent union of the United States with full rights and obligations of citizenship. It would be represented by two members in the U.S. Senate and represented in the U.S. House of Representatives proportionate to the population. Puerto Ricans would be enfranchised to vote in elections for the president and vice president. If enabling legislation similar to H.R. 856 were to be enacted by Congress, Official English-language requirements of the federal government would apply to the same extent in Puerto Rico as federal law requires throughout the other fifty states (Puerto Rico Political Status Act, 1998: sec.3).

There is growing dissatisfaction with present conditions in Puerto Rico, which have deteriorated, partly as a result of changes in American investments and federal tax legislation. In 1976, Congress revamped Section 931 of the Internal Revenue Code, which had granted 100 percent exemption from corporate federal income tax to U.S.-based firm subsidiaries established in any U.S. possession or territory. It was supplanted with Section 936, which permits parent firms to repatriate federally exempted profits at will from their Puerto Rican subsidiaries. In 1997, unemployment was about 20 percent, over three times higher than the United States. Median income in the United States in 1990 was $35,225 compared with $9,988 in Puerto Rico. Poverty is also significantly higher on the island than the United States (Griffin, 1998: A24). The three Puerto Rican parties advocate different status options, but all agree that change is needed to foster the island's economic development and reduce dependence on federal subsidies.

If Puerto Ricans opt for statehood, there are political concerns as well as economic ones. In the current backlash toward linguistic minorities, English-Only proponents in the House as well as U.S. English and other conservative organizations have argued that a Spanish-speaking state, "seeing its culture gradually eroding under the influence of the over-whelming numbers of the English-speaking majority may eventually turn to the same separatist sentiments that have almost torn Quebec from the rest of Canada" (U.S. English, 2000a: 2). Will Puerto Rico become an American Quebec if it is admitted to statehood? Will the admission of a Hispanic state be the first step in creating divisiveness based on language and culture in the United States, much like that which Canada is experiencing?

Puerto Rico: An American Quebec?

On first appearance, there are many similarities between Quebec and Puerto Rico. Both had their own languages and cultures long before becoming part of an English-speaking nation-state. In both Puerto Rico and Quebec, the majority of the population speak languages other than English. In Quebec, 38 percent are bilingual, 5 percent are unilingual English, and 56 percent are unilingual French speakers (Census of Canada, 1996b). In contrast, 24 percent are bilingual in Puerto Rico, 24 percent speak English with difficulty, and 52 percent are unilingual Spanish speakers (U.S. Census, 1993b). In Puerto Rico, 98 percent are native Spanish speakers compared, compared with 82 percent of French speakers in Quebec. The U.S. and Canadian censuses employ different definitions of bilingualism, so the results are not strictly comparable.

Another similarity between Puerto Rico and Quebec relates to the economic elites, which have traditionally been anglophones in both countries. Finally, both countries have experienced independence movements. Upwardly mobile elites were at the forefront of both the Puerto Rican and Québécois nationalist movements. In both cases, the nationalists movements were fuelled by college-educated individuals, whose upward mobility was hampered because of their language (Barreto, 1998).

Despite these similarities there are many differences. While the Quebec sovereignty movement has escalated in the last decade and a half, the Puerto Rican independence movement has waned. In 1980 only 40 percent of Quebecers voted for sovereignty-association; by 1995 49.4 percent voted for the sovereignty option. In contrast, in Puerto Rico the independence status option received less than 5 percent in the 1967, 1993, and 1998 plebiscites. On the island the statehood option has increased significantly in the last decade and a half, with popular opinion currently divided between statehood and enhanced commonwealth status. Independence in Quebec escalated when the Quebecois believed that their language and culture were threatened. Fear of assimilation could also push Puerto Ricans toward a renewed independence movement. If English-Only proponents in Congress force Puerto Ricans to choose between their language and culture and statehood, the independence movement could gain renewed vigor.

Jose Monge, a former chief justice of Puerto Rico, warns,

> Should the people of Puerto Rico feel that their language or sense of identity are threatened by statehood, if, for example, a condition to statehood was that English would be the primary language or that public school instruction would be in English, large numbers of statehood proponents would surely flock to the autonomist and independence options. And, should they be further convinced that the United States has no intention of purging commonwealth status of its colonial features and insists in preserving the status quo, independence could possibly become again the preferred status of a solid majority of Puerto Ricans, although it would take time and understanding for them to overcome their apprehensions. (1997: 183)

Whether Puerto Rico becomes an American Quebec will depend on U.S. domestic policy. If the Puerto Rican situation is allowed to fester, a Quebec response is more likely. The Quebec independence movement was fueled by fear of assimilation, optimism in the profitability of sovereignty, and rejection born from constitutional crisis.[4] The failure of Canadian political institutions to recognize and accommodate the distinct Québécois identity provided more ammunition for separation. Differences in language do not necessarily cause conflict—neglect, inequality, and failure to recognize neocolonial relationships may.

Despite several similarities, there are also significant differences between Quebec and Puerto Rico. A successful language policy must take these into consideration. Unlike Quebec, which is a French-speaking island in a sea of English speakers, Puerto Rico is an island isolated from the mainland United States, located in the northern Caribbean 1,050 miles from Miami. Quebec constitutes approximately a quarter of the Canadian population. If Puerto Rico gained statehood, its 3.8 million inhabitants would roughly equal the population of Kentucky. Puerto Rico's Spanish-speaking population would total less than 2 percent of the continental United States population. This isolation from the mainland, and the comparatively small population, allows the United States solutions that are not available to Canada.

Language policy in Puerto Rico is currently fraught with ambiguity and ambivalence. The history of American involvement in Puerto Rican education in the first four decades of U.S. direct rule does not lead to confidence in the future. Forced linguistic assimilation in the enabling act, if Congress would approve and Puerto Ricans should choose the statehood option, would almost certainly promote a negative reaction on the island. The fact that the majority of Puerto Ricans will retain Spanish as their primary language, with English as a second official language, must be faced squarely by Congress.

Federal courts and agencies are conducted in English in Puerto Rico. Local governmental agencies use both Spanish and English. English is the predominant language of commerce. Local autonomy and providing for English and Spanish as official languages in the enabling legislation, should Congress and Puerto Rico decide to pursue the statehood option, would help to reduce linguistic conflict. Whether English-Only proponents and the other states would accept this territorial solution remains an unanswered question. In May 1998, a Wirthlin Worldwide poll showed that 63 percent of Americans favored a plebiscite bill that would allow Puerto Ricans to choose their political status, and a majority also agreed with arguments in support of statehood, such as that the island's residents would pay federal income taxes (Navarro, 1998). An August 1997 nationwide poll of likely American voters conducted by Mason-Dixon Political/Media Research found that 55 percent of the poll's respondents favored making Puerto Rico the fifty-first state if English and Spanish continued to share equal status as official languages for Puerto Rican state government business (*Puerto Rico Herald*, 1997).

In many ways, Swiss territorial language policy is much more appropriate to Puerto Rico than Canadian language policy, which we have seen attempted to impose a coast-to-coast official bilingualism. It is highly unlikely that the United States will become an official bilingual society on the model of Canada. Proposition 227 in California provides an excellent example of the fragility of bilingual education, even in the state with the largest number of LEP students. Legally, non-English languages have a very precarious existence in most states.

James Bryce warns us that "to create the moral and intellectual conditions that have formed the political character of the [Swiss] people would be, if possible at all, a difficult and extremely slow work (Bryce 1921: 502). . . . Where an institution has succeeded with one particular people and in one set of economic conditions, the presumption that it will suit another people living under different conditions is a weak presumption and affords slight basis for prediction" (Bryce, 1921: 499). Despite the difficulty of transferring attitudes and institutions, and the imperfections in Swiss policy and practice, Switzerland's experience points to a variety of conditions which foster stable and effective democracy in countries with discernible linguistic differences. Switzerland is composed of compact territorial units, where the official language of that unit is given preference in the schools and local government.

In Switzerland, federalism allows Romansch-, Italian-, and French-speaking minorities to

> . . . live within their own culture inside the boundaries of "their" cantons. . . . Linguistic autonomy is guaranteed by the principle of territoriality: the cantons are authorized or even charged to guarantee the traditional language of their regions, so that no commune can be forced to change its language for official use. At the federal level, official documents and correspondence with the federal government acknowledges the principle of personality. Thus important laws are translated in all the major languages and the citizens of the various cantons are able to petition and receive answers from the federal government in their own language. Romansch, which contains less than one percent of the Swiss population and is spoken by only about 50,000 inhabitants, does not figure as an official language and for practical reasons most legal texts are translated only in German, French and Italian. (Linder, 1994: 22)

Second-language learning is widely recognized to be in the national interest in Switzerland. Like the United States, the organization and direction of the public school system in Switzerland is basically local. While the details vary considerably, all cantons in the Swiss confederation require a second official language. Most cantons start a second language by the end of primary school. In the German-speaking cantons, the second national language learned is French, while in the French-speaking cantons, the second national language learned is German. The only group that regularly learns all three official languages is Italian-speaking Swiss gymnasium students.

The small Italian-speaking canton of Ticino, which has less than 5 percent of the Swiss population, has been able to maintain its mother tongue since it incorporation in the Swiss confederation in 1803. It offers an important model of the integration of a small canton, which has successfully been able to maintain its language and identity, while at the same time showing a high level of incorporation in the federal state. In Ticino, school children are taught in their mother tongue of Italian but are required to learn a second national language, usually French. By contrast, in the rest of Switzerland, Italian has fought a losing battle with English as the third language learned in the schools (Schmid, 1981).

A modified version of the Swiss (and particularly Ticino) example would seem to provide an important model for eventual Puerto Rican statehood, particularly in the area of language maintenance. If this model were followed, Puerto Ricans would be assured that their schools could continue to operate in Spanish. English would be a required subject, starting at the latest by the end of primary school. The retention of Spanish as the primary language of Puerto Rico, with English as an official language as well, would be a precondition to statehood. By incorporating this condition in the enabling act, the language issue could be defused. This would assure that only Puerto Rico would maintain official bilingualism. The other states would not be governed by this policy. Furthermore, there would not be a requirement for Spanish to be taught in the other states.

A cornerstone of Swiss language policy toward language minorities, which would seem to be applicable to Puerto Rico, is a system of federal subsidies to public education. In addition to a general grant in Switzerland going to all cantons for every child between the ages of seven and fifteen years, the nine rural "mountain cantons" also receive a supplementary payment per child on account of higher costs and more limited resources. The two mountain cantons of Ticino and Grisons receive a second "linguistic supplement" in recognition of its higher costs for textbook development and teacher training (McRae, 1983: 149). As the only Spanish-speaking state and the only state with English as a required second language, a system of grants recognizing the unique position of a non-English state would be very important for educational success.

In the Swiss cantons of Bern, Fribourg, Valais, and Grisons, official multilingualism is recognized. In Bern, Fribourg, and Valais, the legislature operates in both French and German. The Grissons is trilingual; however, German predominates, with Italian and Romansch also used for limited functions in the districts in which they predominate. In the first three cantons, the printed record, working documents, decrees, and the state judiciary operate in both French and German (see McRae, 1983: 180–183). This model could be applied to Puerto Rico as the only truly bilingual state. Federal institutions would continue to operate in English. Currently, federal courts and agencies are conducted in English in Puerto Rico. Local governmental affairs use both Spanish and English. English is the predominant language of commerce. A combination of local autonomy and providing for English and Spanish as official languages in the enabling legislation would thus help to reduce linguistic conflict. This basic system has operated successfully in Switzerland for almost two hundred years.

Several recent polls have shown that a majority of Americans favor a plebiscite bill that would allow Puerto Ricans to choose their political status. Extensive consultation and resolution of the colonial status is necessary. As former Attorney General Thornburgh (1998: 2) observes, it is extremely important for Congress to realistically define the choices open to Puerto Rico. The problem of Puerto Rico's uncertain and unresolved status will not go away. Without extensive consultation and resolution of the colonial status of Puerto Rico, the United States could be drifting toward its own Quebec. Proposition 227 in California shows that emotion and politics are often able to rapidly sway language policy.

Proposition 227: Californians Reject Bilingual Education

Proposition 227, which essentially limits help to nonnative speakers to a year of intensive English instruction, overwhelmingly passed on June 2, 1998. Immediately after Proposition 227 was approved, the Mexican American Legal Defense and Educational Fund, the American Civil Liberties Foundation, and other concerned civil rights organizations requested a preliminary injunction. The U.S. District Judge and the Ninth U.S. Circuit Court of Appeals refused to grant the court order to block implementation of the initiative statewide. Therefore, Proposition 227 went into effect in the 1998/99 school year.[5]

In the late twentieth century, the English language has taken its place as a symbol of what it means to be an American. Countersymbols that challenge the melting pot, such as the legitimacy of speaking and perhaps even maintaining a language in addition to English, add to the current social conflict. One can vividly see this clash in Proposition 227 in California. The California measure won by a margin of 61 percent to 39 percent in June 1998. Proposition 227 significantly changes the way that LEP students are taught in California. Specifically, it requires that "all children in California public schools shall be taught English by being taught in English." In most cases, this eliminates bilingual classes—programs that provide students with academic instruction in their primary language while they learn English. Although LEP students are entitled to "be taught English . . . as effectively as possible, the initiative shortens the time most LEP students would be able to stay in special classes, prescribing programs of sheltered English immersion during a temporary transition period not normally intended to exceed one year." (English for the Children, 1998: §305).

Proposition 227 contained few exceptions. Schools would be permitted to provide classes in a language other than English if the child's parent or guardian asks the school to put him or her in this type of class and one of the following three conditions occurs: (1) the child is at least ten years old and the school principal and teachers agree that learning in another language would be better for the student; or (2) the child has been in a class using English for at least thirty days and the principal, teachers, and head of the school district agree that learning in another language would be better for the student; or (3) the child is already fluent in English and the parents want the student to take classes in another language. Furthermore, if a school lets twenty or more LEP students in a grade choose to take their lessons in a language other than English, then the school must give such a class. If there are fewer than twenty students, the school must allow the students to attend other schools that have classes in those languages (English for the Children, 1998).

The California measure passed with a majority in all but San Francisco and Alameda counties. San Francisco voters turned down the measure 62 percent to 38 percent and Alameda by a narrower 55 to 45 percent. The initiative received majorities between 52 and 79 percent in all other California counties. Ironically, the strongest vote in favor of Proposition 227 came from the counties that have the fewest number of immigrants. The East Bay cities with the most immigrants, ethnic diversity, and bilingual programs, voted heavily against Proposition 227 (California Primary Election, 1998; Lampros, 1998).

Race and ethnicity played a significant role in support or rejection of Proposition 227. Black support for the initiative fell below 50 percent, according to a Los Angeles/CNN exit poll, with just under half (48 percent) supporting the measure. Fewer than four in ten (37 percent) of Hispanic voters backed the initiative (see Table 8.1). For many Hispanics, an attack on bilingual education became synonymous with prejudice toward the large Mexican American community of new immigrants in California. The proposition failed in two dozen precincts, in which Latinos accounted for at least half of the registered voters. Even though they are the state's fastest growing population, the Hispanic electorate is much smaller (12 percent in 1998) than the group's 29.4 percent share of the California population. According to the exit poll, Latino voters are younger (two-thirds of those polled were under age 50) than the average. Fifteen percent earn less than $20,000 a year, and a third have at most a high school education. Nearly a third voted for the first time in a primary election (*Los Angeles Times* Exit Poll, 1998).

In the 1990 census, at least one-third of Latinos reported that they did not speak English well or at all. Asian Americans tend to be more proficient in English, with only about a quarter reporting poor English skills. This reality was reflected in the referendum vote. On the state level, the initiative was backed by nearly six in ten (57 percent) Asian voters. Exit polls in San Francisco, in contrast, showed that 74 percent of Asian Americans voted against the measure. About 16 percent of registered voters in San Francisco are Chinese Americans, compared with 3.5 percent statewide. As more and more immigrants are naturalized in some districts in San Francisco, foreign-born Asian Americans are starting to outnumber native-born Asian Americans in both voter registration and voter turnout. The first bilingual poll of Chinese American voters in San Francisco tapped a population overlooked in mainstream surveys, which are conducted largely in English and sometimes in Spanish. In the large, non-English-speaking Asian populations in San Jose, oppo-

Table 8.1   Support for Proposition 227 by Group Affiliation (%)

All Voters	Group Affiliation	Yes	No
Race/Ethnicity			
69	White	67	33
14	Black	48	52
12	Latino	37	63
3	Asian	57	43
Education			
20	High school graduate or less	56	44
27	Some College	65	35
28	College graduate	63	37
25	Postgraduate study	57	43
Party Registration			
48	Democrats	47	53
6	Independents	59	41
40	Republicans	77	23
Political Ideology			
20	Liberal	36	64
43	Moderate	59	41
37	Conservative	77	23
Party and Ideology			
13	Liberal Democrat	35	65
29	Other Democrat	55	45
12	Other Republican	68	32
24	Conservative Republican	82	18
Total Voting Population		61	39

Source: Adapted from *Los Angeles Times* Poll, California Primary Election, June 2, 1998, Study #413 / Exit Poll (http://www.latimes.com/news/timespoll/stats/pdfs/413ss.pdf). 28 July 2000.

sition to the referendum was also the case. Where individuals, both Hispanic and Asian, were most directly affected by the initiative, they tended to vote against it (Chao, 1998; McLeod and Gaura, 1998).

Non-Hispanic whites, by contrast, overwhelmingly supported the measure. Almost seven in ten whites (67 percent) supported Proposition 227. Endorsement of the initiative was particularly strong among Republicans, who provided the major support (77 percent). The only other groups besides blacks and Hispanics who voted against the initiative were self-proclaimed Liberals (64 percent), Democrats (53 percent), and those with a family income of less than $20,000 (51 percent) (*Los Angeles Times* Exit Poll, 1998) (see Table 8.1). The California vote against bilingualism in the schools mirrors support and opposition of English-Only laws that we have discussed in chapter 5. Unfortunately, the question of what is the best method to teach children English, especially from less privileged backgrounds, was lost in the noise of the campaign.

The reception of bilingual education is not equally negative in all parts of the country. Perceived economic incentives, especially in the business community, and a sense that bilingual education is "enrichment" rather than "remedial" education are two very important variables explaining why bilingual education is better received in some states. In Florida, a new push for bilingual education has come from the Miami business community. A 1995 survey of businesses in Miami and surrounding Dade County found that more than half of the businesses worked at least 25 percent in Spanish. In addition, 95 percent of the businesses surveyed agreed on the importance of a bilingual work force. A University of Miami study found bilingual Hispanics who are fluent in both English and Spanish earned more—about $3,000 a year more, on the average, than unilingual English speakers. These conditions contrast sharply with California where bilingual education has become equated with remedial education rather than an enrichment program. Businesses in California have been slow to recognize the advantage of bilingual employees (Anderson, 1998).

Despite significant opposition to bilingual education in California, most LEP students do not study in bilingual classes. There are simply not enough classes to accommodate the rapidly growing numbers. California's public schools serve 5.6 million students in kindergarten through twelfth grade. In 1996–97, schools identified 1.4 million LEP students. Only 30 percent of California students with limited English ability are taught in bilingual classes. These students receive some or all of their academic subjects in their home languages. Opposition to bilingual education was at the heart of the Unz initiative, even though a majority of Hispanics are not in bilingual classes. About 40 percent of all LEP students are taught their academic subjects in English, with specially designed materials for students who lack fluency in English. The remaining 30 percent of LEP students do not receive special help in their academic subjects, either because they do not need it or because the school does not provide it (English Language in Public Schools, 1998).

Latino parents and their children were at the heart of the Unz initiative. Ron Unz, a wealthy software developer who initiated and funded the California initiative, has compared today's Spanish speakers unfavorably to his own grandparents, who he wrote in a campaign letter "came to work and become successful . . . not to sit back and be a burden on those who were already here!" Although he did not explicitly name Hispanic immigrants, the only ethnic group referred to was Latinos (Barabak, 1997).

The June 2 outcome appears to follow other recent elections in California. Latinos were in a minority and voted against the non-Hispanic majority on measures that were more likely to affect them personally: the anti-illegal immigrant Proposition 187, and the anti-affirmative action Proposition 209. Latinos opposed both measures passed by state voters. Proposition 227 is the third racially divisive ballot measure in as many election years in California.

The decisive success of Proposition 227 is likely to reverberate across the country. Bilingual education emerged from the civil rights era and was supported by the 1974 U.S. Supreme Court decision, *Lau vs. Nichols*, which held that it is a violation of public students' civil rights to restrict effective help in overcoming language barriers that impede students' access to the school curriculum (see chapter 4). Aside from California, ten states mandate bilingual education (although this is not a federal requirement), and most others permit it. Since 1968, when Congress first passed the Bilingual Education Act, the federal government has helped to finance bilingual education. Federal money for bilingual education, however, amounts to only $400 million annually, which is approximately 6 percent of the states' bilingual budget. California receives approximately $61 million in federal bilingual funding. Many states also provide additional funding. State funding is a small amount of the total education budget. In California in 1997, bilingual education claimed only 96 million in state funds, or less than one-half of 1 percent of the total K-12 budget of $26.8 billion (Bronner, 1998a and 1998b; Gomez and Harders, 1998).

Only a few of the bilingual programs in other states face the sweeping initiative passed by California. Still many are under debate and some under outright attack. In Arizona, Ron Unz financed a California-like initiative to abolish bilingual education.[6] Members of "English for the Children of Arizona" launched a signature campaign. The group in July 2000 announced it had collected 165,000 signatures (González, 2000). The initiative was passed on November 7, 2000. Unz said that Colorado and Massachusetts are also possible future targets of initiatives against bilingual education. He is currently lobbying the New York legislature for a bilingual education ban as well (McCloy, 1999). In Chicago and Denver, school boards in 1999 voted to limit bilingual classes to three years. The legislature in Arizona has voted to limit funding for bilingual classes to four years.

On June 4, 1998, two days after Californians voted to dismantle bilingual education, a U.S. House of Representatives committee voted to overhaul federal aid for teaching LEP students. Riding the antibilingual education coattails of the Unz Initiative in California, Representative Frank Riggs, a California Republican, introduced legislation that would significantly alter the way LEP students throughout the United States are educated. The bill, entitled the "English Language Fluency Act" H.R. 3892, favored programs that teach students in English and limit to two years the time individuals could be taught in a native language other than English. Federal law currently sets no time limit. The Clinton administration opposed the bill partly because of time limits, but also because the Republican-sponsored bill converted competitively awarded grants to block grants. This provision would eliminate federal money to train teachers in bilingual education. By 1997–98, the California Department of Education estimated there was a shortage of twenty-seven thousand bilingual teachers. Under the proposed legislation, Puerto Rico would be allotted only 1.5 percent of the total amount appropriated under the bill (Bronner, 1998a; English Language Fluency Act, 1998; Greene, 1998). On September 30, 1998, the House passed the English Fluency Act by a vote of 221–189. The legislation did not receive Senate action, however, and, therefore, the legislation failed to become law.

Demographics Adds Urgency to California and
National Debate on Education

Demographic shift has played into the rhetorics of Proposition 227. One out of three high school students in California is of Hispanic origin, and the proportion will continue to grow. Less than half of the Spanish-speaking students in California schools are limited English proficient (Han, Baker, and Rodriguez, 1997). As most of the children in California's schools who speak limited English are Hispanic, however, bilingual education is often made to stand for the whole question of educating foreign-language children. The failure of the schools to educate Hispanic youths is often discussed interchangeably with bilingual education as if they were the same thing.

In California alone, one hundred thousand Mexicans arrive legally each year. California's schools currently educate more than two out of five of the country's immigrant children and youths. Nationally, by the year 2008, demographers estimate that Hispanic Americans will outnumber blacks and form the nation's single largest minority group. Within half a century, Latinos are expected to constitute 25 percent of the U.S. population. The education of Latinos, therefore, will have an enormous long-term consequence in California and the nation as a whole (Bronner, 1998a; Vernez and Abrahamse, 1996).

Critics of bilingual education have cited the high Hispanic dropout rate as evidence against bilingual education. The low educational achievement of Hispanics is by far more complex than has been painted by the Unz campaign. The latest U.S. government figures, covering the 1994–95 academic year, conclude that Hispanic students have a higher dropout rate than either whites or blacks. The dropout rate is defined as the proportion of young adults (ages 16 to 24) who are not enrolled in a high school program and who have not completed high school. During the 1994/95 school year, 30 percent of Hispanic young adults were classified as dropouts, as compared with 8.6 percent of non-Hispanic whites and 12.1 percent of non-Hispanic blacks (McMillen, Kaufman, and Klein, 1997).

Among Hispanic adults, dropout rates include many individuals who never enrolled in school. Several studies have shown that the relatively low in-school participation of Mexican immigrants of high school age is primarily due to their not "dropping in" to the school system in the first place, rather than their "dropping out" of school. About one-third of the 30 percent dropout rate for Hispanic young adults is due to nonenrollees. The true dropout figure is about 20 percent. In 1990, one out of every four immigrants from Mexico in the 15–17 age group was not in school. By age 15, Mexican immigrants had already been out of school in Mexico for two years on average (McMillen, Kaufman, and Klein, 1997). The high rate of dropouts among Hispanics is related primarily to economic factors. Russell Rumberger (1983) found that among Hispanic male dropouts, only 4 percent said that the reason for dropping out was "poor performance in school," compared with 8 percent of male non-Hispanic white students. Economic reasons were given by 38 percent of the Hispanic students in contrast to 22 percent of the non-Hispanic white students.

Several factors have been identified as predictors of dropping out among Hispanic students. These include lack of English language speaking ability, low socioeconomic class, and presence of only one parent, recent immigration, and lack of a family support system (in terms of monitoring homework). When these factors are controlled between racial and ethnic groups, there is no difference in dropout rates between Hispanics and other groups. The stark reality is that Hispanic children are much more likely to find themselves in dire economic conditions. Approximately 40 percent of Hispanic children live in poverty, compared to 15 percent of white non-Hispanic children, and only 45 percent live with parents who have completed high school, compared to 81 percent of non-Hispanic white children. Only 68 percent live with both parents, compared to 81 percent of non-Hispanic white children (Rumberger, 1991, 1995).

Bilingual education is certainly not the cause of the high Hispanic dropout rate. At least two recent studies have shown that maintenance of the Spanish language and culture in addition to English either does not make a difference in dropout rates or may actually lower the dropout rate. In their analysis of 1994–95 data, Marilyn McMillen, Phillip Kaufman, and Steve Klein (1997) found that there was no difference in dropout rates between those who spoke Spanish at home (20.3 percent) and those who said they spoke English as their home language (17.5 percent). Rubén Rumbaut (1995), in a study of fifteen thousand high school students in San Diego, observed that the group classified as bilingual (fluent in both English and another language), actually had better grades and slightly lower dropout rates than students who were monolingual in English. This was the case, even though parents of English only students were of higher socioeconomic status than parents of the bilingual students.

The Unz approach appears to contradict current research, which shows there is a strong correlation between proficiency in a child's native tongue and long-term academic success. In well-designed bilingual programs, learning the native language does not slow down the acquisition of English. In fact, learning the first language makes it easier to learn additional languages (Krashen, 1996). Contrary to the popular idea emphasized by the Unz campaign that it takes just a short time to acquire a second language, studies by social linguists have found that it often takes a minimum of four years of second-language learning for the most advantaged students to reach deep academic proficiency and compete successfully with native speakers (Collier, 1995).

Bilingual education became a scapegoat for significant problems that plagued California's classrooms. Many voters found it difficult to justify pouring money and scarce resources into bilingualism education, when the rest of the system was suffering from untrained and understaffed classrooms. More than thirty-one thousand California classrooms are presided over by men and women who do not have teaching certificates. On any given day, two thousand classes are headed by "long-term" substitutes who work a maximum of a month and move on. Several thousand other teachers are hired under waivers allowing them to remain in the classroom although they lack a college degree or have been unable to pass a test at about the tenth grade level in arithmetic, reading, and writing (Colvin, 1998).

In the 1992/93 academic year, California trailed all the states—except New York and Hawaii—in the percentage of teachers with full credentials. In 1997 11 percent of teachers in California lacked regular credentials. The Los Angeles Unified School District, which is also home to a large population of LEP students, has six thousand teachers holding emergency permits. In a dozen other districts in Los Angeles County, more than 20 percent of the teachers do not possess regular credentials (Colvin, 1998). In general, elite schools still have their pick of teachers. LEP students, however, are concentrated in the poorest school districts.

Politics was at the heart of Proposition 227 rather than the best way to teach limited English students. Frustration with the declining quality of California schools was clearly related to the opposition to bilingual education. The media did little to oppose this message.

A study by Media Alliance (1998) of coverage of Proposition 227 found that California's leading newspapers generally failed to provide the California public with the information needed to understand the initiative. A study of media coverage in the *Los Angeles Times, Sacramento Bee,* and *San Francisco Chronicle* on bilingual education between November 1, 1997 and January 31, 1998 found that few articles thoroughly covered the education issues. None of the stories in the three newspapers was about successful or failed bilingual, sheltered English immersion, or other educational programs. The reporters failed to even visit a classroom. Two-thirds of the stories did not even include a definition of bilingual education. Furthermore, the articles neglected to examine the academic research on bilingual education and the effectiveness of bilingual education in teaching English or other subjects.

The California initiative provides another example of the polarization of the American population. Two separate Americas are emerging, one white and middle-aged and less urban, which votes to maintain the status quo and the dominate culture, and another America, often of recent immigrant roots, which is more urban, younger, and less likely to be white. One America cares deeply about preserving English as the official language and eliminating "preferences" in the form of affirmative action. The other cares about bilingual education and retaining programs that they perceive as opening doors to better education and upward mobility, yet preserving their identity.

Summary

In the late twentieth century, the English-Only movement gained widespread political momentum, often with racial overtones. The ability to speak standard English has become a symbol of what it means to be a "true" American. As ethnic and cultural identities attain greater importance in present-day political movements, cultural nationalism has taken on a linguistic cover. Cultural nationalism emphasizes the cultural rather than the politically defined boundaries of a nation. As we have seen in this chapter, majority groups and minority groups use language to promote and mobilize cultural nationalism. Language binds groups together and it is a powerful instrument for promoting internal cohesion and providing an ethnic or national identity.

The Ebonics controversy, although narrowly waged in one school district in California, hinged on much broader questions of language, culture, and power. The decision about whether to use AAVE as the basis for learning standard English became embroiled in an emotional debate. How to teach poor African American students was transformed from an educational issue into a political one. The Ebonics debate illustrates power relations between dominant and subordinate groups. Black dialect became a proxy for class, race and power relations in late twentieth century America. As Noam Chomsky (1979: 191) observed, language issues are often questions of power rather a means of symbolic communication. The tensions apparent in the Ebonics argument exemplify the tensions that characterize urban education, class, race relations, and tolerance of cultural pluralism today.

The debate over Puerto Rican self-determination presents another aspect of the current conflict over language and culture in the United States. Puerto Rico has been under American sovereignty for one hundred years. Although the 3.8 million persons born on the island have U.S. nationality, they are disfranchised in the federal political process. Internal self-government under a local constitution was authorized by Congress and approved by the residents in 1952, but U.S federal law is supreme. The conflict between Puerto Rico and the United States over self-determination illustrates the complex process through which national identity and nations are modeled, imagined, and manipulated. H.R. 856 has intensified the debate over what constitutes the American "nation." English-Only proponents who almost derailed the bill argued that allowing Puerto Rico to become an official bilingual state was "unpatriotic" and divisive. During the House debate on the legislation, Rep. Solomon observed:

> There are many things that have held this country together over the last 200 years. . . . "E pluribus unum" means out of many one. It means patriotism, it means pride, it means volunteerism. But above all it means that we speak a common language in this country. We are a melting pot of the world, of every ethnic background in the entire world, and we are proud of that. But had we let these various languages become part of our American culture, this democracy would not be here. (Congressional Record, 1998)

Proposition 227, which officially ended most bilingual classes in California, is another illustration of the dubious symbolic value of non-English languages at the end of the twentieth century. Opposition to bilingual education was at the heart of the Unz initiative, even though only three of every ten limited English-speaking students receive some or all of their academic subjects in their home languages. The controversy over how best to teach LEP students, however, was about more than what was printed in the initiative. More than 1.4 million children—about a quarter of California's state elementary and secondary students—are labeled as LEP, with only a limited ability to speak or understand English. No state has more students for whom English is a second language. The large Hispanic population was singled out, as it encompasses the majority of students receiving bilingual education. Language and bilingual education became a proxy for race, class, culture, shifting demographics, politics, and, to a much more limited extent, education.

9

CONCLUSION

The Future of Language Politics in the United States

> For the first 180 years of our Nation, we were bound together
> by a common language. Immigrants came to this country
> knowing they had to learn English. Twenty-five years ago we
> went away from this.   (Rep. Pete King, Republican—
>   New York, cited in Crawford, 1997b)

> Language is the blind spot in the debates about multicultural-
> ism in the United States. Though perhaps the most significant
> and fascinating form of diversity...the history and continued
> existence of multilingualism in the United States remain
> virtually unexplored.   (Werner Sollars, 1997)

Our Imagined Monolingual History

A sense of shared experience is an important dimension of national identity (Anderson, 1991). This leads to an imagined construction of a shared past and a vision
of the future to represent the nation. Shared identity in the United States has been
imagined around a monolingual past. Multilingualism and bilingual education do
not figure in the immigrant myth. The melting pot did not immediately turn non-
English speakers into accentless speakers of English. Myths, however, die hard. The
melting pot mythology obscures the hardship that often lasted several generations
and the diversity of cultures that have flourished in the United States despite aggressive efforts to eliminate them. Several events, policies, politics, and wars in the
second half of the nineteenth and early twentieth century forged an ideological
link between political loyalty to the American "nation" and speaking accentless
English to the detriment of other languages.

In contrast to the late nineteenth century, most of the founding fathers were
pragmatists on the language question. They considered language an individual
matter in the new republic, as long as the newcomers did not want to sustain their
language for a prolonged period of time. Fluency in English, while certainly highly
prized in the early American republic, did not carry the same weight. In fact, to se-

cure loyalty to the new nation, many documents were published in languages other than English. Language was not yet a national ideological symbol, indelibly tied to American identity and loyalty to the state. There were, however, early indications that English would be the only medium allowed in the new frontier states. The enabling act of Louisiana, which was admitted as the eighteenth state in 1812, required that judicial and legislative proceedings be conducted in English, although a large part of the population still spoke French.

Past History: The Linking of American National Identity
and the English Language

During the Mexican War in 1848 and its aftermath, the United States was confronted with large non-English speaking populations. The territory won from Mexico contained a majority Spanish-speaking population. Statehood was only granted, however, when English speakers were the majority and dominant group. This happened much sooner in California than New Mexico and helps explain why California became a state in 1850; New Mexico, however, did not receive statehood until 1912, when Anglos finally outnumbered Hispanics, thereby putting an end to the possibility of a bilingual state. Language laws and practices restricted Native Americans and Spanish speakers, so there was never a threat to the predominance of the English language.

After the Spanish-American War, English was prescribed as the medium of instruction in the new colonies of Puerto Rico, Hawaii, and the Philippines. In Puerto Rico, English was imposed through a policy of "Americanization." Language became a vehicle to convert the island's Spanish speakers into anglophones. Little thought was given to how best to make Puerto Ricans bilingual. The policy was an educational catastrophe. As a consequence, the school dropout rate was very high and many Puerto Ricans ended up half-literate in both languages. The current debate over Puerto Rican self-determination continues to be tinged with English language learning and Americanization issues. After one hundred years of American sovereignty over the island, the status of Puerto Rico is still in limbo. The population is almost evenly split between those favoring statehood and a renewed commonwealth status. The recent passage of H.R. 856 and the Puerto Rico referendum in December 1998 have intensified the debate over what constitutes American identity and the American "nation." Whether the Puerto Rican people or federal legislators from the other fifty states would be willing to accept a predominantly Hispanic, Spanish-speaking state remains an unanswered question.

High immigration provided a third and perhaps the strongest strand that wedded proficiency in English and political loyalty to the American nation. Between 1880 and 1910, nine million immigrants entered the United States. Southern and central Europe were the main sources of newcomers. Huge numbers of Italians, Poles, and eastern European Jews flocked to the United States. Although the absolute number was smaller than in the post-1965 wave of immigrants, the percentage of the total population was much higher. In the 1890s, slightly less than 15 percent of the population was foreign born. In the 1990s, it was approximately 10 percent.

The Americanization movement was primarily a reaction against the large immigrant population. In 1919, fifteen states decreed that English was to be the sole language of instruction in all primary schools, both public and private. Idaho and Utah went so far as to require all non-English-speaking aliens to attend Americanization classes. Several states insisted that all public school teachers be citizens. California in 1920 ordered every adult male alien to register and to pay a special poll tax. Oregon came close to outlawing the foreign press by requiring that all foreign-language publications display an English translation of the entire contents of all articles (Higham, 1967). The California and Oregon laws were ruled unconstitutional by the mid-1920s.

The Red Scare and anti-German hysteria prior to World War I sealed the relationship between language and American nationalism. During the second decade of the twentieth century, many patriots clamored for suppression of all German-language newspapers. There was a campaign to eliminate German from the public school curricula, which made considerable headway. Before the end of the war, many states completely banned the teaching of German. In the decades of the 1850s through the 1880s, Germany provided the single largest proportion of immigrants, similar to the mass wave from Mexico after 1965.

Before World War I, immigrant groups often convinced public schools to teach children in their native languages. The group's success, in particular the Germans, depended more on the political power of immigrant groups than on a pedagogical consensus. The immigrants' objective was, according to Richard Rothstein, "to preserve part of their ethnic identity in children for whom the pull of American culture seemed dangerously irresistible" (1998: 104).

At the end of the nineteenth century, Germans were considered a culturally distinct and, therefore, a threatening immigrant group. There was a fierce anti-German reaction during and after World War I, which succeeded in removing native immigrant languages from American classrooms. Native language instruction was absent from 1920 until the mid-1960s. Americans have always been ambivalent about other languages, but events set in motion at the end of the nineteenth century led to a new era of language relations. What was new about the end of the nineteenth century was the wedding of American national identity and loyalty with the speaking of accentless English. The merger of national identity and English language proficiency was a phenomenon born of conflict with non-English speaking populations. This merger was consolidated through colonialization of new American colonies abroad, war with Mexico, and the confrontation with large waves of immigrants that were considered significantly different from earlier waves of British and northern Europeans. World War I sealed the importance of language and national identity with the Americanization movement and hysteria against the German language and culture. As Higham astutely concluded in his study of early American nativism "The new equation between national loyalty and a large measure of political and social conformity would outlive the generation that established it" (Higham, 1967: 330). The ability to speak English was made a condition for citizenship in 1906 and in 1915 an English-literacy requirement was added.

The Americanization movement culminated in legislation in 1921 and 1924, creating the national origins quota system, effectively closing the gates to mass immigration. Immigration restriction marked the conclusion of an era of nativistic legislation in the mid-1920s. This was also a time when the consolidation of "Caucasian" or whiteness was accomplished among the European immigrants and their descendents. Matthew Frye Jacobson concluded that "in the decades following the 1924 immigration legislation, emergent civil rights agitation—a new politics of black and white—was among the social and political phenomena that hastened the reunification of whiteness or papered over it presumed faultlines" (Jacobson, 1998: 202).

Language and immigration issues then lay largely dormant as a public issue for the next half century until the next large wave of immigrants brought a new Americanization movement. The Immigration and Nationality Act of 1965 significantly changed immigration policy. It repealed the national origin quotas, established a preference system based on family unification and skills, and imposed a ceiling for the first time on immigration from the Western Hemisphere, thus opening the gates to large-scale immigration.

Late-Twentieth-Century Nativism: Race, Class, and Non-English Languages

By the time bilingual education began to reemerge in the 1970s, encouraged by the *Lau* decision, the nation's memory of bilingual education had been forgotten. Recent organizing has targeted the language and culture of newcomers to the United States, particularly Spanish speakers, who are the largest single language minority. The United States is now experiencing the largest numerical wave of immigrants in the country's history. Immigration in the 1980s reached almost ten million newcomers. Asian and Latin American countries, taken together, sent 85 percent of all immigrants during the 1980s. From the 1960s through the 1990s, Mexico provided the most immigrants of any single state.

The significant change in United States admissions policy was the product of the civil rights revolution of the 1960s. New laws made it illegal to discriminate against individuals on the basis of race, ethnicity, and nationality. In general, language is not covered under antidiscrimination statutes unless it bears a very close relationship to nationality. Perhaps for this reason, and because of the enduring connection between the English language and American identity that came about at the end of the nineteenth century, language was easier to target than other characteristics, when a mass wave of immigrants came to American shores. While non-English-speaking immigrants in the second half of the twentieth century do have more legal protections than those who entered before them, there are no entitlements to rights in languages other than English either under the Constitution or under the major federal statutes.

Other factors also contributed to the post-1965 emergence of language conflict. These included limited government recognition of bilingualism, a high concentration of non-English-speaking immigrant groups in a few metropolitan areas, and a heightened sense of defensive nationalism. The Bilingual Education Act reversed the American two hundred-year-old tradition of a laissez-faire attitude toward language and seemed to contradict ingrained assumptions about the role of second languages in the United States. The recent entry of so many immigrants who speak languages other than English makes them more visible and distorts perceptions of how well immigrants are learning English and adapting to the United States. English-language ability and incomes tend to increase with time spent in the country.

Finally, speaking accentless English has been identified as an essential component of loyalty to the nation and American identity. Language and culture define the American nation. To be a member of the American "cultural nation" it is necessary to speak English idiomatically, "without a significant accent, with the fluency of a native, to be alive to all the subtle nuances in intonation and vocabulary, [and] to recognize the allusions that make any nation's language a repository of its past" (Lind, 1995: 265). "The fact that questions of loyalty assume such a prominent place in the American identity could be taken as an indication of the degree to which patriotism is a strongly inscribed American moral value" (Wolfe, 1998: 133). Symbols that equate the exclusive use of English with being a loyal American have increased the conflict between old and new Americans. In his sample of middle-class Americans, Alan Wolfe (1998) found that when given a series of statements about the obligations of citizenship—voting, keeping informed, serving in war, and so on—being able to speak and understand English was placed second in importance. Moreover, the California exit poll after the June 2, 1998, primary, which ended bilingual education, found that 65 percent of Proposition 227 voters agreed that "If you live in America, you should speak English" and 57 percent agreed that "Bilingual education is not effective" (Los Angeles Times Poll 1998: 3).

California's Experience, America's Future?

Proposition 227, which officially ended most bilingual classes in California, provides an important illustration of the symbolic value of non-English languages. Negative feelings toward bilingualism are difficult to change through reasoned arguments because hostility to bilingualism is primarily symbolic in nature. Even if programs worked effectively, many non-Hispanic American citizens would be likely to oppose such measures.

Collectively, immigrants and their children have changed the landscape of California. As recently as 1970, 78 percent of California's twenty million people were white, 7 percent were black, 12 percent were Hispanic, and 3 percent were "other." By 1996, only 52 percent of the state's 52 million people were white, 7 percent were black, 30 percent were Hispanic, and 11 percent were "other," most of them Asian (Schrag, 1999). Non-Hispanic whites now account for about three-quarters of the deaths in California and approximately one-third of the births (Purdum 2000). The impact of immigrants and their children and the relentless population growth has had an especially dramatic effect in the public schools, where LEP students now make up more than 25 percent of the enrollment. Although only three of every ten limited English-speaking students in California receive some or all of their academic subjects in their home language, opposition to bilingual education was at the core of Proposition 227. The characterization of bilingual education as an expensive inefficient method found an echo among many non-Hispanic whites.

Bilingual education for Hispanics was a very salient issue. This attitude was dramatically seen in the California vote on Proposition 227. Only slightly more than a third of the Hispanic voters backed the initiative. Latinos deviate significantly from the views of most middle-class Americans on bilingual education and services. Most Hispanics regard bilingualism positively, as a value for individuals, for the community, and for the nation. The evidence of numerous referenda is consistent and compelling. Time and again Latinos have rejected English-Only and antibilingual measures as the general electorate has endorsed them.

Conservatives and some white ethnics resented the expense of bilingual education. They asserted that past generations of immigrants learned English without the help of special programs. This imagined reconstruction of American history ignores two important facts. First, many immigrant groups maintained bilingual schools until World War I. At the turn of the century, Heinz Kloss (1977) estimates, more than 6 percent of American schoolchildren were receiving most or all of their primary education in German. These bilingual schools were often maintained with the help of public funding. Second, contrary to widespread belief, new immigrants did not learn English without significant difficulty. Dropout rates were often much higher for newcomers than for other older ethnic groups. The correlation between immigrant status and poor performance in education is not a new one, especially for newcomers from rural and less privileged backgrounds. Richard Rothstein (1998: 102–103) observes that "Test after test in the 1920s found that Italian immigrant students had an average IQ of about 85, compared to an average for native-born students of 102. . . . The challenge of educating Italian immigrant children was so severe that New York established its first special education classes to confront it. A 1921 survey disclosed half of all special education children in New York had Italian-born fathers."

Italians eventually did find their way into the American mainstream. This process, however, often took at least two or more generations. Education is an even more important dividing line today than in the early twentieth century. For Hispanics to duplicate the progress made by Italians and other white ethnic groups who arrived at the start of the twentieth century, innovative and culturally sensitive education is imperative. In the early twentieth century, factory and other semiskilled jobs provided entry into the middle class. Industrial restructuring and globalization have eroded many opportunities for unskilled workers. Education at the end of the millennium provides a sharp dividing line between "haves" and "have-nots" (see Tienda, 1999).

Proposition 227 was about much more than what was printed in the initiative. More than 1.4 million children—about a quarter of California's state elementary and secondary students—are labeled as LEP, with only a limited ability to speak or understand English. No state has more students for whom English is a second language. About three-fourths of LEP students attend high poverty schools. The large Hispanic population was singled out because it encompasses the majority of students who receive bilingual education. Language and bilingual education became a proxy for race, class, culture, and shifting demographics. The controversy was primarily over a political agenda rather than education and the most effective way to teach LEP students English. Many critical issues intersect in the controversy of Official English. These include immigration; the rights of linguistic minorities— in particular, Spanish-speaking minorities; the pros and cons of bilingual education; tolerance; and how best to educate children of immigrants and the place of cultural diversity in school curricula and in American society in general. In the last two decades of the twentieth century, there has been no more potent symbol of the tension over immigrants and how they assimilate than that seen in the debate over bilingual education.

Legislators and organizations such as U.S. English and the "Save the Children" campaign have taken advantage of this symbolic issue even in states with few language minorities. In states with large Hispanic origin populations, referendums initiated by U.S. English and similar groups have won constitutional amendments. Official English statutes have been passed in twenty-five states. Twenty-two of the constitutional amendments and statutes have been enacted since 1980. The majority of these are largely symbolic, like the 1987 law signed by Bill Clinton when he was governor of Arkansas, which states that "the English language shall be the official language of the state of Arkansas." But a few are more restrictive, notably the state constitutional amendment adopted by Arizona voters in 1988, which barred the state or its employees from conducting business in any language other than English. The Arizona amendment has been the only Official English amendment or statute to be held unconstitutional by a state court since 1980.

Unable to pass a federal constitutional amendment restricting non-English languages, U.S. English changed their strategy at the beginning of the 1990s. They promoted a statutory form of Official English that would apply to the federal government and only require a simple majority of the Congress and the president's approval. In 1996, the U.S. House of Representatives approved H.R. 123, which would have made English the official language of the United States. The debate was intense, acrid, and partisan. The U.S. Senate failed to act on the bill, so it did not become law. Although the federal law was defeated, the success of the English-Only movement is best measured by its ability in persuading a majority of American citizens to accept large parts of the movement's fictious account of the history and situation of non-English-language minorities in America.

The United States is testing its future through California. Because of its large immigrant population, resources, and enormous wealth, California may indeed be a model of the future. In the arena of bilingual education and the absorption of language minorities, this future is at best mixed. California represents the first major test of the democratic viability and potential of a major society where white Europeans may soon be a minority of the population. If the last decade of initiatives in California demonstrates anything, it is that direct democracy almost inevitably reinforces a hostile attitude toward minority rights. This situation is reinforced by the relatively low minority turnout at the polls and the fact that many newcomers are not registered voters.

The fallout from Proposition 227 is spreading beyond California's borders. In several states with the ballot initiative process (currently twenty-four states have the initiative and referendum), bilingual education is vulnerable to English-Only forces. Ron Unz financed an antibilingual initiative in Arizona, which passed by a margin of 63 to 37 percent in November 2000. It is closely patterned after California's Proposition 227. He has announced plans to continue his assault against bilingual education in Colorado, New York, and Massachusetts. In addition to bilingual education and Official English, the status of Puerto Rico also remains a contentious and undecided issue on the language landscape of the twenty-first century.

The Case of Puerto Rico Revisited

The linguistic and political status of Puerto Rico provides one of the biggest challenges to language policy in the new millennium. The incorporation of Puerto Rico as a state would make the United States more ethnically and linguistically diverse. It would be the first state to have a non-English majority. Spanish remains the native tongue of almost all Puerto Ricans. In this sense, Puerto Rico would be a "distinct society" similar to Quebec, whose claims for official recognition of its language could lay the basis for wider efforts to make the United States—like Canada—a bilingual country. Unlike the admissions of formerly sparsely settled Spanish territories of New Mexico and California, admitting Puerto Rico as a state would raise more basic questions about the essence of the American nation.

Whether Puerto Rico becomes the next American Quebec depends on how and to what extent Congress acts on the status question. The local elites have succeeded in defining Puerto Rican identity on the basis of language. A few months before the 1993 referendum vote, the *New York Times* baptized the exercise "the vote of identity." Language is inextricably tied to nationalism and identity in Puerto Rico and the struggle for a viable future.

Although Puerto Ricans accord the English language a great deal of prestige, especially among the socioeconomic elites, there has been a persistent resistance to the language throughout much of the century. Language relations between the United States and Puerto Rico have been troubled ever since Puerto Rico was acquired by the United States in the aftermath of the Spanish-American War. The English language became a symbol of U.S. domination and the erosion of Puerto Rican cultural identity. The introduction of English into the education system exacerbated the growing sense of Puerto Rico as a distinctive culture.

From the time that Puerto Rico was ceded to the United States in 1898, U.S. policy was openly and, at times, coercively assimilationist. The military government's goal was to eliminate Spanish and Anglicize the island's population. From 1900 to 1949, language policy was characterized by significant swings. At first, English was taught as a separate subject, with the core curriculum taught in Spanish. From 1903 to 1915, English was imposed as the language of instruction at all levels and for all subjects, except for Spanish. The period from 1915 to 1942 was marked by disruptive shifts from English to Spanish as the medium of instruction. At times, Spanish was used in the early grades followed by English in later grades, after which English was used as the language half of the day and Spanish the other half. In 1942, Washington made English instruction a condition for receiving federal aid (Clachar, 1997; Resnick, 1993).

Puerto Rican teachers felt threatened by the immense changes in language policy without their input. This policy had a significant effect on social mobility among teachers in Puerto Rico. Amilcar Barreto observes that "promoting the English language in the classroom meant that Americans had priority over locals when it came to magisterial positions and when hired they received higher salaries than their insular counterparts. Thus, not surprisingly, teachers were at the forefront of abolishing the Americanization policy and promoting their language—Spanish—as the medium of instruction in the public schools" (Barreto, 1998: 118).

The Organic Act finally gave Puerto Ricans the right to elect their own governor, who in turn would elect the secretary of education. Luis Muñoz Marín, the first elected governor of Puerto Rico, abolished the Americanization policy by way of an executive order. His education commissioner, Mariano Villaronga, signed a departmental directive initiating a policy of Spanish-language instruction. With that directive, language ceased to be a major issue in Puerto Rico until the 1990s.

In the 1990s, language has increasingly become a component of the status debate. While in power, the procommonwealth Popular Democratic Party, with the support of the separatist Puerto Rican Independence Party, passed Bill 417, making Spanish the only official language of Puerto Rico. The 1991 language law declared that Spanish would henceforth be the official language of all branches, agencies, and departments of the Puerto Rican government. The law did not make or attempt to affect the operations of the U.S. federal government in Puerto Rico, which operates exclusively in English. Individuals could still speak, write, and advertise in any language they preferred. Thus, Bill 417 was mostly symbolic, merely codifying the status quo.

The language law was changed again after the New Progressive Party, which advocates statehood for Puerto Rico, gained power in 1992. The New Progressive Party, under Governor Pedro Rosselló, believed that the promotion of English would gain favor in the U.S. Congress. The new legislation, like its predecessor from 1902, made Spanish and English the official languages of the Puerto Rican government. In reality, nothing had changed. In fact, the law made allowances for the legislature and judiciary to determine how they would implement the law for their branches of government.

Language is a salient part of the status debate. Each of the island's three major parties aligns itself with a different language alternative. The New Progressive Party, as a champion of admitting Puerto Rico into the American union, favors increasing political, economic, and cultural ties with the United States. It also favors bilingual education in the schools in order to make the island more acceptable to the U.S. Congress. On the other end of the spectrum is the separatist Puerto Rican Independence Party. It generally encourages stronger links with Latin America at the expense of links with Anglo North America and supports Spanish as the dominant language in an independent Puerto Rico. The autonomist Popular Democratic Party, which supports enhanced commonwealth status, lies somewhere in between. The language debate is more about laying the framework for a plebiscite on the status question than it is about culture. Spanish will continue to be the dominant language of Puerto Rico in the same way English is the undisputed language of the United States.

U.S. domestic policy will largely determine whether Puerto Rico will legally and peacefully take the road to statehood, enhanced commonwealth, or independence. A successful language policy must take the significant differences between Puerto Rico and the United States into consideration. A territorial language policy, as practiced in Switzerland, would be one possible solution, should the Congress and Puerto Rico choose the statehood option.

Language Minorities and the Future

Global trends and mass immigration have called into question American national identity. The United States is not an isolated case in the new search for a national identity at the turn of the twenty-first century. As Edward Tiryakian (1997) observes, the new era of modernity has made almost all postmodern countries redefine their collective identity. In the United States, language has become a defining characteristic of what it means to be an American at the end of the twentieth century. This is not a new phenomenon, but its reappearance has been exacerbated by the large wave of newcomers and a collective amnesia of the important role played by language minorities in the United States.

Multiculturalism as a discipline has generally neglected to treat this important chapter in American history. In an odd way, it contributed to the notion of "imagined" linguistic homogeneity of the population. Very few departments at universities require fluency in languages other than English among students of ethnic and racial studies. As Werner Sollars (1997) observes, language continues to be a "blind spot" in the debates about multiculturalism and national identity in the United States.

Two concepts recently coined in Germany help explain the American attitude toward language minorities. Werner Bergman and Rainer Erb (1997) conclude that the xenophobia in Germany is a form of "defensive nationalism." Its primary objective is to define the "other," so that Germans can maintain their own affluence. Many Germans believe their country is being overwhelmed by large numbers of refugees and the demands from other countries for financial aid from Germany. In contrast to defensive nationalism, which they find prevalent in Germany in the 1990s, Bergman and Erb observe that an "aggressive, nationalistic sense of mission with respect to other peoples is far less common" (1997: 322). Ignatz Bubis, the leader of Germany's small Jewish community, speaks of what he calls "spreading intellectual nationalism." By this, he is referring to Germany's intense quest for a "normalcy" unburdened by history (Cohen, 1998).

Although the history, policies, and structural integration of minorities is significantly different in Germany and the United States, the attempt to redefine national identity at the end of the twentieth century has many parallels. The United States is also engaged in a "spreading intellectual nationalism" with respect to language minorities. Both U.S. English and many politicians have perpetuated the myth of a monolingual past and have become vocal enthusiasts of an English-Only policy. Senator Dole endorsed English-Only in the 1996 presidential campaign, and Newt Gingrich recently described bilingualism as a menace to American civilization. The focus on language has become a convenient way of underscoring the difference between *us* and *them* (Nunberg, 1997).

The controversies over English-Only laws, Ebonics, Proposition 227, and Puerto Rican statehood are recent manifestations of defensive nationalism in the United States. The intertwined debates at the end of the twentieth century over bilingual education and Official English reflect a cultural conflict over the meaning of American identity. A large proportion of the American public believes that becoming American means speaking only English. Regardless of the current push for immigration restrictions, the Latino population in the United States will continue to be a major force reshaping the American social and political landscape. Early in the twenty-first century, it is estimated that the United States will have the second largest number of Spanish speakers in the world. Most of these individuals, however, will be bilingual. By the second or third generation, most individuals have native fluency in English, with the exception of islanders in Puerto Rico. More than 97 percent of Americans speak English well, a level of linguistic homogeneity that Geoffrey Nunberg calls "unsurpassed by any other large nation in history" (Nunberg, 1997: 4). The irony of the recent growth in linguistic defensive nationalism in the United States is that there was never a language so little in need of official support as English at the end of the twentieth century.

Bilingualism should be seen as a complement to American pluralism rather than a challenge to English. In an age of globalization, bilingualism is an asset rather than a liability. The pressure to be American without "foreign" languages is increasing, especially in places such as California. Whatever the variations on the themes of English-Only, cultural diversity, and identity in the United States at the turn of the millennium, majorities of new immigrants and their children still identify with the American dream. At the same time, newcomers are questioning the exclusive identification of the nation with Anglo/European cultures and the English-Only ideology. The American story is a constant battle between the quest for new immigrants, on the one hand, and a desire for linguistic homogeneity and control and domination, on the other.

NOTES

Chapter 1

1. The total fertility rate or average lifetime births per woman in 1980 was 2.9 children for foreign-born Hispanics, 2.4 children for American-born Hispanics, and 1.8 children for non-Hispanics. By 1996, because of the large influx of Mexicans, the Mexican-American fertility rate stood at 3.3 children. Therefore, from a demographic perspective, the Hispanics' young age structure means that Latino youth are a greater proportion of young people in the United States (Valdivieso and Davis, 1988:3, Pinal and Singer, 1997).

2. "Language minority groups" meant "Spanish heritage," Asian (Japanese, Chinese, Filipino and Korean), American Indian, and Native Alaskan. Illiteracy was defined as fewer than five years of schooling. By this criterion, the national illiteracy rate was 4.6 percent. Illiteracy in English was intended, although never specified by Congress (Woolard, 1990).

3. Grant (1966: 105) observes that the reasons for the omission are essentially twofold. The United States is a "nation of immigrants" and therefore lacks the ethnic homogeneity that sustains many modern European nations. Moreover, the "core of the American nation has since the late-nineteenth century become obscured as American society has continued to diversify and expand."

4. See chapters 2 and 3. In 1978, Hawaii recognized both English and Native Hawaiian as official languages. Arizona passed a very restrictive English-Only state constitutional amendment in 1988, which was ruled unconstitutional by federal and appellate courts, vacated in 1997 by the U.S. Supreme Court, and then held unconstitutional in 1998 by the Arizona State Supreme Court. Alaska passed an Official English constitutional amendment in 1998, which was stayed by the state superior court in March 1999. In November 2000, Utah passed a ballot initiative making English the Official Language for state business, although the legislature had previously rejected a similar provision. The measure passed by an overwhelming 67 percent to 33 percent. U.S. English financed the campaign and said it hoped to pass similar measures in still more states.

Chapter 2

1. Perhaps because of his own inadequacy in speaking French, Jefferson was particularly concerned that Randolph learn oral as well as written French. In his letter, Jefferson specifically recommended that Randolph associate with a French family, suggesting that he would "learn to speak better from women and children in three months than from men in a year" (Lipscomb, 1904: vol. 6, 166). In a diary entry during his stay in Paris in April 1778, John Adams wrote that he "could derive little advantage from Dr. Franklin in acquiring French" (Butterfield, 1961: vol. 4, 60). According to Adams, Franklin understood and spoke French with great difficulty.

2. The *Journals of the Continental Congress* made reference to publication in both French and German. "Extracts from Votes and Proceedings of the Congress" (1774), "Declaration of Articles Setting Forth Causes of Taking up Arms" (1775), and "Resolves of Congress" (1776), for example, were printed in German (see Heath, 1976).

Chapter 3

1. This term is borrowed from Meissner, Hormats, Walker, and Ogata (1993), whose book is entitled *International Migration Challenges in a New Era*. The term "new era immigration" will be used in this chapter to differentiate the post-1965 waves of immigration from the "new immigration" that took place from the 1890s through the 1920s.

2. In Hawaii, both English and Hawaiian are official languages.

3. The Arizona amendment was overturned by the courts in 1990 and was appealed by U.S. English. The ruling, which was reviewed by the U.S. Supreme Court and the Arizona Supreme Court, is discussed in chapter 3. The Arizona Supreme Court held the Official English constitutional amendment unconstitutional in 1998.

4. In 1960, Monterey Park, a city of sixty-two thousand residents just east of Los Angeles, was 85 percent non-Hispanic, whites and blacks, 12 percent Latino, and 3 percent Asian. By 1980, the arrival of second- and third-generation Chicanos, Nisei, and Asian immigrants changed the ethnic composition of the city to 25 percent white Anglos, 39 percent Latino, and 35 percent Asian. During the 1980s, these proportions continued to change, and by 1986 Asian residents increased to become a 51 percent majority, with whites comprising 15.8 percent of the city population, Latinos 30.5 percent, and blacks 1.9 percent (Horton and Calderón, 1992).

Chapter 4

1. Only two states, Nebraska in 1920 and Illinois in 1923, declared English as their only official language before the beginning of the English-Only movement, which was set in motion at the beginning of the 1980s by U.S. English.

2. Following passage of Official English initiatives in Arizona, Colorado, and Florida, in 1989 there were several instances of language discrimination, including the suspension of a supermarket clerk for answering a fellow employee in Spanish, denial of parole to non-English-speaking prisoners in Arizona until confusion over the Official English law was cleared up, and an instance of a school-bus driver in Colorado reprimanding children for speaking Spanish on the school bus (Epic Events, 1989). In North Carolina, after the passage of the Official English statute, the Department of Motor Vehicles stopped giving driver's license tests in languages other than English, as it had previously. It was not until the intervention of the North Carolina Civil Liberties Union that the statute was amended to read that the Division of Motor Vehicles "shall not be permitted to . . . discontinue providing drivers' li-

cense examinations in any language previously administered." N.C.G.S. 145-11 1.1 (private correspondence from the North Carolina Civil Liberties Union, August 21, 1987). Using 1980 and 1990 Census data, Zavodny (1998) concluded that men who speak English "not well" or "not at all" suffer a disadvantage in states that adopt English-Only laws. The annual earnings of limited-English-proficient men in these states fell about 12 percent lower than other male workers. The effect does not appear to be due to an increased number of limited-English-proficient workers or to selective migration after passage of English-Only laws.

3. Louisiana had one of the most restrictive laws, which stated: It shall be unlawful for any teacher, professor, lecturer, person or persons employed in the public, private, elementary or high schools, colleges, universities, or other institutions . . . that in any way form part of the public or private educational system or educational work in the state of Louisiana, to teach the German language to any pupils or class (Ross, 1988: 130, 133).

4. In 1954, discrimination on the basis of "ancestry or national origin" was held to be prohibited by the Fourteenth Amendment by the U.S. Supreme Court in *Hernandez v. Texas* (1954).

5. In their Supreme Court brief, Arizonans for Official English argued that the government, when speaking, has the right to choose both the content of its speech and the manner in which it is delivered. They emphasized that a government's choice about which language or languages that it will use has traditionally been viewed as a political rather than a constitutional question. They also relied on cases holding that non-English citizens do not have a right to have government services delivered in a language other than English. Finally, they argued that the government, as an employer, may constitutionally require that its employee speak only English while working because such a requirement furthers the state's interests in providing effective and efficient services and encouraging a public language (Supreme Court Files, 1996). It is significant that the U.S. Supreme Court asserted nearly identical justifications in support of laws restricting language rights in the 1920s that were ruled unconstitutional.

In her Supreme Court brief, *Yniguez* by contrast, argued that the amendment is content-based and discriminates against a particular type of speech. Therefore, the Court should apply strict scrutiny when reviewing the amendment. If the Court concludes that the amendment is not content-based, she urged the Court to apply a "heightened" balancing test, weighing the employees' interests in communicating freely and the public's interest in receiving these communications. Finally, *Yniguez* argued that the Court should dismiss the appeal on the ground that Arizonans for Official English did not have standing to appeal. The state of Arizona, which was also a respondent, agreed that Arizonans for Official English did not have standing to appeal and that the whole case was moot and should be dismissed, since Yniguez was no longer a state employee (Supreme Court Files, 1996). The Supreme Court case is of particular interest, as it is the first examination of English-Only laws since the Americanization movement in the early twentieth century.

6. The Native American Languages Act, which was passed by Congress in 1990, affirmed a policy of protecting indigenous languages and authorizing some federal help for language renewal. The law does not give Native Americans an absolute right to use their language in schools and other public forums. Although the federal government awarded $1 million to fund eighteen indigenous language renewal programs in 1994, in general, the impact of the act has been limited (Crawford, 1998). The Alaska Official English law provides an exception to use non-English languages to the extent necessary to comply with federal law, including the Native American Languages Act.

7. Civil Rights Act of 1964 (codified as amended at 42 U.S.C. 2000e to 2000e-17 (1981 & Supp. 1990). Workers who are employed by firms with fifteen or more employees are protected under Title VII.

8. EEOC Guidelines on Discrimination because of National Origin, C.F.R. 1606.1–.7 (1987).

9. Although Title VII does not explicitly authorize the EEOC to issue guidelines, the Supreme Court has confirmed the EEOC's authority to do so. EEOC guidelines are generally entitled to deference, as long as they are not inconsistent with congressional intent. The EEOC in response to *Garcia v. Gloor* (1980)—where the court held that language, at least for bilingual individuals, was a matter of individual preference—issued guidelines specifically addressing English-Only workplace rules. These guidelines have been broken down into two categories: when employees are expected to speak English at all times and when English-Only rules are applied at specific times (EEOC Guidelines on Speak English-Only: Rules. 1987):

> (a) *When applied at all times.* A rule requiring employees to speak only English at all times in the workplace is a burdensome term and condition of employment. The primary language of an individual is often an essential national origin characteristic. Prohibiting employees at all times, in the workplace, from speaking their primary language or the language they speak most comfortably, disadvantages an individual's employment opportunities on the basis of national origin, which could result in a discriminatory working environment. Therefore, the commission will presume that such a rule violates Title VII and will closely scrutinize it.
>
> (b) *When applied only at certain times.* An employer may have a rule requiring that employees speak only in English at certain times where the employer can show that the rule is justified by business necessity.

10. Under Title VII, two theories exist whereby employees can show national origin discrimination: disparate impact and disparate treatment. Disparate treatment analysis is applicable to employment situations where similarly situated individuals are treated differently because of race, sex, religion, or national origin. Relatively few language cases have been litigated employing disparate treatment theory. The cases that most often use this analysis allege discrimination on the basis of manner of speaking or accent. A charging party using disparate treatment will typically allege the denial of an employment opportunity because of his or her accent or manner of speaking is discrimination on the basis of national origin.

11. In 1995, for example, California received only 30 percent of the Title VII funding, although it educated approximately 46 percent of the nation's limited-English-proficient students (Dutcher, 1995; Kindler, 1996).

12. 42 U.S.C. 1973b (f). Under section b(f)(3–4), a jurisdiction is covered if over 5 percent of the voting-age citizens are members of a single-language minority group and if the previous presidential election was conducted only in English and less than 50 percent of voting-age citizens were registered. Section 42 U.S.C. 1973b (f)(c) also requires that more than 5 percent of voting-age citizens belong to a single-language minority group. Coverage is triggered under this provision if either the jurisdiction-wide or statewide illiteracy rate exceeds the national rate.

13. The court concluded that New York City's practice of conducting elections by preparing ballots, voting instructions, and other election materials only in English constituted a condition on the right to vote under the Voting Rights Act and deprived Puerto Ricans of their right to vote.

Chapter 5

1. In the statutory states, U.S. English literature was often important in swaying conservative legislators to propose Official English legislation. The white Republican I interviewed in North Carolina said his inspiration for proposing an Official English statute that met with very little opposition in the legislature, was literature and phone calls from U.S. English.

2. How illegal immigrants entered each state varied greatly. In California, three out of four undocumented residents entered the state without proper papers. Illegal residents make up about 6 percent of California's population. In New York, in contrast, 490,000 of the 540,000 undocumented residents overstayed their visa (Schmitt, 1997).

3. The 1996 Survey of American Political Culture is based on two thousand face-to-face interviews. The survey explores citizens' beliefs and feelings toward public institutions and probes our national understanding of America's past and future. The Gallup Organization using a national probability sampling administered the survey. The survey is subject to a sampling error of plus or minus 2 percent.

4. The Latino National Political Survey included 1,546 Mexicans, 589 Puerto Ricans, and 682 Cubans from forty Standard Metropolitan Statistical Areas in eighteen states. The sample is representative of 91 percent of the Mexican, Puerto Rican, and Cuban populations in the United States (de la Garza, DeSipio, Garcia, Garcia, and Falcon, 1992).

5. In the early 1990s, there were sixty Spanish TV channels, 850 radio stations, and thirty-six newspapers that used Spanish full-time or part-time. No other language group had its own TV channel. However, there were 190 Polish, one-hundred German, eighty Italian, seventy French, and thirty-one Portuguese radio stations that used the respective language either full-time or part time. Other language groups had fewer than sixteen stations (Dutcher 1995).

6. The Latino National Political Survey found a similar result. Over 70 percent of Mexican Americans (70.3), Puerto Rican Americans (73.6 percent) and Cuban Americans (77.3 percent) believed the objective of bilingual education was to learn two languages. Fewer than 10 percent answered that the objective of bilingual education was to maintain Spanish language/culture (de la Garza, et al., 1992).

7. The survey was systematically administered by trained phone interviewers in both English and Spanish. A sample of random digit–dialed numbers were drawn in each target state. The random sample used included approximately 50 percent of self-identified Latino households. The questionnaire was constructed to investigate various dimensions of pluralism and attitudes toward social issues, including language, immigration, education, affirmative action, welfare, and crime. The sample consisted of 1,802 citizens (79 percent) and 483 noncitizens (21 percent) (Southwest Voter Research Institute, 1996).

8. The LNPS study found a similar result: 51 percent of Puerto Rican Americans, 56 percent of Mexican Americans, and 60 percent of Cuban Americans disagreed that "English should be the Official Language of the United States." The result for noncitizens of the three nationality groups are not reported (de la Garza et al., 1992: 96).

9. The study did not report comparative levels of pride or love in the country by non-residents (de la Garza et al., 1992).

Chapter 6

1. The Supreme Court of Canada ruled this section of Bill 101 violated the British North America Act, which guarantees the equal status of the French and English languages at the federal level and in the province of Quebec.

2. Under this provision, children could enroll in an English-speaking school only if their parents had been educated in Quebec, if they had a sibling already going to an English school, if their parents were educated in English outside of Quebec but were living in Quebec when the law was passed in 1997, or if they were already enrolled in an English-speaking school when the law came into effect.

3. The Canadian Supreme Court in August 1998 ruled that a simple vote in Quebec is not enough to allow the French-speaking province to legally separate from the rest of Canada. The Supreme Court of Canada, including three justices from Quebec, in an unanimous opinion also found that there is no right to unilateral secession in international law except for colonies and oppressed people, which it said does not apply to the Quebec case. The case does not go as far as to completely rule out the ability of Quebec to separate from Canada. If a clear majority of the people in Quebec want to secede, the rest of Canada would be obliged to negotiate the terms of secession. The Supreme Court of Canada held that "since Confederation, the people of the provinces and territories have created close ties of interdependence (economic, social, political and cultural) based on shared values that include federalism, democracy, constitutionalism and the rule of law and respect for minorities. A democratic decision of Quebec in favor of secession would put these relationships at risk. . . . The Constitution vouchsafes order and stability, and accordingly secession of a province 'under the Constitution' could not be achieved unilaterally, that is, without principled negotiation with other participants in Confederation within the existing constitutional framework" (*Reference re Secession of Quebec*, 1998: 2)

Quebec refused to participate in the case and was represented by a court-appointed lawyer. Those advocating sovereignty for Quebec, however, took heart that the decision did not completely close off the possibility of separation from Canada. The Supreme Court of Canada held that "the clear repudiation by the people of Quebec of the existing constitutional order would confer legitimacy on demands for secession, and place an obligation on the other provinces and the federal government to acknowledge and respect that expression of democratic will by entering into negotiations and conducting them in accordance with the underlying constitutional principles" (*Reference re Secession of Quebec*, 1998: sec. 88).

Young (1999) observed that Canadians supporting federalism and Quebecers advocating sovereignty received the decision positively. The opinion did not answer the question of what type of majority Quebec would need to enter negotiation with the rest of Canada. At the end of 1999, the separatist cause is in a free fall. The reasons for the decline of support for separatism are related to the ideology of globalization, a robust Canadian economy, and weariness with the issue of separation by the Quebec populace.

4. The recognition of First Peoples and maintenance of aboriginal languages may be another important distinguishing characteristic between Canada and the United States. The Constitution Act of 1982 recognizes three main groups of Aboriginal peoples in Canada: First Nations (or Indians), Inuit (Eskimo), and Métis, who emerged after the settlement of Canada. Today, there are more than fifty-three distinct languages spoken by Aboriginal peoples, most of which are spoken only in Canada. In contrast to the United States, in Canada about 30 percent of the indigenous languages are still spoken by children. In Canada's northern region, the territorial governments have given several Aboriginal languages the same official status as English and French. This is true for the new northern territory of Nunavut, which was established on April 1, 1999. Inukititut, English, and French are the three official languages of the territory (Citizenship and Immigration Canada, 1999a, 1999b; Nunavut, 1999).

5. Lester Pearson (1963-1968) was Canada's last unilingual head of state. The Quiet Revolution and a strong nationalist movement, as well as the advent of television, have greatly changed the unwritten rules of politics, making the ability to speak French a necessity for

high visibility politicians. There are currently seventy-five federal ridings (voting districts), where French-speakers are in the majority.

6. According to a Maclean's/Decima poll conducted between June 9 and 13, 1994, of 1,000 Canadians—including 257 Quebecers, 222 of them francophones—there is an untapped and unexpected reservoir of attachment for Canada. Ninety-four percent of respondents agree that Canada is the best country in the world to live. Among Quebecers, the figure is 90 percent—with 83 percent of them confirming they meant *all* of Canada (Maclean's/Decima Poll, 1994: 16).

7. Multiculturalism is named by only 6 percent nationally and 2 percent of Quebecers as "the thing that most divides us" (Maclean's/Decima Poll, 1994: 18).

8. Canadians do have some core values that are shared. Spicer (1995: 18-19) names the following: a belief in equality and fairness in a democratic society, a belief in accommodation and tolerance, a commitment for diversity, an attachment to a social safety net of universal healthcare and pensions, a respect for Canada's natural beauty, and Canada's world image of being committed to freedom. The question remains whether these core values are strong enough to keep the Canadian federation together.

Chapter 7

1. In a similar fashion, French and English Canada were divided on the North American Free Trade Agreement (NAFTA), with Quebec being more favorable than English Canada toward it. Identity and American dominance of English Canada were important considerations in the initial lack of support of NAFTA among many anglophone Canadians.

2. Article 70 of the 1999 revised Swiss Constitution states:

1 The official languages of the Confederation are German, French, and Italian. Romansch shall be an official language for communicating with persons of Romansch language.

2 The Cantons shall designate their official languages. In order to preserve harmony between linguistic communities, they shall respect the traditional territorial distribution of languages and take into account the indigenous linguistic minorities.

3 The Confederation and the Cantons shall encourage understanding and exchange between the linguistic communities.

4 The Confederation shall support the plurilingual Cantons in the fulfillment of their particular tasks.

5 The Confederation shall support the measures taken by the Cantons of Grissons and Ticino to maintain and to promote Romansch and Italian. (Swiss Embassy, 1999: 21)

3. Robert Schläpfer led one of the most comprehensive studies of attitudes between the four Swiss national language groups in 1985. Approximately thirty-four thousand Swiss male recruits, born between 1964 and 1966, were polled on their attitudes toward many aspects of language relations (Kreis, 1993: 96). Switzerland has a militia system in which all able-bodied Swiss men are required to do basic training between nineteen and twenty-one years old. This is an excellent cross-section, with close to a 100 percent return of Swiss young men in all language groups and cantons. The survey's major drawback is that it excludes older men and women (although a nonrepresentative sample of 3,500 young women was obtained for purposes of comparison). In contrast with Canada, there have been few attitude studies of the relationship between the language groups in Switzerland.

4. Only the 1994 survey gave the sample a choice of three responses with respect to different levels of identity. The cumulative totals are shown in Table 7.2.

5. The extreme variety of Jurassian nationalism is certainly an exception, however. This is not the first partition in Swiss history. Switzerland has been the site of three other partitions. The canton of Appenzell was partitioned in 1597 as a way of ending religious strife between Catholics and Protestants, which had driven the canton to the brink of civil war. Unterwalden was partitioned into two halves in the fourteenth century. Basel was partitioned in 1833 as a result of severe tension between rural and urban areas.

6. A seldomly discussed "solution" to Quebec separation, following the Swiss example, would be to separate Quebec and the surrounding francophone areas into two or more predominantly French-speaking provinces.

7. In the October 24, 1999 parliamentary election, the right-wing Swiss People's Party scored a large victory with a gain of fifteen additional seats. The Swiss People's Party combined with other right-wing parties that had little ability to influence domestic and international policy by themselves. The "tilt to the right" (Olsen, 1999) was oversimplified in some American papers. On closer examination, the vote was more complex. If the Greens and Social Democrats are included as the Swiss left, then it may be said that the left managed to more or less hold its position as the victor of the 1999 vote. The Social Democrats lost three seats but remain the largest single faction. The Free Democrats lost two seats, while the Christian Democrats won one seat (Swiss Week in Review, 1999a).

The gains in seats and votes of the Swiss People's Party came primarily from small far-right parties. Christoph Blocher, the People's Party's most visible spokesman and millionaire industrialist, appealed to voters worried about taxes, immigrants and asylum seekers, and closer ties with the rest of Europe. The party became a refuge for homeless center-right protest votes. In many ways, the vote was about Swiss identity shaped by furor over Switzerland's role in World War II and its uncertainty over what path to take in the future in the wake of a large foreign population, globalization, and a unified Europe. With more parliamentary seats, the Swiss People's Party will be able to push harder for the planks in its platform, which focus on the abuse of asylum, the demand for tax cuts, and the rejection of Swiss membership in the European Union and the United Nations (Olsen, 1999; Swiss Week in Review, 1999a).

8. Language alone does not promote closeness with one's cultural kin. German Swiss are much more likely to see themselves as distinct from the German culture and Germans than French Swiss see themselves as distinct from the French and the French culture (Schmid, 1981: 90-91).

9. The proportion of Canadian francophones residing in Quebec increased from 78 percent in 1921 to about 90 percent by the mid-1990s (Brooks, 1993: 250). The explanation of overlapping cleavages neglects the role of anglophone Catholics, who have played a bridging role between English-speaking Protestants and French-speaking Catholics. Cross-cutting cleavages have been less successful in reducing intergroup tensions in Canada than in Switzerland.

10. The increased salience of language and decline in the importance of religion in both countries can be traced to similar factors. These include a decreased interest in religion, especially among younger adults (for Switzerland, see Schmid, 1981: 109-111; Kreis, 1993: 219-237), a climate of ecumenism, increased urbanization, industrialization, and federal intervention in cantonal and provincial affairs.

11. Federalism has also helped reduce the intensity of conflict in the Canadian context in two major ways: (1) by relegating some elements of intergroup conflict to various provincial areas or to joint federal and provincial level and (2) by providing a substantial political separation between a primarily French-speaking Quebec and several primarily English-speaking provinces (McRae, 1990: 199-200). The territorial principle is less ingrained in Canadian law and political and civic culture than in Switzerland, and, therefore, it is less ef-

fective in maintaining demographic stability and reducing language conflict on the federal level. The Canadian federal solution to the Quebec "problem" has leaned toward power sharing at the center rather than decentralization and formal recognition of language territories.

12. The territorial solution in Switzerland has been important in assimilating the large second generation of the foreign worker population, at the same time maintaining the relative proportions of the three official language groups in Switzerland. The children of foreign workers in Switzerland face more problems than their counterpart in Canada, as Switzerland does not think of itself as an immigrant country. Citizenship is not automatically granted when a child is born on Swiss soil, and it is possible for foreign worker families to live several generations in Switzerland without the privileges of citizenship.

13. The practice of having all or most major parties represented on the seven-member Federal Council (the executive branch) has a long tradition in Swiss political history. The last step was taken in 1959, when the Social Democrats were accorded a proportionate share of seats. The October 1999 victory of the Swiss People's Party (see note 7 to this chapter) has intensified the discussion about the composition of the Federal Council, which was elected by the joint houses of parliament in December 1999. Although the Swiss People's Party has openly laid claim to a second Federal Council seat, this request evoked little resonance with the other government parties (Swiss Week in Review, 1999b).

14. This was the case, for instance, with women's right to vote, which was first introduced in 1959, but was not approved until 1971. At the cantonal level, the majority of French-speaking cantons allowed women suffrage before most German-speaking cantons did. Another recent example was maternity insurance. The proposal was turned down for the third time in fifteen years on June 13, 1999. There was a sharp division between the German-speaking and French-speaking parts of Switzerland. All the German-speaking cantons turned the proposal down, with between 57 percent and 86 percent against the measure, whereas all francophone cantons except for Valais approved it (Buess, 1999: A1).

Chapter 8

1. By the 1970s, there were two or three pilot sets of textbooks in AAVE, including the Bridge reading program. The Bridge materials included texts and exercises written in AAVE, a transitional variety, and Standard English. The experimental use of the Bridge program with 417 seventh to twelfth graders across the United States showed significantly larger gains on the Iowa Test of Basic Skills in Reading Comprehension than did the control group of 123 students, who were taught with their regularly scheduled remedial reading materials. Despite this initial success, the program did not survive (Rickford, 1997).

2. Only 28 percent of black parents considered standard tests to be culturally biased against blacks. Nearly eight black parents in ten wanted results of such tests made public as a way to spur school reforms. Black and white parents have strikingly similar visions of what should be taught in the schools: 91 percent of black parents and 95 percent of white parents considered mastery of reading, writing, and arithmetic absolutely essential (*News and Record*, 1998).

3. There are also preliminary international examples to support "dialect readers" as a preliminary aid in teaching the standard form of the language. In a Swedish-dialect context, Töre Österberg found that the teaching of reading skills to primary students in dialect increased reading proficiency both in the elementary and later grades (Rickford, 1997).

4. Thornburgh observes that in many ways the situation in Puerto Rico is worse than that in Quebec. Inequality, rather than language conflict is contributing to "tribalism and separatism" within the American political culture. "If a comparison is to be made, imagine how the vote would go in Quebec if—in addition over the French language question—the

Canadian federal government denied the people of that province voting representation in the national parliament and disenfranchised residents of Quebec in national elections. That is the Puerto Rican experience in America today. Compared to this denial of equal rights, language is hardly the real issue which divides our fellow citizens in Puerto Rico from the rest of the nation" (Statement of Richard Thornburgh, 1998: 5).

5. Several school districts applied for waivers from the state board of education in order to preserve their bilingual education programs. In December 1999, the California supreme court unanimously refused to allow districts to seek exemptions from the state board of education in the case *McLaughlin v. State Board of Education*. The narrow parental exception analyzed in chapter 8 remains in effect (Egelko, 1999).

6. The Arizona initiative passed in November 2000 reversed the states' bilingual education law. Instead of teaching LEP students in their native language, there is a one-year required immersion program similar to that required in California (McCloy, 1999). Native American tribes came out strongly against the measure. The Navajo Nation Council voted 64 to 0 in July 1999 to strongly oppose the measure. The council observed that it was much more concerned about the continuing loss of the Navaho language and the relative lack of quality Navaho and English bilingual education programs than about English immersion programs (Shebala, 1999). The initiative forbids the teaching of any subject, including reading and writing, in a language other than English, subject to narrow exceptions, similar to the initiatives in California.

BIBLIOGRAPHY

Abelmann, Nancy, and John Lie. 1995. *Blue Dreams: Korean Americans and the Los Angeles Riots*. Cambridge: Harvard University Press.

Adams, John. 1992. "Proposal for an American Language Academy." In *Language Loyalties*, ed. James Crawford. Chicago: University of Chicago Press.

Adams, Mark L. 1995. "Fear of Foreigners: Nativism and Workplace Language Restrictions." *Oregon Law Review* 74:849–908.

Adley-SantaMaria, Bernadette. 1997. "White Mountain Apache Language: Issues in Language Shift, Textbook Development, and Native Speaker-University Collaboration." In *Teaching Indigenous Languages*, ed. Jon Reyhner. Flagstaff: Northern Arizona University.

Alatis, James E. 1986. "Comment: The Question of Language Policy." *International Journal of the Sociology of Language* 60:197–200.

Alba, Richard D., Douglas Massey, and Rubén G. Rumbaut. 1999. *The Immigration Experience for Families and Children*. Washington, DC: American Sociological Association.

Almond, Gabriel, and Sidney Verba. 1963. *The Civic Culture*. New York: Little, Brown.

"American Voters Support Puerto Rico Statehood with English and Spanish as State's Official Languages." 1997. *Puerto Rico Herald*. October 8 (http//:www.puertorico-herald.org/issues/971008/top-story-971008.shtml). Accessed 30 July 2000.

Anderson, Benedict. 1991. *Imagined Communities*. London: Verso.

Anderson, Nick. 1998. "A Boomtown of Bilingual Education." *Los Angeles Times*. May 25 (http://www.humnet.ucla.edu/humnet/linguistics/people/grads/macswan/LAT86.htm). Accessed 31 July 2000.

Annuaire statistique de la Suisse. 1994. Zurich: Verlag Neue Zürcher Zeitung.

Annual Report on Official Languages 1998–99. 1999. BT 23-1/1999. Ottawa: Treasury Board of Canada.

Applebome, Peter. 1996. "English Unique to Blacks Is Officially Recognized." *New York Times*. December 20: A20.

———. 1997. "Dispute over Ebonics Reflects a Volatile Mix." *New York Times*, March 1: sec 1, p. 10.

Ayres, B. Drummond, Jr. 1994. "Anti-Alien Sentiment Spreading in Wake of California's Measure." *New York Times*, December 4: A1, 42.

Barabak, Mark Z. 1997. "GOP Bid to Mend Rift with Latinos Still Strained." *Los Angeles Times*, August 31 (http:/ourworld.compuserve.com/homepages/jwcrawford/LAT6. htm). Accessed 27 July 2000.

Baron, Dennis. 1990. *The English-Only Question*. New Haven: Yale University Press.

Barrera, Mario. 1979. *Race and Class in the Southwest*. Notre Dame: University of Notre Dame Press.

Barreto, Amilcar A. 1995. "Nationalism and Linguistic Security in Contemporary Puerto Rico." *Canadian Review of Studies in Nationalism* 22:67–74.

———. 1998. *Language, Elites and the State: Nationalism in Puerto Rico and Quebec*. Westport, CT: Praeger.

Bauch, Hubert. 1998. "Blessed Calm: Neither a Constitutional Crisis nor an Economic Disaster looms on the Canadian Horizon This New Year." *Montreal Gazette*, December 26.

Bell, Daniel, ed. 1964. *The Radical Right*. New York: Doubleday.

Bennet, James. 1996. "White House Rejects Federal Aid for Black English Courses." *New York Times*, December 25: A22.

Bennett, David H. 1988. *The Party of Fear: From Nativist Movements to the New Right in American History*. Chapel Hill: University of North Carolina Press.

Bennici, Frank J., and William E. Strang. 1995. *An Analysis of Language Minority and Limited English Students*. NELS 88. Arlington, VA: Developmental Associates.

Bergman, Werner, and Rainer Erb. 1997. *Anti-Semitism in Germany*. Trans. Belinda Cooper and Allison Brown. New Brunswick, NJ: Transaction.

Bickel, Hans. 1994. "Räumliche Mobilität." In *Mehrsprachigkeit—eine Herausforderung*, ed. Hans Bickel and Robert Schläpfer. Basel: Helbing and Lichtenhahn.

Blais, André, and Richard Nadeau. 1992. "To Be or Not to Be Sovereignist: Quebecers' Perennial Dilemma." *Canadian Public Policy* 18:89–103.

Bohnenblust, Ernst. 1974. *Geschichte der Schweiz*. Erlenbach-Zurich: Eugen Rentsch.

Bonjour, Edgar. 1952. *A Short History of Switzerland*. Oxford: Clarendon.

Breton, Raymond. 1984. "The Production and Allocation of Symbolic Resources: An Analysis of the Linguistic and Ethnocultural Fields in Canada." *Canadian Review of Sociology and Anthropology* 21:123–140.

———. 1986. "Multiculturalism and Canadian Nation-Building." In *The Politics of Gender, Ethnicity and Language in Canada*, ed. Alan Cairns and Cynthia Williams. Toronto: University of Toronto Press.

———. 1992. *Why Meech Failed*. Toronto: C. H. Howe Institute.

Briggs, Vernon M. Jr. and Stephen Moore. 1994. *Still an Open Door? U.S. Immigration Policy and the American Economy*. Washington, DC: Urban Institute.

Brimelow, Peter. 1995. *Alien Nation: Common Sense about America's Immigration Disaster*. New York: Random House.

Bronner, Ethan. 1998a. "Bilingual Education Is Facing Push toward Abandonment." *New York Times*, May 30: A1.

———. 1998b. "Bilingual Education is Challenged in Federal Court." *New York Times*, June 4: A25.

Brooke, James. 1999a. "Clinton Jolts Canadians with a Plea on Federalism." *New York Times*, October 10: sec. 1. p. 4.

———. 1999b. "Quebe Gains as a Language Lab." *New York Times*, October 16: A16.

Brooks, Stephen. 1993. *Social Policy in Canada*. Toronto: McClelland and Stewart.

———. 1996. *Canadian Democracy*. Toronto: Oxford University Press.

Brubaker, William Rodgers. 1992. *Citizenship and Nationhood in France and Germany*. Cambridge: Harvard University Press.

Bruni, Frank. 1998. "California Townsfolk Speak Different Languages over Education." *New York Times*, May 27: A12.

Brunner, Matthias, and Lea Sgier. 1997. "Crise de confiance dans les institutions politiques suisses? Quelques résultats d'une enquête d'opinion." *Swiss Political Science Review* 3:105–113.

Bryce, James. 1921. *Modern Democracies*, vol. 1. London: Macmillan.

Buess, Urs. 1999. "Die Romandie wurde überstimmt." *Tages Anzeiger*, June 15:A1 (foreign edition).

Butterfield, L. H., ed. 1951. *Letters of Benjamin Rush*. Vol. 1. Princeton: Princeton University Press.

Califa, Antonio J. 1989. "Declaring English the Official Language: Prejudice Spoken Here." *Harvard Civil Rights—Civil Liberties Law Review* 24:293–348.

California Primary Election. 1998. "Proposition 227—Bilingual Education." (http://primary98. ss.ca.gov/Returns/prop/mapR227.htm). Accessed 31 July 2000.

Camarota, Steven. 1999. "Immigrants in the United States—1998: A Snapshot of America's Foreign-born Population." *Backgrounder*. Washington, DC: Center for Immigration Studies.

Camartin, Iso. 1996. "A Land of Many Languages, A Multicultural Nation?" In *The New Switzerland: Problems and Policies*, ed. Rolf Kieser and Kurt R. Spillmann. Palo Alto, CA: Society for the Promotion of Science and Scholarship.

Carter, Bob, Marci Green, and Rick Halpern. 1996. "Immigration Policy and the Racialization of Migrant Labour: The Construction of National Identities in the USA and Britain." *Ethnic and Racial Studies* 19:135–157.

Castellanos, Diego. 1992. "A Polyglot Nation." In *Language Loyalties*, ed. James Crawford. Chicago: University of Chicago Press.

Census of Canada. 1983. *Nuptiality and Fertility*. Ottawa: Statistics Canada.

———. 1996a. *Population by Home Language*. Ottawa: Statistics Canada.

———. 1996b. *Population by Knowledge of Official Language*. Ottawa: Statistics Canada.

Chao, Julie. 1998. "Bilingual Poll: S.F. Chinese Back Fong, Oppose Prop. 227." *San Francisco Chronicle*. May 27 (http://www.humnet.ucla.edu/humnet/linguistics/people/grads/ macswan/SFEx21.htm). Accessed 31 July 2000.

Chen, Edward M. 1992. "Language Rights in the Private Sector." In *Language Loyalties*, ed. James Crawford. Chicago: University of Chicago Press.

Chomsky, Noam. 1979. *Language and Responsibility*. Brighton, East Sussex: Harvester Press.

Citizenship and Immigration Canada. 1999a. "A Look at Canada: Aboriginal Peoples of Canada" (http://www.cic.gc.ca/english/citizen/look/look-06e.html). Accessed 31 July 2000.

———. 1999b. "A Look at Canada: The North" (http://www.cic.gc.ca/english/citizen/look/ look-14e.html). Accessed 31 July 2000.

Citrin, Jack, Beth Reingold, Evelyn Walters, and Donald P. Green. 1990. "The 'Official English' Movement and the Symbolic Politics of Language in the United States." *Western Political Quarterly* 43:535–559.

Clachar, Arlene. 1997. "Students's Reflections on the Social, Political, and Ideological Role of English in Puerto Rico." *Hispanic Journal of Behavioral Sciences* 19:461–479.

Clarke, Harold D., and Allan Kornberg. 1996. "Choosing Canada? The 1995 Quebec Sovereignty Referendum." *Political Science and Politics*, pp. 676–682.

Cohen, Rodger. 1998. "Anniversary Sets Germany to Quarreling over Holocaust." *New York Times* November 10: A16.

Collier, Virginia P. 1995. "Acquiring a Second Lanugage for School." *Directions in Language and Education* Fall 1 (Fall): 1–9. (http://www.ncbe.gwu.edu/ncbepubs/directions/04.htm). Accessed 31 July 2000.

Colvin, Richard Lee. 1998. "Too Many Teachers Are Ill-Prepared." *Los Angeles Times*, May 19.

Commission on Behavioral and Social Science and Education. 1997. *The New American: Economic, Demographic, and Fiscal Effects of Immigration*. Washington, DC: National Academy Press.

Congressional Record. 1998. "Providing for Consideration of H.R. 856, United States–Puerto Rico Political Status Act." House of Representatives. March 4: H765 (http://thomas.loc.gov/cgi-bin/query/D?r105:2:./temp/~r1056i6Aon::). Accessed 31 July 2000.

Conklin, Nancy Faires, and Margaret A. Lourie. 1983. *A Host of Tongues*. New York: Free Press.

Crawford, James. 1989. *Bilingual Education: History, Politics, Theory and Practice*. Trenton: Crane.

———. 1992. *Hold Your Tongue: Bilingualism and the Politics of "English Only."* Reading, MA: Addison-Wesley.

———. 1997a. *Best Evidence: Research Foundations of the Bilingual Education Act*. Washington, DC: National Clearinghouse for Bilingual Education.

———. 1997b. "Opinion Polls on Official English" (http://ourworld. compuserve.com/homepages/JWCRAWFORD/can-poll.htm). Accessed 31 July 2000.

———. 1998. "Endangered Native American Languages: What Is to Be Done, and Why?" In *Language and Politics in the United States and Canada: Myths and Realities*, ed. Thomas Ricento and Barbara Burnaby. Mahwah, NJ: Lawrence Erlbaum.

———. 2000. "Language Legislation in the U.S.A." (http://ourworld.compuserve.com/homepages/jwcrawford/langleg.htm). Accessed 31 July 2000.

Danforth, Loring. 1995. The Macedonia Conflict: Ethnic Nationalism in a Transnational World. Princeton, NJ: Princeton University Press.

de la Garza, Rodolfo O., Louis DeSipio, F. Chris Garcia, John Garcia, and Angelo Falcon. 1992. *Latino Voices: Mexican, Puerto Rican, and Cuban Perspectives on American Politics*. Boulder, CO: Westview.

de la Garza, Rodolfo O., Angelo Falcon, F. Chris Garcia, and John Garcia. 1994. "Mexican Immigrants, Mexican Americans, and American Political Culture." In *Immigration and Ethnicity: The Integration of America's Newest Arrivals*, ed. Barry Edmonston and Jeffrey S. Passel. Washington, DC: Urban Institute.

de la Peña, Fernando. 1991. *Democracy or Babel? The Case for Official English*. Washington, DC: U.S. English.

DePalma, Anthony. 1998. "Quebec's Election Failed to Give Clear Idea of Where Province Is Heading." *New York Times*, December 2. E2.

DeSipio, Louis, and Rodolfo O. de la Garza. 1998. *Making Americans, Remaking America*. Boulder, CO: Westview.

Dion, Stéphane. 1992. "Explaining Québec Nationalism." In *The Collapse of Canada*, ed. R. Kent Weaver. Washington, DC: Brookings Institution.

Domínguez, Jorge I. 1995. "Do 'Latinos' Exist?" *Contemporary Sociology* 24:354–357.

Données démolinguistiques. 1997. Table 1.6 in "Indice synthétique de fécondité, par langue maternelle, ensemble du Québec, 1956–1961 à 1986–1991" (http://www.olf.gouv.qc.ca). Accessed 31 July 2000.

Donneur, André. 1984. "Un nationalisme romand est-il possible?" In *Vous avez dit "Suisse romande"?*, ed. René Knusel and Daniel L. Seiler. Lausanne: Institut de Science Politique.

Driedger, Leo. 1996. *Multi-Ethnic Canada*. Toronto: Oxford University Press.

Durkheim, Emile. 1961. *Moral Education*. New York: Free Press.

Dutcher, Nadine. 1995. "Overview of Foreign Language Education in the United States." Center for Applied Linguistics, Washington, DC: NCBE Resource Collection Series, No. 6, spring (http://www.ncbe.gwu.edu/ncbepubs/resource/foreign.htm). Accessed July 31 2000.

Edmonston, Barry, and Jeffrey S. Passel, eds. 1994. *Immigration and Ethnicity: The Integration of America's Newest Arrivals*. Washington, DC: Urban Institute.

Edwards, John. 1985. *Language, Society and Identity*. New York: Basil Blackwell.

———. 1994. *Multilingualism*. London: Routledge.

EEOC Guidelines on Speak English-Only Rules. 1987. 2 CFR sec. 1606.7.

Egelko, Bob. 1999. "Court won't let Districts keep Bilingual Programs." Associated Press, December 22 (http://www.yeson227.org/9912/122299.html). Accessed 31 July 2000.

Eljera, Bert. 1996. "Bilingual Voting under Attack." *Asian Week News*, 17: May 31 (http://www.asianweek.cbilingualVote53196.html). Accessed 31 July 2000.

Ellis, Joseph J. 1997. *American Sphinx: The Character of Thomas Jefferson*. New York: Knopf.

Elon, Amos. 1998. "Switzerland's Lasting Demon." *New York Times Magazine*, April 12:40–44.

Elshtain, Jean Bethke. 1995. *Democracy on Trial*. New York. Basic Books.

English for the Children. 1998. "English Language Education for Immigrant Children." English Language in Public Schools. Initiative Statute Proposition 227 passed June 2, 1998. Section 1, Chapter 3 (commencing with Section 300) as added to Part 1 of the California Education Code. (http://primary98.ss.ca.gov/VoterGuide/Propositions/227text.htm). Accessed 31 July 2000.

English Language Fluency Act. 1998. H.R. 3892, 105th Congress, House of Representatives, introduced May 19, 1998.

English Language in Public Schools. 1998. Initiative Statute, California Secretary of State Analysis (http://primary98.ss.ca.gov/VoterGuide/Propositions/227analysis.htm). Accessed 31 July 2000.

Epic Events. 1989. *Newsletter of the English Plus Clearing House*. March/April.

Esman, Milton J. 1985. "The Politics of Official Bilingualism in Canada." In *Language Policy and National Unity*, ed. William R. Beer and James E. Jacob. Totowa, NJ: Rowman and Allanheld.

Espenshade, Thomas J., and Haishau Fu. 1997. "An Analysis of English-Language Proficiency among U.S. Immigrants." *American Sociological Review* 62:288–305.

Faust, Albert. 1909. *The German Element in the United States*. Vols. 1 and 2. Boston: Houghton Mifflin.

Feagin, Joe R. 1997. "Old Poison in New Bottles, Deep Roots of Modern Nativism." In *Immigrants Out*, ed. Juan F. Perea. New York: New York University Press.

Feldman, Paul. 1995. "Most Call Prop. 187 Good, Want It Implemented Now. *Los Angeles Times*, March 13.

Fischer, Hardi, and Uri P. Trier. 1962. *Das Verhältnis zwischen Deutschschweizer und Westschweizer: Eine socialpsychologische Untersuchung*. Berne: Verlag Huber.

Fishman, Joshua. 1981. "Language Policy: Past, Present and Future." In *Language in the USA*, ed. Charles A. Ferguson and Shirley Heath. Cambridge: Cambridge University Press.

———. 1988. "English Only: Its Ghosts, Myths and Dangers." *International Journal of Sociology of Language* 74:124–142.

———. 1989. *Language and Ethnicity in Minority Sociolinguistic Perspective*. Clevedon: Multilingual Matters.

———. 1991. *Reversing Language Shift*. Clevedon: Multilingual Matters.

Fix, Michael, and Jeffrey S. Passel. 1994. *Immigration and Immigrants: Setting the Record Straight*. Washington, DC: Urban Institute

Fleras, Augie, and Jean Leonard Elliott. 1992. *Multiculturalism in Canada*. Scarborough: Nelson.

Folk, Mark. 1995. "Brains over Brawn: Jobs Require Higher Level of Competence." *Greensboro News and Record*, July 24:B5, 8.

Frendreis, John, and Raymond Tatalovich. 1997. "Who Supports English-Only Language Laws? Evidence from the 1992 National Election Study." *Social Science Quarterly* 78:354–368.

Fuchs, Lawrence. 1990. *The American Kaleidoscope: Race, Ethnicity, and the Civic Culture*. Hanover: University Press of New England.

Gagnon, Jean-Louis. 1989. "Bilingualism in Canada: The Past and the Future." *Language and Society* Summer: 5–6.

Gagnon, Lysiane. 1993. "Inside Quebec—Bilingualism Cuts Deeply into the Canadian Psyche." *Globe and Mail*, April 10.

Gill, Robert M. 1980. "Quebec and the Politics of Language." In *Encounter with Canada: Essays in the Social Sciences*, ed. Wayne G. Reilly. Occasional Papers Series, No. 7. Durham, NC: Duke Center for International Studies.

Gingras, Francois-Pierre, and Neil Nevitte. 1983. "Nationalism in Quebec: The Transition of Ideology and Political Support." In *Political Support in Canada: The Crisis Years*, ed. Allan Kornberg and Harald D. Clark. Durham, NC: Duke University Press.

Glazer, Nathan. 1995. "Debate on Aliens Flares beyond the Melting Pot." *New York Times*, April 23:E3.

Golden, Tim. 1997. "Oakland Revamps Plan to Teach Black English." *New York Times*, January 14: A10.

Gomez, Manuel N., and Robin L. Harders. 1998. "End Bilingual Schooling? It Hasn't Even Been Fully Implemented Yet." *Los Angeles Times*, May 3 (http://www.humnet.ucla.edu/humnet/linguistics/people/grads/macswan/LAT68.htm). Accessed 31 July 2000.

González, Daniel. 2000. "Group organizes to fight English-Only Initiative." Arizona Republic, July 6 (http://www.onenation.org/0007/070600.html). Accessed 31 July 2000.

Government of Quebec. 1972. *Report of the Commission of Inquiry on the Position of the French Language and French Language Rights in Quebec*. Montreal: Government of Quebec.

Graham, Otis L., Jr. and Elizabeth Koed. 1993. "Americanizing of the Immigrant, Past and Future: History and Implications of a Social Movement." *Public Historian* 15:24–45.

Grant, Susan-Mary. 1996. "When Is a Nation not a Nation? The Crisis of American Nationality in the Mid-nineteenth Century." *Nations and Nationalism* 2:105–129.

Greene, Robert. 1998. "Panel Overhalls Bilingual Education Aid." *Associated Press*. June 4 (http://www.humnet.ucla.edu/humnet/linguistics/people/grads/macswan/AP7.htm). Accessed 31 July 2000.

Griffin, Clifford. 1998. "Colonial Relationship Obsolete." *News and Observer* (Raleigh), April 5:A24.

Guerra, Sandra. 1988. "Voting Rights and the Constitution: The Case of Disenfranchisement of Non-English Speaking Citizens." *Yale Law Journal* 97:1419–1437.

Gusfield, J. R. 1963. *Symbolic Crusade: Status Politics and the American Temperance Movement*. Urbana: University of Illinois Press.

Haas, Walter. 1982. "Sprachgeschichte der Schweiz." In *Die viersprachige Schweiz*, ed. Robert Schläpfer. Zurich: Benziger Verlag.

Hakuta, Kenji. 1986. *Mirror of Language: The Debate on Bilingualism*. New York: Basic Books.

Han, M., D. Baker, and C. Rodriguez. 1997. *A Profile of Policies and Practices for Limited English Proficient Students: Screening Methods, Program Support, and Teacher Training.* NCES 97–472. Washington, DC: U.S. Department of Education.

Hancock, LynNell. 1995. "History Lessons: What Should We Teach Our Kids and How Should It Be Taught?" *Newsweek,* July 10:28–32.

Handlin, Oscar. 1957. *Race and Nationality in American Life.* Boston: Little, Brown.

Hansen, Lee O. 1988. "The Political and Socioeconomic Context of Legal and Illegal Mexican Migration to the United States, 1942–1984." *International Migration* 26:95–107.

Hartmann, Edward George. 1948. *The Movement to Americanize the Immigrant.* New York: Columbia University Press.

Heath, Shirley Brice. 1976. "A National Language Academy? Debate in the New Nation." *International Journal of the Sociology of Language* 11:9–43.

———.1981. "English in Our Language Heritage." In *Language in the USA*, ed. Charles A. Ferguson and Shirley Price Heath. Cambridge: Cambridge University Press.

Heath, Shirley Brice, and Lawrence Krasner. 1986. "Comment." *International Journal of the Sociology of Language* 60:157–162.

Heath, Shirley Brice, and Frederick Mandabach. 1983. "Language Status Decisions and the Law in the United States." In *Progress in Language Planning*, ed. Juan Cobarrubias and Joshua A. Fishman. Berlin: Mouton.

Heer, David M. 1996. *Immigration in America's Future.* Boulder, CO: Westview.

Heiman, G. 1966. "The 19th Century Legacy: Nationalism and Patriotism in Canada." In *Nationalism in Canada*, ed. Peter Russell. Toronto: McGraw-Hill.

Hernández-Chávez. Eduardo. 1994. "Language Policy in the United States: A History of Cultural Genocide." In *Linguistic Human Rights: Overcoming Linguistic Discrimination*, ed. Tove Skutnabb-Kangas and Robert Phillioson. Berlin: Mouton.

———. 1997. "Revival and Maintenance of Chicano Spanish in New Mexico: An Imperative for Cultural Survival." Paper presented at the Symposium on the Relocation of Languages and Culture in a Changing World, Duke University, May 6–10.

Higham, John. 1967. *Strangers in the Land.* New York: Atheneum.

Hill, Howard C. 1919. "The Americanization Movement." *American Journal of Sociology* 24:609–642.

Hofstadter, Richard. 1967. *The Paranoid Style in American Politics and Other Essays.* New York: Vintage.

Holloway, Karla F. C. 1995. *Codes of Conduct: Race, Ethics, and the Color of Our Character.* New Brunswick, NJ: Rutgers University Press.

Holm, Agnes, and Wayne Holm. 1995. "Navajo Language Education: Retrospective and Prospects." *Bilingual Research Journal* 19:169–178.

Holmes, Steven. 1996. "Black English Debate: No Standard Assumptions." *New York Times,* December 30: A9.

"Hooked on Ebonics." 1997. *Newsweek.* 129 (January 13):78.

Hornblower, Margot. 1994. "Making and Breaking Law." *Time* 144:68, 73.

Horowitz, Donald L. 1985. *Ethnic Groups in Conflict.* Berkeley: University of California Press.

Horton, John. 1995. *The Politics of Diversity: Immigration, Resistance, and Change in Monterey Park.* Philadelphia: Temple University Press.

Horton, John, and José Calderón. 1992. "Language Struggles in a Changing California Community." In *Language Loyalties*, ed. James Crawford. Chicago: University of Chicago Press.

Hughes, Christopher. 1962. *The Parliament of Switzerland.* London: Cassell.

Huntington, Samuel P. 1981. *American Politics: The Politics of Disharmony*. Cambridge: Harvard University Press.

Hutchinson, E. P. 1981. *Legislative History of American Immigration Policy, 1798–1965.* Philadelphia: University of Pennsylvania Press.

Hutchinson, John. 1994. "Cultural Nationalism and Moral Regeneration." In *Nationalism,* ed. John Hutchinson and Anthony Smith. London: Oxford University Press.

Hutchinson, John, and Anthony Smith, eds. 1994. "Introduction." *Nationalism.* London: Oxford University Press.

Imboden, Max. 1964. *Helvetisches Malaise.* Zurich: EVZ Verlag.

"Immigration and Limited English Proficiency Trends in the Schools: What Is Happening?" 1995. *Urban Indicator,* September:1–2.

Jacobson, Matthew Frye. 1998. *Whiteness of a Different Color: European Immigration and the Alchemy of Race.* Cambridge: Harvard University Press.

Jain, Geneviève. 1977. "Nationalism and Education Politics in Ontario and Quebec, 1867–1914." In *Canadian Schools and Canadian Identity,* ed. Alf Chitin and Neil McDonald. Toronto: Gage.

Jenkins, John R. G. 1986. *Jura Separatism in Switzerland.* Oxford: Clarendon.

Jost, Hans Ulrich, 1983. *Geschichte der Schweiz und der Schweizer.* Basel: Helbing and Lichtenhahn.

Jost, Kenneth. 1995. "Cracking down on Immigration." *Congressional Quarterly Researcher* 5:99–116.

Joy, Richard J. 1992. *Canada's Official Languages: The Progress of Bilingualism.* Toronto: University of Toronto Press.

Judd, Elliot I. 1987. "The English Language Amendment: A Case Study on Language and Politics." *TESOL Quarterly* 21:113–133.

Keller, Morton. 1994. *Regulating a New Society.* Cambridge: Harvard University Press.

Kerr, Henry, Jr. 1974. *Switzerland: Social Cleavages and Partisan Conflict.* Beverly Hills: Sage.

Kibria, Nazli. 1995. "The New Immigration." *Contemporary Sociology* 24:312–314.

Kindler, Anneka L. 1996. "Title VII Funding for States and Territories from 1969 to 1995." *NCBE Policy Analysis Information Report,* July (http://www.ncbe.gwu.edu/askncbe/pairs/states). Accessed 28 July 2000.

King, Robert D. 1997. "Should English Be the Law?" *Atlantic Monthly* 279 (April):55–64.

Kloss, Heinz. 1977. *The American Bilingual Tradition.* Rowley, MA: Newbury House.

Kobach, Kris W. 1994. "Switzerland." In *Referendums around the World,* ed. David Butler and Austin Ranney. Washington, DC: AIE Press.

Kohn, Hans. 1956. *Nationalism and Liberty: The Swiss Example.* London: Allen and Urwin.

Krashen, Stephen. 1996. *Under Attack: The Case against Bilingual Education.* Culver City, CA: Language Education Associates.

Kraus, Michael. 1949. *The Atlantic Civilization.* Ithaca, NY: Cornell University Press.

Krauss, Michael. 1996. "Status of Native American Language Endangerment." In *Stabilizing Indigeneous Languages,* ed. G. Cantoni. Flagstaff: Center for Excellence in Education, Northern Arizona University.

Kreis, Georg. 1993. *Die Schweiz unterwegs: Schlussbericht des NFP 21 "Kulturelle Vielfalt und nationale Identität."* Basel: Helbing and Lichtenhahn,

Kriesi Hanspeter, Boris Wernli, Pascal Sciarini, and Matteo Gianni. 1996. *Le clivage linguistique: Problèmes de compréhension entre les communautés linguistinques en Suisse.* Berne: Office Fédéral de la Statistique.

Labaree, Leonard W., ed. 1961. *The Papers of Benjamin Franklin.* Vol. 4, July 1750–1753. New Haven: Yale University Press.

Labelle, M., F. Rocher, and G. Rocher. 1995. "Pluriethnicité, citoyenneté et intégration: De la souveraineté pour lever les obstacles et les ambiguïtés." *Cahiers de recherche sociologique* 25:213–245.

Labov, William. 1972. *Language in the Inner City: Studies in the Black English Vernacular.* Philadelpia: University of Pennsylvania Press.

———. 1997. "Testimony on Ebonics" before the Subcommittee on Labor, Health and Human Services and Education of the Senate Appropriations Committee, January 23 (http://ling.upenn.edu/~labov/L102/Ebonics_test.html). Accessed 28 July 2000.

Labovitz, Priscilla. 1996. "Immigration—Just the Facts." *New York Times,* March 25.

Lambert, Wallace. D. 1984. *An Overview of Issues in Immersion Education.* Studies in Immersion Education. Sacramento: California State Department of Bilingual Bicultural Education.

Lampros, Andrea. 1998. "Faces of East Bay Reflected Prop. 227." *Contra Contra Times.* June 5 (http://www.humnet/linguistics/people/grads/macswan//CCT17.htm). Accessed 1 August 2000.

Landes, A., C. Cessna, and C. Foster, eds. 1993. *Immigration and Illegal Aliens.* Wylie, TX: Information Plus.

Language Policy Task Force. 1978. "Language Policy and the Puerto Rican Community." *Bilingual Review* 5:1–39.

Leibowicz, Joseph. 1985. "The Proposed English Language Amendment: Shield or Sword?" *Yale Law and Policy Review* 3:519–550.

Leibowitz, Arnold. 1971. *Educational Policy and Political Acceptance: The Imposition of English as the Language of Instruction in America's Schools.* Washington, DC: Center for Applied Linguistics.

Lemco, Jonathan. 1992. "Quebec's 'Distinctive Character' and the Question of Minority Rights." In *Language Loyalties,* ed. James Crawford. Chicago: University of Chicago Press.

Lewis, Neil A. 1996. "Jackson Says Black English Isn't a Separate Language." *New York Times,* December 23: B9.

Lieberson, Stanley, Guy Dalto, and Mary Ellen Johnson. 1975. "The Course of Mother-Tongue Diversity in Nations." *American Journal of Sociology* 81:34–61.

Lind, Michael. 1995. *The Next American Nation.* New York: Free Press.

Linder, Wolf. 1994. *Swiss Democracy: Possible Solutions to Conflict in Multicultural Societies.* New York: St. Martin's.

Lipscomb, Andrew A., ed. 1904. *The Writings of Thomas Jefferson.* Vol. 6. Washington, DC: Thomas Jefferson Memorial Association.

Lipset, Seymour Martin. 1990. *Continental Divide.* New York: Routledge.

Lipset, Seymour Martin, and E. Raab. 1978. *The Politics of Unreason: Right-Wing Extremism in America, 1790–1977.* Chicago: University of Chicago Press.

Lo, Clarence Y. H. 1982. "Countermovements and Conservative Movements in the Contemporary U.S." *Annual Review of Sociology* 8:107–134.

Locke, Steven. 1996. "Language Discrimination and English-Only Rules in the Workplace: The Case for Legislative Amendment of Title VII." *Texas Tech Law Review* 27:33–72.

Lopez, David E. 1996. "Language: Diversity and Assimilation." In *Ethnic Los Angeles,* ed. Roger Waldinger and Mehdi Bozorgmehr. New York: Russell Sage.

Los Angeles Times Poll. 1998. California Primary Election. June 2, 1998. Study 413. (http://www.latimes.com/news/timespoll/stats/pdfs/413ss.pdf). Accessed 28 July 2000.

Lüthy, Herbert. 1962. "Has Switzerland a Future? The Dilemma of the Small Nation." *Encounter* 19:23–34.

Macías, Reynoldo. 1999. "How Has the Limited English Proficient Student Population Changed?" *National Clearinghouse for Bilingual Education* (http://www.ncbe.gwu.edu/askncbe/faqs/08leps.htm). Accessed 28 July 2000.

Mackey, William F. 1983. "U.S. Language Status Policy and the Canadian Experience." In

Progress in Language Planning, ed. Juan Cobarrubias and Joshua A. Fishman. Berlin: Mouton.

Maclean's/CTV Poll. 1994. *Maclean's* 107:10–34.

Maclean's/Decima Poll. 1994. "In Search of Unity." *Maclean's* 107:16–19.

MALDEF (Mexican American Legal Defense and Education Fund). n.d. "Equal Access to Voting: The Need to Protect the Language Assistance Provisions of the Voting Rights Act."

Malinverni, G. 1986. "Art. 116." In *Kommentar zur Bundesverfassung der schweizerischen Eidgenossenschaft.* vol. 3. Basel: Helbing and Lichtenhahn.

Marques, Guilhermina. 1991. "Die Familie." In *Die Werte der Schweizer*, ed. Anna Melich. Bern: Peter Lang.

Marshall, David F. 1986. "The Question of an Official Language: Language Rights and the English Language Amendment." *International Journal of the Sociology of Language* 60:7–75.

Martin, Philip, and Elizabeth Midgley. 1994. "Immigration to the United States: Journey to an Uncertain Destination." *Population Bulletin*, Vol. 49, No. 2. Washington, DC: Population Reference Bureau.

———. 1999. Immigration to the United States." *Population Bulletin*, Vol. 54. No. 2. Washington, DC: Population Reference Bureau.

Martínez García, Alfonso L. 1976. *Idioma y Política.* San Juan: Editorial Cordillera.

Mayer, Kurt. 1952. *The Population of Switzerland.* New York: Columbia University Press.

———. 1968. "The Jura Problem: Ethnic Conflict in Switzerland." *Social Research* 35:707–741.

McCloy, Mike. 1999. "Showdown over Language." *Arizona Republic*, January 7 (http://our-world.compuserve.com/homepages/jwcrawford/AR4.htm). Accessed 28 July 2000.

McFadden, Bernard J. 1983. "Bilingual Education and the Law." *Journal of Law and Education* 12:1–27.

McLeod, Ramon, and Maria Gaura. 1998. "Prop 227 Got Few Latino Votes." *San Franscisco Chronicle*, June 5 (http://www.humnet.ucla.edu/humnet/linguistics/people/grads/mac-swan/SFChr31.htm). Accessed 31 July 2000.

McMillen, Marilyn, Phillip Kaufman, and Steve Klein. 1997. *Dropout Rates in the United States: 1995.* NCES 97-473. Washington, DC: United States Department of Education.

McRae, Kenneth D. 1964. *Switzerland: Example of Cultural Coexistence.* Toronto: Canadian Institute of Internal Affairs.

———. 1983. *Conflict and Compromise in Multilingual Societies: Switzerland.* Waterloo, Ontario, Canada: Wilfrid Laurier University Press.

———. 1990. "Canada: Reflections on Two Conflicts." In *Conflict and Peacemaking in Multiethnic Societies*, ed. Joseph V. Montville. Lexington, KY: Lexington Books.

McRoberts, Kenneth. 1988. *Quebec: Social Change and Political Crisis.* Toronto: McClelland and Stewart.

———. 1997. *Misconceiving Canada: The Struggle for National Unity.* Toronto: Oxford University Press Canada.

Mealey, Linda. 1989. "English-Only Rules and 'Innocent Employers: Clarifying National Origin Discrimination and Disparate Impact Theory under Title VII.'" *Minnesota Law Review* 74:387–434.

Media Alliance. 1998. *New Study Finds Omissions in California Media Coverage of Proposition 227* (http://www.humnet.ucla.edu/humnet/linguistics/people/grads/macswan/mediall.htm). Accessed 31 July 2000.

Meissner, Doris, Robert D. Hormats, Antonio Garrigues Walker, and Shijuro Ogata. 1993. *International Migration Challenges in a New Era: Policy Perspectives and Priorities for Europe, Japan, North America and the International Community.* New York: Trilateral Commission.

Melich, Anna. 1991. "Nationale Identität." In *Die Werte der Schweizer*, ed. Anna Melich. Bern: Peter Lang.

Mitchell, Alanna. 1997. "French Ratio Reaches New Low: Census Figures Fan Assimilation Issue." *Globe and Mail*, December 3: A1.

Moore, Joan, and Harry Pachon. 1985. *Hispanics in the United States*. Englewood Cliffs, NJ: Prentice Hall.

Monge, Jose Trias. 1997. *Puerto Rico: The Trials of the Oldest Colony in the World*. New Haven: Yale University Press.

Moran, Rachel F. 1981. "Quasi-Suspect Classes and Proof of Discriminatory Intent: A New Model." *Yale Law Journal* 90:912–931.

Moss, Marc, and Michael Puma. 1995. *Prospects: The Congressionally Mandated Study of Educational Growth and Opportunity. First Year Report on Language Minority and Limited English Proficient Students*. Cambridge, MA: Abt Associates.

Muller, Thomas. 1997. "Nativism in the Mid-1990s—Why Now?" In *Immigrants Out*, ed. Juan F. Perea. New York: New York University Press.

Multiculturalism and Canadians: Attitude Study. 1991. Angus Reid Group. Ottawa: Multiculturalism and Citizenship Canada.

National Clearinghouse for Bilingual Education. 1995. "What are the Most Common Language Groups for LEP Students?" (http://www.ncbe.gwu.edu/askncbe/faqs/05toplangs.htm). Accessed 28 July 2000.

———. 1998. Summary Report of the Survey of the States' Limited English Proficient Students and Available Educational Programs and Services, 1996–97 (http:www.ncbe.gwu.edu/ncbepubs/seareports/96-97/index.htm).

National Immigration Forum. 1997a. "New Requirement will Cut Legal Immigration Through the Back Door." (http://www.immigrationforum.org/Press/102097pr.htm). Accessed 28 July 2000.

———. 1997b. "New Poll Shows Americans Becoming More Tolerant of Immigrants, Diversity" (http://www.immigrationforum.org/FACTS/USATodayPol.html). Accessed 28 July 2000.

———. 1999. "Chronology: Changes in Immigration and Naturalization Law" (http://www.immigrationforum.org/Facts/ChronRestrict.htm). Accessed 28 July 2000.

Navarro, Mireya. 1998. "Marking a Puerto Rican Anniversary." *New York Times*, July 26: sec. 1, p 24.

Negron de Montilla, Aida. 1971. *Americanization in Puerto Rico and the Public School System, 1900–1930*. Río Piedras: Editorial Edil.

Negrón-Muntaner, Frances. 1997. "English Only *Jamás* but Spanish Only *Cuidado*: Language and Nationalism in Contemporary Puerto Rico." In *Puerto Rican Jam: Rethinking Colonialism and Nationalism*, ed. Frances Negrón-Muntaner and Ramón Grosfoguel. Minneapolis: University of Minnesota Press.

Nelde, Peter H., Normand Labrie, and Colin H. Williams. 1992. "The Principle of Territoriality and Personality in the Solution of Linguistic Conflicts." *Journal of Multilingual and Multicultural Development* 13:387–406.

"Not Quite So Welcome Anymore." *Time*, 1993. Fall: 10–12.

Nunberg, Geoffrey. 1997. "Lingo Jungo: English-Only and the New Nativism." *American Prospect*, no. 33 (July–August):40–47.

Nunavut. 1999. "Our Language, Our Selves" (http://www.nunavut.com/nunavut99/english/our.html). Accessed 29 July 2000.

Oakland Board of Education. 1996. "Original Oakland Board of Education Ebonics Resolution of December 18, 1996" (http://linguistlist.org/issues/8/8–53.html). Accessed 29 July 2000.

———. 1997a. "Revised Oakland Board of Education Resolution of January 19" (http://linguistlist.org/8/8-56.html). Accessed 29 July 2000.

———. 1997b. "Oakland clarifies its Ebonic Policy." (http://horizons.educ.ksu.edu/winter97/oakland.html). Accessed 30 July 2000.

"Obligations of Citizenship." 1985. *Public Opinion*, October/November: 32–33.

"Official English: Federal Limits on Efforts to Curtail Bilingual Services in the States." 1987. *Harvard Law Review* 100:1345–1362.

Olson, Elizabeth. 1999. "Swiss Voters, Tilting Right, Unsettle Traditions." *New York Times*, October 28: A9.

Ong, Paul, Edna Bonacich, and Lucie Cheng, eds. 1994. *The New Asian Immigration in Los Angeles and Global Restructuring*. Philadelphia: Temple Press.

Orfield, Gary, Sara Schley, Diane Glass, and Sean Reardon. 1993. *The Growth of Segregation in American Schools: Changing Patterns of Separation and Poverty since 1968*. Alexandria, VA: National School Boards Association.

Osuna, Juan José. 1949. *A History of Education in Puerto Rico*. Río Piedras: Universidad de Puerto Rico.

Ortiz, Alba A. 1992. *Assessing Appropriate and Inappropriate Referral Systems for LEP Special Education Students. Proceedings of the National Research Symposium on Limited English Proficient Student Issues*. Vol. 1: *Focus on Evaluation and Measurement*. Washington, DC: Office of Bilingual Education and Minority Languages Affairs.

Paltiel, Khayyam Zev. 1987. "Group Rights in the Canadian Constitution and Aboriginal Claims to Self-determination." In *Contemporary Canadian Politics*, ed. Robert J. Jackson, Doreen Jackson, and Nicolas Baster-Moore. Scarborough, Ontario: Prentice Hall Canada.

"Parents Value Standards more than Integration." 1998. *News and Record* (Greensboro, NC), July 29:A3.

Park, James. 1982. "Historical Foundations of Language Policy: The Nez-Perce Case." In *Language Renewal among American Indian Tribes*, ed. Robert St. Clair and William Leap. Rosslyn, VA: National Clearing House for Bilingual Education.

Peal, Elizabeth, and Wallace E. Lambert. 1962. "The Relation of Bilingualism to Intelligence." *Psychological Monographs: General and Applied* 76:1–23.

Pedretti, Bruno. 1994. "Die Beziehungen zwischen den einzelnen Sprachregionen der Schweiz." In *Mehrsprachigkeit—eine Herausforderung*, ed. Hans Bickel and Robert Schläpfer. Basel: Helbing and Lichtenhahn.

Perea, Juan. 1992. "Demography and Distrust: An Essay on American Languages, Cultural Pluralism and Official English." *Minnesota Law Review* 77:269–373.

Perlmann, Joel. 1990. "Historical Legacies: 1840–1920." *Annals of the American Academy of Political and Social Science* 508:27–37.

Piatt, Bill. 1986. "Toward Domestic Recognition of a Human Right to Language." *Houston Law Review* 23:885–906.

Pichard, Alain. 1975. *Vingt Suisses à decouvrir*. Lausanne: Editions 24 Heures.

Pinal, Jorge del, and Audrey Singer. 1997. "Generation of Diversity: Latinos in the United States." *Population Bulletin*, vol. 52, no. 3. Washington, DC: Population Reference Bureau.

Pitt, Leonard. 1966. *The Decline of the Californios: A Social History of the Spanish-Speaking Californians, 1846–1890*. Berkeley: University of California Press.

Population Reference Bureau. 1999. *United States Population Data Sheet*. Washington D.C.: Population Reference Bureau.

Portes, Alejandro. 1990. "From South of the Border: Hispanic Minorities in the United States." In *Immigration Reconsidered*, ed. Virginia Yans-McLaughlin. New York: Oxford University Press.

Portes, Alejandro, and Lingxin Hao. 1998. *E Pluribus Unum*: Bilingualism and Loss of Language in the Second Generation. *Sociology of Education* 77:269–294.

Portes, Alejandro, and Rubén G. Rumbaut. 1996. *Immigrant America.* Berkeley: University of California Press.

Portes, Alejandro, and Richard Schauffler. 1994. "Language and the Second Generation: Bilingualism Yesterday and Today." *International Migration Review* 4:640–661.

Prucha, Frances Paul, ed. 1973. *Americanizing the American Indians: Writings by the "Friends of the Indian" 1880–1900.* Cambridge: Harvard University Press.

Public Agenda Online. 1999a. "Immigration: A Nation Divided?—Most People Think Immigrants Are Here Illegally" (http://www.publicagenda.org/issues/nation_divided_detail.cfm?issue_type=immigration&list=7). Accessed 30 July 2000.

———. 1999b. "Immigration: People's Chief Concerns—Immigration Should Be a Priority for American Foreign Policy" (http://www.publicagenda.org/issues/issues/pcc_detail.cfm?issue_type=immigration&list=4). Accessed 30 July 2000.

———. 1999c. "Immigration: People's Chief Concerns—Immigration Burdens the Country Socially and Economically" (http://www.publicagenda.org/issues/pcc_detail.cfm?issue_type=immigration&list=10). Accessed 30 July 2000.

———. 1999d. "Immigration: A Nation Divided?—Spanish Should Become the U.S.'s Second Language" (http://www.publicagenda.org/issues/nation_divided_detail.cfm?issue_type=immigration&list=10). Accessed 30 July 2000.

———. 1999e. "Immigration: Major Proposals—Not Trying to Learn English Means an Immigrant Is a Bad Citizen." (http://www.publicagenda.org/issues/major_proposals_detail.cfm?issue_type=immigration&list=8). Accessed 30 July 2000.

Puerto Rico Political Status Act. 1998. H. R. 856. Accessed 31 July 2000. (http://thomas.loc.gov/cgi-bin/bdquery/z?d105:HR00856:@@@L).

Purdum, Todd S, 2000. "Shift in the Mix Alters the Face of California." *New York Times,* July 4:A1.

Ramírez, J. David, Sandra D. Yuen, Dena R. Ramsey, David J. Pasta, and David K. Billings. 1991. "Executive Summary." *Final Report: Longitudinal Study of Structured Immersion Strategy, Early-Exit, and Late-Exit Transitional Bilingual Programs for Language Minority Children.* San Mateo, CA: Aguirre International.

Rash, Felicity. 1998. *The German Language in Switzerland: Multilingualism, Diglossia and Variation.* German Linguistic and Cultural Studies, 3. Bern: Peter Lang.

Read, Allen Walker. 1937. "Bilingualism in the Middle Colonies, 1725–1775," *American Speech* 12:93–99.

Reference re Secession of Quebec. 1998. 2 S.C.R. 217: 161 D.L.R (4th) 385 (http://www.lexum.umontreal.ca/csc-scc/en/pub/1998/vol2/html/1998scr2_0217.html). Accessed 1 August 2000.

Reitz, Jeffrey G., and Raymond Breton. 1994. *The Illusion of Difference: Realities of Ethnicity in Canada and the United States.* Toronto: C. D. Howe Institute.

Remak, Joachim. 1992. *Swiss Cohesion: An Analysis of the Largely Historic Kind.* Working Paper 2.9. European Political Relations and Institutions Research Group. Berkeley: University of California at Berkeley, International and Area Studies.

Renan, Ernest. 1970. "What Is a Nation?" In *The Poetry of the Celtic Races and Other Studies,* ed. Ernest Renan. London: Kenikat Press.

Resnick, M. 1993. "ESL and Language Planning in Puerto Rico." *TESOL Quarterly* 27:259–275.

Rethinking Government 1995. 1996. Final Report. Toronto: Ekos Research Associates.

Reyhner, Jon. 1990. "A Description of the Rock Point Community School Bilingual Education Program." In *Effective Language Education Practices and Native Language Survival,* ed. Jon Reyhner. Choctaw, OK: Native American Language Issues.

———.1992. "Policies toward American Indian Languages: A Historical Sketch." In *Language Loyalties,* ed. James Crawford. Chicago: University of Chicago Press.

———.1998. "Two Higher Education Programs Which Promote Navajo and Hawaiian." *NABE News* 21 (June 15):1–2.

Rickford, John R. 1997. "Unequal Partnership: Sociolinguistics and the African American Speech Community." *Language in Society* 26:161–197.

Rickford, John R., 1999. *African American Vernacular English.* Oxford: Blackwell.

Rischin, Moses. 1966. *Immigration and the American Tradition.* Indianapolis: Bobbs-Merrill.

Roberts, Sam. 1995. *Who We Are: A Portrait of America Based on the Latest U.S. Census.* New York: Times Books.

Rohter, Larry. 1996. "In Spanish, It's Another Story." *New York Times*, December 15: sec. 4:1, 6.

Rosier, Paul, and Wayne Holm. 1980. *The Rock Point Experience: A Longitudinal Study of a Navajo School Program.* Bilingual Education Series, 8. Washington, DC: Center for Applied Linguistics.

Ross, William G. 1988. "A Judicial Janus: *Meyer v. Nebraska* in Historical Perspective." *University of Cincinnati Law Review* 57:125–204.

Rossiter, Clinton, ed. 1961. *The Federalist Papers.* New York: Mentor Books.

Rothstein, Richard. 1998. *The Way We Were? The Myths and Realities of America's Student Achievement.* New York: Century Foundation Press.

Rumbaut, Rubén G. 1995. "The New Immigration." *Contemporary Sociology* 24:307–311.

Rumberger, Russell. 1983. "Dropping out of High School: The Influence of Race, Sex, and Family Background." *American Educational Research Journal* 20:199–200.

———. 1991. "Chicano Dropouts: A Review of Research and Policy Issues." In *Chicano School Failure and Success*, ed. Richard Valencia. New York: Falmer Press.

———. 1995. "Dropping Out of Middle School: A Multilevel Analysis of Students and Schools." *American Educational Research Journal* 32:583–625.

Russell, Peter H. 1992. *Constitutional Odyssey: Can Canadians Be a Sovereign People?* Toronto: University of Toronto Press.

Sack, Kevin. 1999. "Don't Speak English? No Tax Break, Alabama Official Declares." *New York Times*, April 4: A24.

Sandmeyer, Elmer Clarence. 1939. *The Anti-Chinese Movement in California.* Urbana: University of Illinois Press.

Schäppi, Peter. 1971. *Der Schultz sprachlicher und konfessioneller Minderheiten im Recht von Bund und Kantonen.* Zurich: Polygraphischer Verlag.

Schläpfer, Robert, Jürg Gutzwiller, and Beat Schmid. 1991. *Das Spannungsfeld zwischen Mundart und Standardsprache in der deutschen Schweiz.* Aarau: Verlag Sauerländer.

Schlesinger, Arthur M., Jr. 1992. *The Disuniting of America.* New York: Norton.

Schlossman, Steven. 1983. "Is There an American Tradition of Bilingual Education? German in the Public Elementary Schools, 1840–1919." *American Journal of Education* 91:139–186.

Schmid, Carol. 1981. *Conflict and Consensus in Switzerland.* Berkeley: University of California Press.

———. 1987. "Language and Education Rights in the United States and Canada." *International and Comparative Law Quarterly* 36:903–908.

———. 1990. "Quebec in the 1970s–80s: Submerged Nation or Canadian Fringe?" In *The Political Sociology of the State*, ed. Richard G. Braungart and Margaret M. Braungart. Greenwich, CT: JAI Press.

———. 1992a. "The English-Only Movement: Social Bases of Support and Opposition among Anglos and Latinos." In *Language Loyalties*, ed. James Crawford. Chicago: University of Chicago Press.

———. 1992b. "Language Rights and the Legal Status of English-Only Laws in the Public and Private Sector." *North Carolina Central Law Journal* 20:65–91.

Schmitt, Eric. 1997, "Illegal Immigrants Rose to 5 Million in 1996." *New York Times*. February 8: A7.

Schrag, Peter. 1999. *Paradise Lost: California's Experience, America's Future.* Berkeley: University of California Press.

Schwander, Marcel. 1992. "Die Westschweiz: Gipfel und Gräben." In *Handbuch der schweizerischen Volkskultur,* ed. Paul Hugger. Vol. 4. Aristau: Schweizerische Gesellschaft für Volkskunde.

Seper, Jerry. 1995. "Group's 10–point Plan Offers Hill Standard for Immigration Reform." *Washington Times,* March 10: A1.

Shebala, Marley. 1999. "Council Slams Door on 'English-Only.'" *Navajo Times,* July 22 (http://ourworld.compuserve.com/homepages/jwcrawford/NT1.htm).

Simon, Rita. 1984. *American Opinion and the Immigrant.* Lexington, KY: Lexington Books.

Smith, Anthony. 1971. *Theories of Nationalism.* London: Duckworth.

———. 1991. *National Identity.* Reno: University of Nevada Press.

Sollars, Werner. 1997. "For a Multilingual Turn in American Studies." *American Studies Newsletter,* June (http://www.georgetown.edu/crossroads/interroads/sollors1.html). Accessed on 31 July 2000.

Southwest Voter Research Institute. 1996. "Latino Issues Survey." San Antonio: Southwest Voter Research Institute.

Spicer, Keith. 1995. "Canada: Values in Search of a Vision." In *Identities in North America,* ed. Robert L. Earle and John D. Wirth. Stanford: Stanford University Press.

Spring, Joel. 1996. *The Cultural Transformation of a Native American Family and Its Tribe, 1763–1995.* Mahwah, NJ: Lawrence Erlbaum.

Stamp, Robert M. 1977. "Canadian Education and National Identity." In *Canadian Schools and Canadian Identity,* ed. Alf Chaiton and Neil McDonald. Toronto: Gage.

Stark, Andrew. 1992. "English-Canadian Opposition to Quebec Nationalism." In *The Collapse of Canada?,* ed. Kent Weaver. Washington, DC: Brookings Institute.

State of Disunion: 1996 Survey of American Political Culture. 1996. 2 vols. Ivy, VA: In Media Res Educational Foundation.

"Statement of Richard Thornburgh, The National Interest in Self Determination for Puerto Rico." 1998. *Puerto Rico Herald,* April 28 (http//www.puertorico-herald.org/issues/vol2n07/thornburgh-980428–AtYaleUniv.shtml). Accessed 30 July 2000.

Stefancic, Jean. 1997. "Funding the Nativist Agenda." In *Immigrants Out,* ed. Juan F. Perea. New York: New York University Press.

Steiner, Jürg. 1974. *Amicable Agreement versus Majority Rule.* Chapel Hill: University of North Carolina Press

———. 1990. "Power Sharing: Another Swiss 'Export Product.'" In *Conflict and Peacemaking in Multiethnic Societies,* ed. Joseph V. Montville. Lexington, KY: Lexington Books.

———. 1999. "Switzerland and the European Union —A Puzzle." Paper presented at the Conference on Ethnicity, University of Western Ontario, November 1997 (revised August 1999).

Stepick, Alex, and Guillermo Grenier. 1993. "Cubans in Miami." In *In the Barrios: Latinos and the Underclass Debate,* ed. Joan Moore and Racquel Penderhughes. New York: Russell Sage.

Stevenson, Patrick. 1990. "Political Culture and Intergroup Relations in Plurilingual Switzerland." *Journal of Multilingual and Multicultural Development* 11:227–255.

Stewart, Donald. 1998. "Why Hispanic Students Need to Take the SAT." *Chronicle of Higher Education* 44 (January 30):A48.

Supreme Court Files. 1996. Freedom of Speech, 96–97 Terms, "Arizonans for Official English v. Arizona" (http://www.fac.org/legal/supcourt/96-97/Ariz_sum.htm). Accessed 30 July 2000.

Suro, Roberto. 1994. *Remembering the American Dream: Hispanic Immigration and National Policy*. New York: Twentieth Century Fund.

Swiss Embassy. 1999. "The Federal Constitution of the Swiss Confederation, April 18, 1999." (http://www.swissemb.org/legal/html/constitution.html). Accessed 1 August 2000.

Swiss Review of World Affairs. 1996. "Protecting the Mother Tongues." April 31.

Swiss Week in Review. 1999a. "People's Party Emerges Second Strongest." *Neue Zürcher Zeitung* Online, English Window, 18 to 24 October (http://www.nzz.ch/online/04_english/swissweek/swissweek1999/sw9910.htm #18 to 24 October 1999). Accessed 1 August 2000.

———. 1999b. " 'Magic Formula' under Attack." *Neue Zürcher Zeitung* Online, English Window, 25 to 31 October (http://www.nzz.ch/online/04_english/swissweek/swissweek1999/sw9910.htm #25 to 31 October 1999).

Takaki, Ronald. 1987. "Reflections on Racial Patterns in America." In *From Different Shores*, ed. Ronald Takaki. New York: Oxford University Press.

Tatalovich, Raymond. 1995. *Nativism Reborn?* Lexington: University of Kentucky Press.

———. 1997. "Official English as Nativist Backlash." In *Immigrants Out*, ed. Juan F. Perea. New York: New York University Press.

Terry, Don. 1998. "Arizona Court Strikes down Law Requiring English Use." *New York Times*, April 29: A14.

Tetley, William. 1982. "Language and Education Rights in Quebec and Canada." *Law and Contemporary Problems* 45:177–217.

Thompson, John Herd, and Stephen J. Randall. 1994. *Canada and the United States: Ambivalent Allies*. Athens: University of Georgia Press.

Thornburgh, Dick. 1998. "The Status Vote in Puerto Rico: Clarifying the Ballot Choices." *Puerto Rico Herald* 2 (21) (http://www.puertorico-herald.org/issues/vol2n19/Thornburgh_en.shtml). Accessed 30 July 2000.

Tienda. Marta. 1999. "Immigration, Opportunity, and Social Cohesion." In *Diversity and Its Disconents*, ed. Neil J. Smelser and Jeffrey C. Alexander. Princeton, NJ: Princeton University Press.

Tiryakian, Edward A. 1997. "The Wild Cards of Modernity." *Daedalus* 126:147–181.

Tocqueville, Alexis de. 1969. *Democracy in America*, ed. J. P Mayer. Garden City, NY: Anchor Books.

Toomey, Sheila. 1999. "English: Judge Says Law Unclear, Puts Debut on Hold." *Anchorage Daily News*, March 4 (http://ourworld.compuserve.com/homepages/jwcrawford/ADN2.htm). Accessed 30 July 2000.

Tribe, Lawrence. 1978. *American Constitutional Law*. Mineola, NY: Foundation Press.

Tyack, David. 1967. *Turning Points in American Educational History*. Waltham, MA: Blaisdell.

U.S. Bureau of the Census. 1993a. *Language Spoken at Home and Ability to Speak English for United States, Regions and States*:1990 CPH-L-96 and 133. Washington, DC: U.S. Government Printing Office.

———. 1993b. *Ability to Speak Spanish and English: Social and Economic Charactistics: Puerto Rico*. 1990 CP-2-53. Washington, DC: U.S. Government Printing Office.

———. 1993c. *The Foreign-Born Population of the United States*, CP-3-1. Washington, DC: U.S. Government Printing Office.

U.S. Civil Rights Commission. 1972. *The Excluded Student: Educational Practices Affecting Mexicans in the Southwest*. Mexican American Education Study, Report 3. Washington, D.C.: U.S. Government Printing Office.

U.S. English/Gallup Opinion Poll. 1991. *A Gallup Study of Attitudes toward English as the Official Language of the U.S. Government,"* January 10.

———. U.S. English 2000a. "Avoiding an American Quebec: The Future of Puerto Rico and the United States." Issue Briefing (http://www.us-english.org/foundation/issues/prbriefing.asp). Accessed 30 July 2000.

———. 2000b. "U.S. English Home Page" (http://www.us-english.org/inc). Accessed 30 July 2000.

U.S. Immigration and Naturalization Service. 1997. *Statistical Yearbook of the Immigration and Naturalization Service, 1996.* Washington, DC: U.S. Government Printing Office.

———. 1998 *Annual Report.* 1999. Washington, DC: U.S. Government Printing Office.

Valdivieso, Rafael, and Cary Davis. 1988. *U.S. Hispanics: Challenging Issues for the 1990s.* Washington, DC: Population Reference Bureau.

Vanoni, Bruno. 1999. "Zitterpartie um neue Verfassung." *Tages Anzeiger,* April 20:A1 (foreign edition).

Veltman, Calvin. 1988. *The Future of the Spanish Language in the United States.* Washington, DC: Hispanic Policy Development Project.

Vernez, Georges, and Allan Abrahamse. 1996. *How Immigrants Fare in U.S. Education.* MR-718-AMF. Santa Monica, CA: Rand.

Volksabstimmung vom 10 März. 1996. "Referendum on Romanish" (http://www.admin.ch/ch/d/pore/va/19960310/explic/d-pp0300.html). Accessed 30 July 2000.

Waddell, Eric. 1986. "State, Language and Society: The Vicissitudes of French in Quebec and Canada." In *The Politics of Gender, Ethnicity and Languages in Canada,* ed. Alan Cairns and Cynthia Williams. Toronto: University of Toronto Press.

Wagner, Stephen T. 1981. "The Historical Background of Bilingualism and Biculturalism in the United States." In *The New Bilingualism,* ed. Martin Ridge. Los Angeles: University of Southern California Press.

Wardhaugh, Ronald. 1983. *Language and Nationhood: The Canadian Experience.* Vancouver: New Star Books.

———. 1987. *Languages in Competition.* New York: Basil Blackwell.

Weaver, Glenn. 1970. "Benjamin Franklin and the Pennsylvania Germans." In *The Aliens: A History of Ethnic Minorities in America,* ed. Leonard Dinnerstein and Frederick Cople Jaher. New York: Appleton-Century-Crofts.

Weaver, R. Kent. 1992. "Political Institutions and Canada's Constitutional Crisis." In *The Collapse of Canada,* ed. R. Kent Weaver. Washington, DC: Brookings Institution.

Weber, Max. 1978. "The Nation." In *Economy and Society,* ed. Guenther Roth and Claus Wittich. New York. Bedminister Press.

Webster, Noah. 1992. "Declaration of Linguistic Independence." In *Language Loyalties,* ed. James Crawford. Chicago: University of Chicago Press.

Weibel, Ernst. 1986. "Les rapports entre les groupes linguistiques." In *Handbuch Politisches System der Schweiz,* ed. Raimund E. Germann and Ernest Weibel. Bern: Paul Haupt.

Weilenmann, Herman. 1925. *Die vielsprachige Schweiz: Eine Lösung des Nationalitäten-problems.* Basel: Am Rhein Verlag.

Wertenbaker, Thomas J. 1937. *The Founding of American Civilization: The Middle Colonies.* New York: Scribner's.

Williams, Cynthia. 1985. "The Changing Nature of Citizen Rights." In *Constitutionalism, Citizenship and Society,* ed. Alan Cairns and Cynthia Williams. Toronto: University of Toronto Press.

Wilson, Kenneth L., and Alejandro Portes. 1980. "Immigrant Enclaves: An Analysis of Labor Market Experiences of Cubans in Miami." *American Journal of Sociology* 86:295–319.

Wittke, Carl. 1936. *German-Americans and the World War.* Columbus: Ohio State Archeological and Historical Society.

Wolfe, Alan. 1998. *One Nation, After All.* New York: Viking.

Wollenberg, Charles. 1976. *All Deliberate Speed: Segregation and Exclusion in California Schools, 1855–1975.* Berkeley: University of California Press.

Woolard, Kathryn A. 1990. "Voting Rights: Liberal Voters and the Official English Movement—An Analysis of Campaign Rhetoric in San Francisco's Proposition "O."" In *Perspectives on Official English,* ed. Karen L. Adams and Daniel T. Brink. New York: Mouton.

Wright, Louis B. 1957. *The Cultural Life of the American Colonies.* New York: Harper.

Wyler, Alfred. 1990. *Dialect and High German in German-Speaking Switzerland.* Zurich: Pro Helvetia.

"The Young Bill: Puerto Rico Self-Determination History, Issues and House Passage." 1998. *Puerto Rico Herald,* March 28 (http://www.puertorico-herald.org/issues/vol2n06/Young-Bill-History.shtml). Accessed 30 July 2000.

Young, Brian Jeffrey. 1999. "Canadian Politics, the Supreme Court, and the Québec Secession Referendum of 1998." Talk presented at Duke University, Canadian Studies Program, November 2.

Zavodny, Madeline. 1998. "The Effects of Official English Laws on Limited-English-Proficient Workers." Working Paper 98-4a. Atlanta: Federal Reserve Bank.

Zipperer, John. 1995. "Immigration Divides Christians." *Christianity Today* 39 (February 6):42–43.

Legal Cases

Alaskans for a Common Language Inc. v. Kritz. 2000. sp. 5284.

Arizonans for Official English v. Arizona. 1997. U.S. 95–974. 117 S.Ct. 1055.

Asian American Business Group v. City of Pomona. 1989. 716 F. Supp. 1328 (C.D. Cal.).

Bartels v. Iowa. 1923. 262 U.S. 404.

Carbajal v. Albuquerque Public School District. 1999. CIV 98–279 MV/DS.

Carmona v. Sheffield. 1973. 475 F.2d 738 (9th Cir.).

Castaneda v. Pickard. 1981. 648 F.2d 989 (5th Cir.).

Cintron v. Brentwood Union Free School District. 1978. 455 F. Supp. 56 (E.D.N.Y.).

Espinoza v. Farah Manufacturing Co. 1973. 414 U.S. 86.

Frontera v. Sindell. 1975. 522 F.2d 1215.

Garcia v. Gloor. 1980. 618 F.2nd 264 (5th Cir.), cert. denied, 449 U.S. 1113 (1981).

Garcia v. Spun Steak Co. 1993. 998 F.2d 1480 (9th Cir.), cert. denied, 114 S.Ct. 2726 (1994).

Guadalupe Organization, Inc. v. Tempe Elementary School. 1978. 587 F.2d 1022 (9th Cir.).

Gutierrez v. Municipal Court. 1988. 838 F.2d 1031 (9th Cir.), vacated as moot, 490 U.S. 1016 (1989).

Hernandez v. Texas. 1954. 347 U.S. 475.

Keyes v. School District No. 1. 1983. 576 F.Supp. 1503 (D. Colo.).

Lau v. Nichols. 1974. 414 U.S. 563.

Meyer v. Nebraska. 1923. 262 U.S. 390.

Morales v. Shannon. (1975). 516 F.2d 411 (5th Cir.).

Pabon v. MacIntosh. 1982. 546 F. Supp. 1328 (E.D. Pa)

Puerto Rican Organization for Political Action v. Kusper. 1973. 490 F.2d 575 (7th Cir.)

Ruiz v. Hull. 1998. __Ariz. ___, ___P.2d___ (App. 1996).

Sandoval v. Hagan. 1999. 197 F.3d 484 (11th Cir.)

Serna v. Portales. 1974. 499 F.2d 1147 (10th Cir.).

Soberal-Perez v. Heckler. 1983. 717 F.2d 36 (2d Cir.).
Toure v. the United States. 1994. 24 F.3d 444 (2d Cir.).
Yniguez v. Mofford. 1990. 730 F. Supp. 309 (D. Ariz.).
Yniguez v. Arizonans for Official English. 1995. 53 F.3rd 1084 (9th Cir.).
Yu Cong Eng v. Trinidad. 1926. 271 *U.S. 500.*

INDEX